I0061675

WAR REMAINS

Contemporary Issues in the Middle East
Mehran Kamrava, *Series Editor*

Select Titles in Contemporary Issues in the Middle East

Being There, Being Here: Palestinian Writings in the World
Maurice Ebileeni

Kurds in Dark Times: New Perspectives on Violence and Resistance in Turkey
Ayça Alemdaroglu and Fatma Müge Göçek, eds.

Life on Drugs in Iran: Between Prison and Rehab
Nahid Rahimipour Anaraki

The Lost Orchard: The Palestinian–Arab Citrus Industry, 1850–1950
Mustafa Kabha and Nahum Karlinsky

Readings in Syrian Prison Literature: The Poetics of Human Rights
R. Shareah Taleghani

Turkey's State Crisis: Institutions, Reform, and Conflict
Bülent Aras

Understanding Hezbollah: The Hegemony of Resistance
Abed T. Kanaaneh

Victims of Commemoration: The Architecture and Violence of Confronting the Past in Turkey
Eray Çaylı

For a full list of titles in this series, visit https://press.syr.edu/supressbook-series/contemporary-issues-in-the-middle-east.

WAR REMAINS

Ruination and Resistance in Lebanon

YASMINE KHAYYAT

Syracuse University Press

Syracuse University Press
Syracuse, New York 13244-5290

First Edition 2023

23 24 25 26 27 28 6 5 4 3 2 1

∞ The paper used in this publication meets the minimum requirements of the American National Standard for Information Sciences—Permanence of Paper for Printed Library Materials, ANSI Z39.48-1992.

For a listing of books published and distributed by Syracuse University Press, visit https://press.syr.edu.

ISBN: 978-0-8156-3800-1 (hardcover)
978-0-8156-3793-6 (paperback)
978-0-8156-5578-7 (e-book)

Library of Congress Cataloging-in-Publication Data

Names: Khayyat, Yasmine, author.
Title: War remains : ruination and resistance in Lebanon / Yasmine Khayyat.
Description: First edition. | Syracuse, New York : Syracuse University Press, 2023. |
Series: Contemporary issues in the Middle East | Includes bibliographical references and index.
Identifiers: LCCN 2022050560 (print) | LCCN 2022050561 (ebook) | ISBN 9780815638001 (hardcover) |
ISBN 9780815637936 (paperback) | ISBN 9780815655787 (ebook)
Subjects: LCSH: Arabic literature—Lebanon—History and criticism. | Arabic literature—
20th century—History and criticism. | War in literature. | Ruins in literature. | Underground
movements in literature. | Collective memory in literature. | LCGFT: Literary criticism.
Classification: LCC PJ8078 .K47 2023 (print) | LCC PJ8078 (ebook) |
DDC 892.7/0995692—dc23/eng/20230302
LC record available at https://lccn.loc.gov/2022050560
LC ebook record available at https://lccn.loc.gov/2022050561

Manufactured in the United States of America

For my mother, Fadia Basrawi,
who wove a world of wondrous love around me.

For my father,
Mohammad Adnan Salaheddine Khayyat (1949–2021),
whose undying love for South Lebanon
is immortalized in his favorite saying:
"The sun rises from the South:
الشمس تشرق من الجنوب."

I remember war, but as a sepia photograph.
—Ilyās Khūrī, Yālū

Contents

Illustrations

Preface

The Aṭlāl *of Memory*

War has remained a fixture of curiosity, horror, and fascination for me since childhood. I grew up south of Beirut during the grueling Lebanese Civil War (1975–90) and still find myself opening and closing doors onto new memories as well as weaving experiences into an exceedingly elaborate textual canvas that I call memory. The Civil War ended when I was nine years old, and this "memory" of war that I had quilted from the fabric of experiences and stories began to take on a texture of its own, especially at certain *wuqūf ʿalā l-aṭlāl* (standing before the ruins) moments. In those moments, I am suddenly transported back to a place and time alive with giggles, musty makeshift bomb shelters, electricity cuts, stockpiles of candles for midday blackouts, extended family slumber parties, sudden school closures (*iḍrāb*), interminable bottleneck traffic jams, pockmarked buildings, derelict and abandoned houses. And, of course, there was the soundtrack of war—the constant thud, sometimes louder, sometimes softer, sometimes inaudible, that continued to play throughout my young life.

Growing up with war meant imagination wielded great power over reality, transmuting bombs into thunder and fear into adrenaline. Midday evacuations to the school basement remain one of my most powerful recollections. Giggling schoolchildren herded into a musty basement strewn with rusty tables, old chairs, and discarded props became the backdrop to much-anticipated sibling reunions. The real backdrop was the war, of course—the danger of stray shrapnel necessitated our hasty evacuation to subterranean quarters at odd hours of the day. We excitedly chattered to each other in our little underworld, while our teachers nervously accommodated our misguided excitement. As these recurrences became the norm, we slowly experienced boredom, that fertile breeding ground for questions.

On a seemingly normal day to visit the dentist in 1988, I witnessed, as I now understand it, a "scuffle" break out between militia fighters. Gunfire erupted in the crisp December air, and my mother, abandoning her usual composure, hurled my twin sister, Rola, and me against a dilapidated wall and ordered us to be still. An elderly lady witnessing the scene unfolding beneath her balcony gestured to my mother frantically: "Come on up! Are you crazy? You have children!" Smiling wanly, my mother replied: "Thank you, we're fine. We're just visiting the dentist." Unyielding to the kind offer of shelter, we waited until the coast had cleared before our mother herded us back into our car, and we promptly returned home. Questions about a failed dentist visit met with a watered-down version of events. A scuffle between people who cannot control their anger became the moral lesson of the day.

Destruction and chaos were the norm; we often climbed into the ruins of abandoned homes and, along with a slew of cousins, mimicked checkpoints and hunted for wayward shrapnel and spent bullets in the thickets surrounding our house. We even reinvented popular song lyrics to reflect the times: "Bombs are falling, all around us. . . . Merry Christmas, Lebanon." When said bombs fell too close for comfort, we knew the drill: huddle together in the hallway of the ground-floor bedroom and call the cousins—yet another reunion! We even enjoyed the palpable uncertainty of driving to school and the sudden adrenaline rush of a gas pedal pressed for dear life as we flew across Beirut to the "safety" of our home. Laughing childish faces greeted ashen adult expressions as we stumbled over our words to narrate the day's events. Life as (un)usual persisted.

Such adrenaline-packed moments were punctuated by more somber realities that slowly penetrated our gossamer childish worlds: a schoolmate who never made it to school; a yearbook dedicated to the missing; young teachers with spouses caught up in the web of war inexplicably bursting into tears; the daily news we were barred from watching; the instruction to stay away from parked cars; and the tangible destruction we met with daily. The Civil War ended when I was nine, but "other" wars continued to reverberate throughout my adolescence. I was actively involved in civilian relief efforts in the wake of major Israeli operations in South Lebanon in 1993 and 1996, and in May 2000 I witnessed and documented the collapse of the Israeli occupation (1978–2000) and the explosive war of July 2006 and its aftermath.

These remnants of war have found a snug place in my memory, where they remain, sometimes ripe for the picking, sometimes cozily stored away. But once I crack open the door to that storehouse, a tapestry of images, recollections, and emotions come cascading into my present life, both disturbing and enriching it. We know now that memories are usually prompted by visceral encounters—such as the scent of a kerosene lamp, a scene in a Lebanese war novel, the taste of a chocolate-covered macaroon, and that infamous school auditorium—an ever-powerful sensorium that prompts the ghosts of the past to reemerge. Perhaps, then, my fascination with ruins stems from a memory I am still piecing together. Standing before the ruins of my own memory, I am continually confronting a past that is at the heart of this book.

Acknowledgments

As I sit down to write my acknowledgments—with my cats, Angel and Minyas, purring synchronously on my lap—my mind wanders to all the loving friends, family, and nonhumans who have made this book possible.

My heartfelt gratitude goes to my lifelong brilliant mentor, Muhsin al-Musawi, whose unwavering intellectual and spiritual guidance in my journey from graduate student to published author has left an indelible mark on this book. Tarek El-Ariss is a magnanimous scholar and dear friend who has seen me through every single stage of the book. At Columbia University, where the kernel of this book's idea was planted, I benefited from shapeshifting feedback from Timothy Mitchell, Partha Chatterjee, Marianne Hirsch, miriam cooke, and Rashid Khalidi. As a graduate student, I met my lifelong friend Jessica Rechtschaffer, who has always reminded me that a done book is a good book.

At Syracuse University Press, I owe my gratitude to Mehran Kamrava, the editor of Syracuse's series Contemporary Issues in the Middle East, for believing in this project from its inception. I give thanks to Peggy Solic for her patient guidance at the start of the writing and to Kelly Balenske for effortlessly shepherding the book to its finish. The feedback from two anonymous reviewers for the press was insightful and generative, and to them I owe my thanks. I wish to thank Syracuse's exceptional editorial and production team, Kay Steinmetz, Miranda Kristine Baur, and Meghan Cafarelli, for their valuable editorial insights throughout the book's production process. I am ever so grateful to Annie Barva for her thoughtful feedback and copyediting in the final stages of writing. I give warm thanks to Jessica LeTourneur Bax for her impeccable proofreading of the book, and Elise Hess for carefully preparing the index. I am thankful for Lisa Renee Kuerbis's important work on the book's future publicity.

I am beyond thankful to Petra Shenk and Edith Klein for their developmental feedback on early drafts of the book.

At Rutgers, I am lucky to be surrounded by warm colleagues in the Department of African, Middle Eastern, and South Asian Languages and Literatures. Alamin Mazrui took me under his wing when I was first hired and has outdone his duties by being a true mentor, friend, and confidante. I am especially grateful to my friend, colleague, and former chair, Charles Haberl, for his unceasing academic and personal support throughout my academic travails and to my current chair, Anjali Nerlekar, for navigating the pandemic academic waters while constantly offering support. Deans Michelle Stephens and Rebecca Walkowitz have generously supported my journey as a tenure-track professor. I owe my gratitude to Dale Koznecki for her support throughout my tenure at Rutgers. My students at Rutgers, especially Mark Morroquin, continually inspire me with their capacious zest for knowledge.

During the early stages of my research, many colleagues and friends made my path a much smoother one. Mona Harb and Mona Fawwaz helped me navigate my research on memorials in South Lebanon, and to them I owe my gratitude. I thank Iman Humaydan for introducing me to Abbas Beydoun and Huda Fakhreddine for introducing me to her father, the fantastic poet Jawdat Fakhreddine. Bilal Orfali graciously pointed me in the direction of important Arabic archives at the American University of Beirut. I am deeply grateful to all my southern interlocutors and friends there, who chose to remain anonymous, and to my interviewees—Adnan Sammur, Mona Ḥallāk, Sāliḥ Barakāt, Nadim Karam, and Monika Borgmann—for generously sharing their stories and experiences with me. I thank Hayat Nazer, Pierre Abboud, and Roula Abdo for graciously allowing me access to their important artistic creations.

This book has benefited enormously from colleagues' and friends' critical feedback, which took time away from their own writing. I owe special thanks to Michael Allan, Michelle Hartmann, Elizabeth Holt, Mehammed Mack, Hatim El-Hibri, Fawwaz Traboulsi, Talal Asad, and

Lila Abu-Lughod, whose piercing insights enriched the book's formative stages. This book has been enhanced by my friendships and conversations with Tahia Abdelnasser, Frances Hasso, David Bond, Suzanne Stetkevych, Nizar Hermes, Ghenwa Hayek, Stefan Sperl, Sami Hermez, Chiara Fontana, Joud Al-Korani, Isa Blumi, and Heiko Wimmen. In the fall of 2019, I had the privilege of being a visiting faculty member at the American University of Beirut, where I enjoyed the camaraderie of my colleagues in the Department of English and Comparative Literature. My dear colleagues and neighbors there—Rana Issa, Livia Wick, Anaheed Hardan, Yaser Shoaib, Eveline Hitti, and Maria Abunasr—made campus life colorful and fun.

Parenting while professoring and writing a book is not for the meek, and I would not have managed this feat without the support of similarly situated friends and family. I am ever so grateful to my amazing sister-in-law, Aspasia Kosmatopoulos and her husband, Andreas Koutsoumbelis, and their lovely twins, my niece, Ioana, and nephew, Christos, for always showering the twins and me with love. I thank Yorgos and Amalia for inviting my family and me to their beautiful island home in Syros. Special thanks to Dania Dandashly, my kindred spirit and neighbor, for welcoming the twins and me into her warm home since their birth so I could have space to write and think. I thank Emily Allen-Hornblower for her camaraderie and support. My friendship with Zainab Mahmoud has traversed the span of this planet—from New York to Shanghai: we shared real and virtual chais, drool-worthy food pictures, and lavender-colored trinkets, and her pithy words of wisdom have uplifted and inspired me. My childhood friends Julia Choucair (and her amazing father, Mahmoud Choucair) and Ramzi Khalaf hold a special place in my heart and deserve special mention for always being a lifeline away. My dear neighbors Mazen Labban and Laura Schneider have my warm thanks for making life in Highland Park feel like home.

This book benefited enormously from the cuddles and purrs of my nonhuman companions, Angel, Minyas, Bello, Taffy, Shnoodles, and Zoe, and from the sun-dappled Mediterrenean and Aegean Seas, which always kept my horizons open when it felt as if the world were caving in.

Caretakers make the world go round, and I am ever so grateful to Cita Barua, Betty Heran, Dennis and Anna Landicho, Lenny, Jeralyn, Ghada Awali, Mona Awali, and Ali Jaafar for their relentless devotion to keeping me, my children, and my parents afloat during these precarious times.

In Athens, I found my home away from home. My nurturing parents-in-law, Vasso and Yanni, *efxaristo para poly* for your unwavering love and support, welcoming affection, and, of course, gracious lessons in Greek. I thank my cousin-in-law Kosta for his sunny temperament, good humor, and ever-ready support no matter where we are.

My trailblazing big sister, Munira Khayyat, has my endless thanks for always plowing the path ahead and letting me ride shotgun on our historic trips to South Lebanon—trips filled with laughter, circuitous detours, and questionable vegetables. Her constant encouragement through thick and thin helped me stay the course of academic motherhood as we proceeded in lockstep. My telepathic twin sister Rola Khayyat's precious mark on this book is obvious through her incredible photographs. Her artistic flair and sensitive eye for the beauty of this world translate into the photographs that adorn this book. She is the one I turn to whenever I falter, or when I am ecstatic about a new idea. Her profound presence in my life precedes and exceeds words: she is in every single sense my better half. I thank my wiser and older brother, Amer Khayyat, for his ever-ready support from the moment I decided to pursue higher education, and for being the calm and collected sibling everyone needs in their life. My musical genius brother Ghassan has my gratitude for jazzing up life with his fierce talent. My indomitable nephews, Nessim and Qais, and multitalented niece, Darya, enrich my life by simply being who they are, delectable slices of sunshine. Aunty Bushra, matriarch of the Khayyats, has plied me with bountiful Lebanese meals, nurturing my body, mind, and soul whenever I need it most. Reem Saffouri, you hold a special place in my heart.

My father, Adnan Khayyat, did not live to see this book come to fruition, but his infectious love for South Lebanon catalyzed its creation. I will forever cherish the moments I spent listening to him reciting the poetry I include in chapter 1. His death at the age of seventy-five, when I was in the final stages of writing, is both a huge personal and intellectual loss, and it is my aspiration that the book will serve as a tribute to him. My mommy's, Fadia Basrawi's, sheltering love through war and shine quite literally brought me to adulthood. She is the guiding light of my life, and I would not be who I am without her exemplary love for literature and all things memory, even as hers began to fade.

When I first met my beloved partner and intellectual companion, Nikolas Kosmatopoulos, we bonded over our book projects: I work on war, he on peace. True to his subject matter (and nature), he remains the most calming force in my life, buoying me up through it all: from baby to book production and all that life has proffered in between (insert: magical Greek islands). Without him, the solitary nature of book writing would have lost its luster. Speaking of luster, our twin forces and eternal loves, Qamar and Leony, burst midway into the book-writing scene, making the journey that much more rambunctious, hilarious, colorful, and—well, let's face it—slow! My hope for a world without war remains with them.

Permission has been granted to reproduce excerpts of translated work in and by the following:

In chapter 1, the extract from Sharif S. Elmusa's translation of "Ṣūr" by 'Abbās Bayḍūn, published in Elisa Salem Manganaro, "Bearing Witness: Recent Literature from Lebanon," *Literary Review* 37, no. 3 (Spring 1994): 382, is reprinted with permission of Sharif S. Elmusa. In chapter 2, the translation of lines from Abū Tammām's panegyric "Lā anta anta walā al- diyāru diyāru" [You Are Not You and the Abodes Are Not Abodes], originally published in *Dīwān Abī Tammām,* 2 vols., ed. Muḥyī al-Dīn Ṣubhī (Beirut: Dār Sādir, 1997), 1:321, is reprinted from Suzanne Stetkevych, *Abu Tammam and the Poetics of the Abbasid Age* (Leiden: Brill, 1990), 81, with the permission of the translator, Suzanne Stetkevych.

Note on Transliteration, Translation, and Spelling

This book follows the transliteration and translation conventions of the *Journal of Arabic Literature*, maintaining diacritical marks for Arabic words and names of authors writing in Arabic.

Except where indicated otherwise, all translations of non-English material quoted in the book's chapters are my own.

W A R
REMAINS

Introduction

Ruins That Matter

In the wake of Ḥarb Tammūz,[1] a thirty-three-day Israeli air and land assault on Lebanon that started on July 12, 2006, the South Lebanese poet ʿAbbās Bayḍūn (b. 1945) penned a prose poem titled "Qaṣīḍa mumkina ʿan al-Ḍāḥiya" (A Possible Poem on Dahiya),[2] inviting his readers to ruminate on the wreckage piling up in the southern suburb of Beirut and prompting one of the most critical reflections on ruination. The Lebanese South, with Ḍāḥiya[3] at its urban reach, has always emerged in juxtaposition to Beirut, the "modern" and "western" capital at the heart of Greater Lebanon. The Israeli war on Lebanon in July 2006 and its ruinous aftermath only exacerbated the exclusionary violence of this discursive divide. Bayḍūn's prose poem sets out to capture this divisiveness[4] through a depiction of the exclusive tally of war's remains. The poem directs our optics to the plight of the so-called margins, where the dislocated and dispossessed have been expelled and remaindered like rubble by ongoing war and neglect:

> I don't know any poet who has written on Dahiya, and I don't think that a poem singing about its destruction is ever possible. We will surely read rhymes and meters, but who will ever give them any attention? The eyes that the rockets have opened in Dahiya's buildings will, for a long time, remain eyes with a dreadful look, which poets will never dare to encounter. They will never know what to do with a broken rib of concrete, how to see a fallen wing of cement, how to contemplate those volumes of cracked stone stacked one after another. Worse still, they will be afraid of those architectural dinosaurs that disappeared without a

> scream. And, of course, they will be unable to find a rhyme for the endless odyssey of rubble; for the tsunami of debris and its waves tumbling over one another; for the quivering sails on the tops of the buildings; for the stone tatters caught in the throes of death on the roofs; and for the vast wasteland that appeared all of a sudden.
>
> Poets and those who are not poets can note that this unnamed city, which spoke in the language of huge measurements and large sizes, was not heard by anyone. We don't know whether it spoke to poets or thought of them. This unnamed city did not ask poets for a single word . . . places born of separations, which can only be treated by a measure of invisibility—such places have no language, of course.
>
> Unnamed we lived—on an unnamed land in an unnamed existence. . . . The lost name became unnamed, and the hated world became vacant. We were the surplus of life, the surplus of human beings, the surplus of overcrowding. And here, where no one had specific features, we have to move without faces in an undetermined and unlimited nebulous existence.
>
> The place consists of heaps upon heaps; of plains of ruined heaps. . . . Can we be deviant and speak about beauty here? Or is the real ruin on our tongues? Can we now think in language's terms about something we had neither given a name nor qualities? Let us at least see . . .[5]

Bayḍūn issues a warning to the ambivalent ruin gazer too easily inured to the rubble (*rakm*) accruing in this "unnamed land":[6] stay sentient to war's remains, to the humans deemed fungible and disposable. Remains, here, signal a dual meaning: both human and nonhuman. Bayḍūn urges us to contemplate these persistent remains of war[7] while in the same breath laments that "no poet will ever dare to encounter" them.[8] In so doing, he expresses outrage at the routine indifference to suffering in the South and casts doubt on the shared sentience of bodies in ruin, uncertain if the human is an expansive category or an exclusive one—if, indeed, a human is perceived at all amid the still-smoldering wreckage.[9]

I have opened with Bayḍūn's imagery of *Ḍāḥiya*'s neglected wreckage because it is expressive of a dominant tendency to overlook the Lebanese South and its myriad encounters with war, whose remains are both real and imagined. South Lebanon[10] encompasses a vast history of war-related violence, including the dispossession of Palestine in 1948, Palestinian guerrilla warfare in the 1960s and 1970s, the Lebanese Civil War from 1975 to 1990, the first and second Israeli invasions in 1978 and 1982, and the Israeli occupation of 1978–2000. The most recent war in July 2006 killed more than a thousand civilians and wreaked infrastructural and ecological damage across Lebanon, especially in the South.

Roughly the size of municipal Beirut and home to more than half a million, mainly Shīʿite Muslim residents, Ḍāḥiya is inextricably tied to the Lebanese South, to which waves of displaced rural migrants came streaming as a result of ongoing war in the southern borderland. Since the 1980s, the name "Ḍāḥiya" has become vernacular for the area extending south of the capital, so that diverse neighborhoods are lumped under a single umbrella label.[11] Ḍāḥiya and its overlooked wreckage are emblematic of the Lebanese South's penumbral positionality in war-related memory, a position that this book attempts to trouble and undo.

Accordingly, Bayḍūn's poem speaks of ruination in terms of the disenfranchised, who are extruded like unwanted accrual and living "nebulous existences not heard by anyone."[12] The sorts of remains he conjures are marked by neglect and abandonment—the accumulated leftovers of violence given flesh as superfluous people. For Bayḍūn, not only war itself but also our neglect of its remains produce "the surplus of human beings"[13] in their subjection to "overcrowding . . . where no one had specific features." Refugees in their own land and abandoned by a negligent state, these still smoldering human remains are in the vortex of destruction and its persistent aftermath. This dangerous divide between valued lives and disposable lives defines the very meaning of war's ruinous if intangible aftermath. In this sense, Bayḍūn's poem not only points to palpable debris but also alludes to seemingly banal yet violent categories of segregation that give rise to places like Ḍāḥiya: "Places born of separations, which can only be treated by a measure of invisibility." Such invisible forms of structural violence in turn define everyday existence on the verge of catastrophe and expected disaster. Such wars and their remains fall from view.

Yet at the center of Bayḍūn's prose poem is a ruin that dares the viewer to encounter its gaze. Heaving like a gathering tide of debris, it stares back at us. "The eyes that the rockets have opened in Dahiya's buildings," warns the poetic voice, "will for a long time remain eyes with a dreadful look." By attributing a haunting human gaze to Ḍāḥiya's ruined buildings, Bayḍūn reframes ruination as a spectral marker of defiance against the inevitable void of oblivion, for to speak of ruination is to trace the tangible and intangible sense in which war remains in bodies, minds, and gazes. The derelict building's gaze betrays not only dread but also accusation. Bayḍūn's provocative question, "Is the real ruin on our tongues?," comes across as a wake-up to acknowledge these forgotten ruins that remain on the margins[14] of existence and, by extension, of public memory. Bayḍūn's outrage at the public silence on the southern ruins strikes me as a call to pursue that which has been neglected far too long. As the poignant question "When is life grievable?" posed by the feminist scholar Judith Butler underscores,[15] there is a fleeting temporality to the recognition of vulnerability and precarity "after" officially designated wartime ends, for this recognition risks burial beneath the suffocating rubble of indifference.

On first reading Bayḍūn's prose poem, I was inspired by his challenge to "think in language's terms about something we had neither given a name nor qualities." That is to say, I began to think of ruins as a glutinous concept that binds together variegated discourses and practices rather than simply as the crumbling aftermath of war's violence. Drawing together multiple perspectives from literature, cultural production, anthropology, ethnography, and contemporary art practice, this book explores the material and metaphorical afterlives of ruins in all their ubiquity, diversity, and persistence. It traces the aesthetics of ruination and resistance in select contemporary Lebanese wartime literature, cultural production, and sites of memory. I analyze war remains and how they matter throughout literary texts and sites of memory stretching from South Lebanon to the capital, Beirut. I ask how war remains manifest as a resistant trope in the intellectual and material spaces of war's aftermath. In other words, I examine the literary and cultural terrain on which wartime processes and discourses of ruination leave their marks. I aim to highlight the centrality of war remains as a medium through which practices of resistance to ruinous discourses can be refracted. This book, then, illuminates an understudied poetics of resistance emanating from South Lebanon. It shifts the focus from melancholic frames of destruction to creative practices of resistance forged from the forgotten ruins of ongoing devastation. I argue that the ruin of war can be thought of as a generative trope for resistant thought and action. Accordingly, in this book the figure of war remains is posited as both a site of protest and a trope for reflexive rebellion.

The term *remains* in the title of this book captures three principal features of war: its persistent presence; its multiple temporalities; and its enduring, if sometimes elusive, traces. My focus is not on inert war remains but on their active appropriation in the present as nodes of resistance in the poetics and politics of contemporary Lebanese literary-cultural production. In my examination of war remains, I underscore the slippage between human and nonhuman ruins as well as between metaphorical and material ruins. I examine what this slippage does to engender the heterogeneous ruins that I explore in the book and investigate the aesthetic, literary, and political sensibilities this slippage harbors. The remains of war highlighted in the book not only serve as mere material signifiers but also evoke a vast archive of silenced affects, narratives, perceptions, memories, and life-worlds. Specifically, the ruins I have in mind are an amalgam of metaphorical and material knots of debris resulting from anthropogenic-related violence and upheaval, such as war (the Lebanese Civil War of 1975–90 and the July War of 2006), occupation (the Israeli occupation of South Lebanon, 1978–2000), protests (the Lebanon uprisings of 2019), and explosions (the port blasts in Beirut on August 4, 2020). In the literary texts and material sites of memory I examine, war remains offer conflicting forms of engagement with the past: between attention and neglect, reality and imagination, aesthetics and politics, remains serve as important portals to an austere and violent past that nevertheless trigger hope through resistance.

South Lebanon's wars, unlike those of prominent Beirut, have been consigned to the margins of memory. I argue that South Lebanon has undergone a triple occlusion: not only historically and structurally owing to the belligerent Israeli occupation and state neglect but also literarily as intellectuals directed their laments toward ruined Beirut, the epicenter of the Civil War, and thus leaving southern voices largely unheard. Despite having resisted Israeli occupation for twenty-two years (from 1978 to 2000), the South has remained strikingly absent from contemporary Lebanese literary-cultural production. The July War of 2006 placed a ruinous yet resilient South back in the public eye, if only fleetingly, for as Bayḍūn intimates in his prose poem, it remained a shadowy presence on the literary scene. Although South Lebanon's chapters of war preceded and were entangled with the Lebanese Civil War, this area, unlike Beirut, has largely been underexplored. Not much work has been conducted on this region, apart from Lucia Volk's *Memorials and Martyrs in Modern Lebanon* (2010),[16] which provides an anthropological study of the politics of memory embedded in three key memorial sites in South Lebanon and their joint interreligious commemorations, and Munira Khayyat's *A Landscape of War: Ecologies of Resistance and Survival in South Lebanon* (2022),[17] which shows how war, a condition dominated by technologies of death, is also a place where life resolutely carries on. Recent scholarship on Lebanon examines the memory culture of the decades following the declared end of the Civil War in 1990, albeit with a Beirut-centered focus. Social scientists and literary critics turn their attention to the ruins of Beirut[18] and, especially, to the celebrated postwar reconstruction of the city's center.[19] Likewise, studies of wartime fiction focus on Lebanon's secular, upper-middle-class writers[20] and tend to privilege urban-centered readings of films,[21] artistic installations,[22] rebuilding projects,[23] and "memory cultures"[24] rather than address the occluded remains of war that continually haunt the edges of the nation-state.

This book turns to what scholarship on Lebanon has largely evaded: how narratives from outside the dominant purview of Beirut draw occluded war remains back into the sphere of public awareness. Each chapter centers on a different set of ruins that have been occluded or denied representation. Occluded war remains take heterogeneous forms in the book and include figures, metaphors, tropes, and material objects. Sometimes they manifest as an invisible trace, a legible mark, a human remainder, or a disquieting presence. These occluded war remains, I argue, have literary and aesthetic afterlives. By questioning the politics and poetics of ruins in relation to experiences of vulnerability and violence, I explore how war remains can be mobilized for change. What roles do literature and culture play in addressing the erasure of traces of past violence and in charting alternative memories for future generations? How can war remains disrupt and counter both public forgetting and dominant forms of remembrance?

To answer these questions, this book teases out a dynamic dialogue among poets, novelists, activists, artists, former detainees, museum architects, and ordinary citizens on the imbrication of ruins, politics, memory, and resistance. In the process, I underscore that the violence wrought by ever-returning cycles of war has left its traces on the material environment and on a corpus of cultural producers and their war-inspired productions. I call this collective of cultural producers and their creative productions "southern counterpublics." Using ruins, they disrupt facile distinctions between politics and poetry, margin and center, memory and oblivion. I show how war remains are central to the aesthetic, literary, and political imaginary of southern counterpublics.

This project has four aims in general: (1) to foreground the aesthetic, literary, and political significance of war remains through my concept of southern counterpublics; (2) to disrupt facile distinctions between margin and center, especially the dominant tendency toward reductionism of the South; (3) to articulate a poetics of resistance outside hegemonic institutions by seeking alternative modalities of memories of past violence that are not tethered to political or national agendas; (4) to trace the continuities and the tensions that southern counterpublics entertain with their classical literary forebears.

Southern Counterpublics

Southern counterpublics constitute a collective of cultural producers and their war-related productions that have emerged from creative practices of reckoning with war remains. This concept allows for seemingly disconnected aspects of the *longue durée* of the Lebanese Civil War to come into active symbiosis and collision with each other. I call this collective "southern counterpublics" to bring out its fertile counterpublic potentialities by thinking through war remains as nodes of creative resistance. I bring together different genres, voices, and practices to emphasize their uniqueness and provide a platform to discuss the tensions that characterize their relationship and resistance to dominant practices of producing and obviating memory in Lebanon. I show how southern counterpublics illuminate the differential power relations and hegemonic exclusions experienced by women, minorities, and southerners, who are largely absent from the archives of public memory, and how they generate an affective attunement to untranslated wartime verses, voices, and experiences.

In an attempt to trouble canonicity and undo facile dichotomies, I include in southern counterpublics the historically neglected Shuʿarāʾ al-Janūb (Poets of the South) ʿAbbās Bayḍūn, Shawqī Bizīʿ (b. 1952), Jawdat Fakhr al-Dīn (b. 1953), Muḥammad ʿAlī Shams al-Dīn (d. 2020), and Ḥasan ʿAbdallāh (b. 1950) alongside prominent Civil War novelists Ilyās Khūrī (b. 1948), Ghādah al-Sammān (b. 1942), and Ḥasan Dāwūd (b. 1950); nonstate public war museums alongside oppositional memoirs of former prisoners; and derelict war relics alongside recognized war remains. By orienting our optics South and by mixing and muddling neglected and acknowledged forms of cultural production, this book challenges the monochromatic conception that cultural resistance is composed of urbane leftist Beiruti writers. Rather, it traces the colorful modalities of memory unbound by state, memorial institution, or dominant center.

Interlacing close reading with long-term research at understudied memorial sites, I show how southern counterpublics transform occluded war remains into a vibrant trope that interrogates issues of marginality and belonging. Southern counterpublics, I argue, do more than represent or depict war remains. They inventory affects, textures, and vulnerabilities of unbelonging by highlighting experiences of forced migration, literary neglect, and the marginalization of women and minorities. Instead of reifying ruins, southern counterpublics address the ruins' capacity to be reappropriated and contested. Each chapter, then, captures resistant practices animated by ruins—practices that have both succeeded and failed to be put in place. I employ the concept of "counterpublics" to illuminate both the breaking points and the creative energies that traverse the works under consideration.

Rather than being a homogenous entity, southern counterpublics resemble what Michael Warner calls "multiple reflexive counterpublics,"[25] a constellation of attempts to resist or chart out alternatives to dominant discourses of silencing. In thinking about southern counterpublics, I extend the contours of Warner's counterpublics "as constituted through a conflictual relation to the dominant public"[26] to include the "South" conceptually in the wider structures of vulnerability that I examine in the book. Southern counterpublics emerge in the recognition of various exclusions of precarious groups from wider publics. In so doing, they offer an alternative platform from which to view the diversity of wartime experiences in Lebanon while sharing a set of commemorative practices, tropes, and motifs.

The counterpoints in this book are arranged to indicate the degree to which the concept of "southern counterpublics" becomes complicated or undermined when dominant discourses enter the picture. I pay particular attention to common cultural forms and the dominant relations that structure them, which requires attention to the ways cultural productions can also be part of hegemonic political projects (see chapters 3 and 4). I turn to southern counterpublics that veer off the manicured museum path to reveal the gaps, fissures, and contradictions inherent in politically motivated modalities of remembrance.

I begin in the literary South with a close reading of the Shuʿarāʾ al-Janūb and of wartime and postwar novels. Part one, "Domestic Detritus," considers the work of poetry and fiction in tarrying over the remains of the wartime concept of "home" through my own translations of Arabic poetry by the Shuʿarāʾ al-Janūb and close readings of three Arabic novels that span from the opening chapter of the Lebanese Civil War in 1975 to the immediate postwar period in 1993. They include the Syrian writer Ghādah al-Sammān's wartime novel *Kawābīs Bayrūt* (*Beirut Nightmares*); the South Lebanese writer Ḥasan Dāwūd's *Bināyat Mātīld* (*The House of Mathilde*); and the Beiruti writer Ilyās Khūrī's postwar novel *Yālū* (*Yalo*). The part title, "Domestic Detritus," alludes to the remains of an allegory of human dwelling, a striving for existence amid the ruins of fracturing social relations. I explore how literary negotiations of the domestic dimension of war lead to the development of a counterpublic conception of unbelonging. In part two, "Resistant Ruins," I take the reader on a visit to the edge of the southern borderland, where two war memorials are located; here I demonstrate that encounters with war remains can provoke competing claims of resistance. Part three, "The People's Right to the Ruin," draws a counterpoint between intended and unintended wartime ruins and their ramifications for mediating public memory and its counterpart, oblivion. In the conclusion, I open up the assemblage of ruins examined in the book to draw parallels with ruins elsewhere in the Global South and to reflect on the interconnections between ruins and global uprisings. On the heels of the massive double explosion in Beirut on August 4, 2020, when 2,750 tons of ammonium nitrate carelessly stored in Beirut's port blew up, I ruminate on the challenges of thinking with ruins in real time in a country still reeling from economic collapse, which itself came on the heels of a planetary pandemic.

My conception of southern counterpublics aligns with Michael Warner's contention that counterpublics are not simply dominated subalterns but "world making discourses with other poetic or textual qualities such as affect and expressivity."[27] In particular, Warner's notion of counterpublics "as poetic world making"[28] aligns with the counterpublic poetics of memory. I show in chapter 1 how an emergent corpus of Shīʿite poets known as Shuʿarāʾ al-Janūb (Poets of the South), frustrated by the silencing of the South, introduced a counterpublic poetics of memory emanating from the occupied South. Part of the larger project of this poetic collective, I argue, is to carve out a unique space of memory in which the South inhabits a central instead of liminal position within the nation's cultural imaginary. In their verses, the counterpublic southern poets transform the occupied South from a muted blank page into one rife with potentialities and alternative futures, expressing a unique metapoesis of memory that resists dominant tropes that have reduced the South and relegated its rich literary production to the margins. Through the poets' rearticulation of the South, a new configuration of memory emerges that makes legible unexamined narratives and experiences of war and occupation stemming from the occluded borderland. In their counterpublic verses, the South emerges not as a backwater battlefield but as a conceptual filter that brings together multiple temporalities, movements, and theoretical intersections. In chapter 2, I show how southern counterpublics open up the possibility of narratives and modes of subjectivity not reducible to the power of the state. The counterpublic novels I examine trace the effects of unbelonging and noncitizenship on precarious subjects and protagonists who embody loss, trauma, and memory of painful pasts by opening up the possibility of imagining alternative relationships between national belonging and home. In chapters 3 and 4, I show how southern counterpublics counter public memory practices and institutions that tout nationalist male-oriented imaginaries. Such possibilities are explored both in feminist historiographies that seek to bring women's private experiences more fully into the purview of history and politics[29] and in diverse forms of scholarship concerned with the experiences of subjects traditionally excluded from historical accounts.

Recent monographs on memory and cultural representation in Lebanon have mapped important terrain for this book. Following on Laleh Khalili's *Heroes and Martyrs of Palestine* (2007), which recounts how Palestinians construct narratives about the past outside the framework of the state,[30] Lucia Volk's *Memorials and Martyrs in Modern Lebanon* is particularly helpful here for thinking beyond sectarian memory politics in South Lebanon to find sustained evidence for cross-community memorial practices after periods of violence by showing how "images, values, or practices can transcend community boundaries and bring people together."[31] Given the relentless ruination that Lebanon has endured over the past century, there is an urgent need for scholarship that reckons with these restive ruins and finds there a generative milieu for resistant thought and practice. In *Standing by the Ruins: Elegiac Humanism in Wartime and Postwar Lebanon* (2011), the literary scholar Ken Seigneurie makes a crucial connection between the ancient-ruins motif in Arabic literature and the trope of "elegiac humanism," which has helped to form "an aesthetic of resistance against a dominant war ethos since the late 1970s.[32] Seigneurie argues that against the backdrop of a dominant aesthetic of ideological and sectarian commitment (*al-adab al-multazim*), a young generation of Lebanese writers and filmmakers began nurturing a contemplative and self-critical ethos that found echoes in popular culture.

My book also draws important insights from Sune Haugbølle's *War and Memory in Lebanon* (2010), which traces the development of the debate about the war by drawing on multiple sources of public culture. Moreover, this book is in conversation with Chad Elias's *Posthumous Images* (2018) and Felix Lang's *The Lebanese Post–Civil War Novel* (2016), which study discursive memory practices across a range of media and cultural production.

Building on these studies, I pay attention to the elisions and biases of certain actors and events from the archive of public memory, especially as they affect minorities' and women's experiences of war. What emerges from my observations is the controlled quality of ruination within the matrix of the museum as distinct from the disorderly resistant ruin in its metaphorical manifestation. The resistant ruin, I contend, charts a new terrain for remembrance, one that cannot be accommodated by a memorial but that must be read on its own terms as a form of affective haunting. I show how southern counterpublics shed light on the intimate qualities and textures of memorial acts outside and beyond the bounds of sectarian affiliation by urging us to think of alternative modes of solidarity and collectivity inspired by the uprisings in Lebanon in 2019. Southern counterpublics cumulatively argue for an acknowledgment of the complexity of memory practices. They do so by foregrounding the role of hegemonic institutions—such as the nation-state, statelike actors, and museums—in the biased representations of certain actors and events and the elision of women's experiences of war from the archive of public memory. As conceptual filter, southern counterpublics encourage us to recognize the powerful potential of creative collectives in an unrelentingly ruinous world. This book, then, follows southern counterpublics as they shore up fragments of their wartime memories and experiences precisely to resist their fracturing worlds.

Through studies of literature and long-term field research at memorial sites, my goal throughout the book is to archive the texture and substance lost to view when studies of memory rely solely on data furnished by "official" narratives and military accounts of war. It is to the so-called margins, then, that we must venture if we are to encounter "only a vague memory or a bare trace . . . visible to those who bothered to look."[33] Indeed, it is only through my encounter with the forgotten nodes of rubble, both textual and material, that I began to grasp the assemblage of ruins described in this book, which have long remained invisible even as they have obviously been in the public eye. As textual ruins entangle with the tangible material forms of debris that I encountered in my fieldwork, I provide a genealogy of the southern borderland as it morphed from periphery to battlefield and interlace that genealogy with my observations of the occupied border starting from 1999.

Unsilencing the South: From Ruination to Resistance

A war-seasoned battlefield, the southern borderland is both bucolic idyll and embattled terrain. A cornucopia of thyme, hawthorn, sage, juniper, buckthorn, olive, and myrtle, this stretch of southern land has awakened and kindled poetic and musical sensibility for many decades. But more than vegetal roots thrive in this pastoral pastiche: the southern border is

1. Minefields fencing off South Lebanon in the forefront from Israel in the background, July 1, 2010. Photograph by the author.

also a subterranean battlefield and base harboring several armed networks, such as Hizbullah (Party of God), the Lebanese Army, the United Nations Interim Force in Lebanon (UNIFIL), the United Nations Truce Supervision Organization (UNTSO), and the Israeli army, to name only a few. The South Lebanon borderland is at once a space riven by recurrent war and bedecked with breathtaking natural beauty, where memories of both violence and conviviality continually pulsate. This seeming contradiction has a complex backstory. Formerly the vibrant region of Jabal 'Āmil,[34] the southern borderland was carved out in 1923 by France and Great Britain, the Great Allied Powers that administered Lebanon and Palestine, respectively, in the wake of the First World War. Present-day Lebanon's southern frontier was formerly the hinterland of Palestine's coastal cities. The arbitrary border divided the predominantly rural hinterland from the affluent coastal cities Acre and Haifa, severing vital historic socioeconomic ties and catalyzing the South's current chapter as remote and impoverished state margin.[35] One account penned a few months before the first Israeli invasion of Lebanon in 1978 illuminates the stark dichotomy between center and periphery: "The South is the poorest area of Lebanon for many reasons: the lack of services and infrastructure, the economic exploitation of its main crop tobacco, and the disinterest, indeed lack of awareness, of the rest of the nation. According to official Lebanese government statistics (1974), the South has about 20 percent of the total population, but it receives less than 0.7 percent of the State budget."[36]

The South has (unwillingly) hosted wars for more than half a century, starting with the Nakba in 1948;[37] Palestinian and Lebanese guerrilla warfare in the 1960s and 1970s;[38] Operation Līṭānī, the first Israeli invasion in April 1978; Operation Peace for Galilee, the second Israeli invasion in June 1982; Operation Accountability in 1993; Operation Grapes of Wrath in 1996; a twenty-two-year grueling Israeli occupation (1978–2000); and, most recently, the July War of 2006. The Israeli occupation exacerbated the disproportionate incorporation of this poor periphery into the increasingly absent modern nation-state and its eventual elision from the purview of public memory with the onslaught of wars. I say "wars" to indicate both the Lebanese Civil War, which officially ended in 1990, and the Israeli occupation of South Lebanon, which overlapped with and outlived the

Civil War. Those temporally overlapping wars are crucial to the texts and sites of memory I examine in the book.

The *sharīṭ al-lubnānī al-muḥtal* (occupied Lebanese border strip) that Israel referred to euphemistically during the occupation as its "security zone" snaked ten to fifteen kilometers along the entire Lebanese side of the border and entrapped around 150 Lebanese towns and villages. Only residents of the occupied zone were begrudgingly permitted to cross the heavily militarized checkpoints manned by the Israeli army and its ally, the South Lebanon Army, a locally recruited proxy militia. The occupation zone was a space rife with surveillance, collaboration, hegemonic militia rule, and illegal detentions, where torture and aggression were endemic in places such as the infamous Khiam Detention Center, which I examine in chapter 3. Lebanese and Palestinian guerilla warfare between the resistance (in its various guises) and the Israeli occupiers and their proxy Lebanese allies continued to flare up until the South's liberation in May 2000, when the occupation finally collapsed. Today, although war has (temporarily) receded, the borderland remains a heavily militarized and precarious place in the penumbra of war.[39] In the words of the South Lebanese novelist Ḥasan Dāwūd, (South) Lebanon "has implicitly accepted a seemingly endless vacillation between war and peace."[40]

Reframing Resistance

Although South Lebanon is most often considered a vortex of destruction, this book argues that it is also a space of unexpected creative resistance forged from the ongoing ruination. Instability on one level breeds resistance on another. The lacunae left neglected by the state bred forms of resistance; the arrested development of state-sponsored projects only accelerated nonstate cultural projects with renewed vigor when war-related violence abated, as I explore in part two. Thus, the Lebanese South is a particularly rich site for exploring varying and vying resistance narratives that emerged from the long Israeli occupation and ongoing conflict between Lebanon and Israel. On the heels of the South's liberation in May 2000 and especially after the July War of 2006, Hizbullah, the Shīʿite militant grassroots organization and Lebanese political party, has unilaterally acquired social, political, economic, and military power in South Lebanon in part through its cultural production. Hizbullah also became a powerful present-day participant in the Lebanese government. Today, the party remains the dominant memorializing power in South Lebanon. It is known in common parlance as al-Muqāwamah (the Resistance), consolidating resistance in its varying iterations.[41]

The Israeli invasion in 1982 and subsequent occupation of Lebanon catalyzed Hizbullah's political and social formation. Hizbullah is the imbrication of multiple Shīʿite mobilizations that began in the 1970s and included several key actors with varying political perspectives, methods, and ideologies. As Lara Deeb aptly explains, "What united [these actors] was an effort to organize Shīʿī Muslims in Lebanon, historically a politically and economically marginalized community, to work toward alleviating poverty and disenfranchisement in their communities. The backdrop for these mobilizations included the Lebanese civil war [*sic*] (1975–1990), the Islamic Revolution in Iran (1979), and most crucially, Israel's two invasions of Lebanon (1978 and 1982) and its continued occupation of South Lebanon until May 2000."[42]

The increasing alienation of Shīʿite villagers gave rise to a movement that rallied around the luminary figure of Mūsa al-Ṣadr, a Shīʿite imam of distant Lebanese descent who emerged in the 1960s. Ṣadr organized his rhetoric around the Shīʿites' historical and ongoing dispossession at the hands of the power-hungry (Sunni) establishment, and their subsequent massacre, suffering and impoverishment, exile, and dispossession. The movement gained traction in tandem with the outbreak of the Lebanese Civil War as the Shīʿites faced increased alienation as a community. Taking over the mantle of the "movement of the dispossessed," Hizbullah led the military resistance against the Israeli occupation in South Lebanon and garnered military, political, and social prominence in the postliberation period. This particular history and war burnished Shīʿite identity and is what Hizbullah has successfully put on ruinous display in Khiam and Mleeta, the two war memorials I examine in part two: one of the party's goals is to target increasingly urbanized youthful constituents who possess no memory of the occupation period.

The historian Augustus Richard Norton has dubbed the period of relative calm between May 25, 2000, and July 12, 2006, the "interregnum."[43] It is during this hiatus that Hizbullah's cultural projects came to fruition and in some cases to destruction. It is important to underscore that although I have long championed and supported Hizbullah's formidable defense and subsequent liberation of the South, I also acknowledge that the party's all-consuming resistance narrative has several strands. My discussion of (resistant) ruins in part two collides with Hizbullah's cultural production because it is my intent in this section to show the "other" side of memory in the South and its many strands of narratives, practices, and poetics that risk occlusion by a singular discourse of memory. To this end, this book provides an alternative site from which to think about resistance or *ṣumūd* (steadfastness). I show how activist-literary-cultural practices of resistance problematize and disrupt the dominance of militarized memorials. In chapters 3 and 4, I draw a counterpoint between what I term "resistance ruins" and "resistant ruins." I equate "resistance ruins" with the heavily politicized war ruin embedded within the memorial practices and politics of institutions and statelike narratives of memory. I trace how the two war memorials located on the southern borderland curate the wreckage of two decades of occupation into a hegemonic narrative expressive of a certain political and cultural project. I argue that the war memorials utilize "resistance ruins" to craft an exclusive culture of memory by overriding other modalities of resistance that repose just beneath the rubble. "Resistant ruins," in contrast, disrupt the politically motivated memorial culture premised on confessional identification. The virtue of the resistant ruin, I emphasize, is in its acknowledgment of memory as constantly in flux rather than being fixed in one form.

As a work that engages and critiques Hizbullah's practices of memory building, this book is in dialogue with Lara Deeb and Mona Harb's *Leisurely Islam: Negotiating Morality and Geography in Shi'i South Beirut* (2013), which examines Hizbullah's creation of an "Islamic milieu" in Lebanon through its cultural productions. Hatim El-Hibri's *Visions of Beirut: The Urban Life of Media Infrastructure* (2021) offers important insights into the politics of visuality and concealment with respect to Hizbullah's cultural production—namely, the Mleeta memorial I explore in part two. Moreover, this book also speaks to Tarek El-Ariss's attunement to the politics of scene making in Arab cultural production in *Trials of Arab Modernity* (2013) and to the essays on the contours of a Shīʿite aesthetic collected in Zeina Halabi's *Unmaking of the Arab Intellectual: Prophecy, Exile, and the Nation*.[44] Relatedly, my specific interest in part two is to explore how Hizbullah's cultivation of resistance memory is galvanized by cultural projects such as Mleeta and Khiam.

Ruins serve as an organizational trope that ties together divergent artistic, literary, and cultural practices. In this sense, the ruin not only resides in ruined buildings, in materiality, but also evokes a more immaterial and resonant space, one of resistance. Throughout my discussion of how the kinds of memories stimulated in "resistant ruins" might be used to critically assess dominant ways of producing and governing memory, I draw on recent work on the theme of life in ruins. Building on Gastón Gordillo's definition of rubble as "textured, affectively charged matter that is intrinsic to all living places,"[45] I consider ruins as a vibrant assemblage of pulsating memories, affects, and perceptions rather than as simply the crumbling aftermath of violence. Thinking through ruins as an assemblage allows for heterogeneous parts of the book—the spectral and tangible—to stay intricately imbricated while remaining independently distinct. Bhakti Shringarpure's *Cold War Assemblages* (2020), specifically her interest in thinking through the postcolony as an extended "Cold War ruin," is useful in this regard. For the scope of my work on the colliding and often contradictory memories of the Lebanese Civil War, I find Shringarpure's understanding of assemblages intriguing because of her interest in connecting them to marginalized histories. The Cold War, she argues, "is an assemblage of the colonial, postcolonial, racial, military, technological, and cultural imaginaries" that "allows multiple vantage points to co-exist and illustrates that we remain in the grip of a tenacious Cold War imaginary."[46] This reference to Shringarpure's work is not meant to conflate the Lebanese Civil War with the Cold War but rather to point to the continuities in thinking through the ruins of the Global South by using an assemblage approach and insisting on the centrality of the war remains charted here, which is essential for excavating heterogeneous and silenced discourses.[47] I draw further insights from Tim Edensor's, Dylan Trigg's, and Yael Navaro-Yashin's work,[48] which attends to affective structures of feeling that emerge through ruin encounters. I also consider Ann Laura Stoler's proposed shift from ruins as inert objects toward processes of ruination that differentially generate the growing piles of "imperial debris" that we are left to contend with.[49] Like Stoler, I view the verb *to ruin, kharaba* in Arabic, as a "vibrantly violent verb,"[50] uniting the disparate texts, events, places, people, and objects I study in this book into a palimpsest of ruin.

Researching Ruins at the Margins of Memory

My first encounter with the southern borderland began twenty-three years ago, when the South was still an occupied place. On February 17, 1999, I traveled to the edge of the "zone" to protest Israel's annexation of Arnūn,[51] a lonely village where only a cluster of elderly villagers continued to live. As I walked up to the scraggly looking barbed wire decorated with forbidding warning signs in Arabic, English, and Hebrew, I tried to fathom how a small strip of earth could affectively and existentially separate me from the remainder of "occupied" Lebanon. One sight has never left me: a 104-year-old man, waiflike, sitting steadfastly in his plastic chair in front of the barbed wire encircling his newly occupied village. When I asked him how he felt on that day, he responded: "Shribit ahiwteh winṣamadit. Naḥnul-ṣāmidūn [I drank my coffee and sat my ground. We are the steadfast]."[52] A few days later I returned to witness throngs of students storm the village and bare-handedly remove what turned out to be flimsy fencing. It was a particularly prescient moment that would be repeated on a much larger scale a little more than a year later when the occupation would finally end. But for the time being, ensconced high up in their occupied ruin, Beaufort Castle,[53] Israeli soldiers incredulously watched the scene of liberation unfolding below. This movement was led by students, but politicians, many of whom had never heard of the village a month earlier, nonetheless flocked to bask in the glow of cameras and deliver bombastic speeches about Arnūn's liberation, embodying how distant, indeed, Beirut was from the occupied South.

My first foray to the edge of the "zone" would remain indelibly etched in the skin of my memory. It was a transformative experience that set me on my path of inquiry as it engendered myriad questions about life lived in this obscured edge of nation. Before Arnūn, my only "contact" with the occupied borderland had been mediated by oral memories, especially in conversations with an interlocutor whose husband was imprisoned in the infamous Khiam Detention Center.[54] My interlocutor would cross the perilous occupied territory to visit her detained husband; a few southerners with special permits (*tasrīh*) were allowed into the borderland following intense interrogation. Gripped by her nightmarish stories about the prison and in search of ways to continue to traverse the occupation zone and penetrate its carceral depths, I sought out a Khiam detainee who had just been released in a prisoner exchange in 1999. This former detainee had been giving Che Guevara's son, Ernesto Guevara, a tour around South Lebanon as part of a campaign to raise awareness of southerners' detainment by the Israeli army. In a private interview, more details emerged about this detainee's life in "the shadows,"[55] filling out the picture of the prison that had transfixed my curiosity.

As I mentioned, the southern borderland is a military zone patrolled by the Lebanese Armed Forces, the Israeli Defense Forces, Hizbullah, the UNIFIL, and the UNTSO. Only Lebanese nationals are allowed in and out of this area without a military pass. Throughout the course of my research on this occupied strip of land, I managed to traverse the borderland not only physically but also literarily through the Poets of the South (Shuʿarāʾ al-Janūb), whose verses powerfully resonated with the South's ruinous rhythms of war. I was struck by the way the ruin stands out as a central metaphor and trope in their verses, a symbol of remembrance and forgetting, a trope for resistance through rumination—a throbbing, violent, and vibrant trope for all that remains of hope despite ruination. I discovered that even though the southern poets had been publishing volumes of poetry since the early 1970s, their publications remained largely untranslated well into the late 1980s, when the cause of the South started hesitantly to grace the printed page. This snub inspired me to take on the task of translating their poetry (see chapter 1). Although these poets were once known as the "Shuʿarāʾ al-Janūb," an umbrella name that denotes significant intersections between them, especially in terms of their leftist sensibilities, they go their own ways with respect to poetic style, as chapter 1 demonstrates. Each poet is distinct beyond the common interest in unsilencing the South through the trope of ruins. The poets, rather, resemble what Michael Warner calls "multiple reflexive counterpublics," which, taken together, compose a constellation of attempts to resist or to chart out alternatives to the silencing of the South. I have chosen to focus on their poetry as it presents a powerful literary response to the experience of the Israeli occupation. By exploring the thematic connections of such a diverse group of poets as well as contemporary Lebanese Arabic novelists and their cultural productions, I hope to disrupt the notion of linear memory and allow the rich assemblage of resistant ruins embedded in each narrative to come to the fore.

It was not until May 25, 2000, liberation day, that I actually set foot in the southern borderland and finally laid eyes on the epistemic and material divide that courses loudly throughout the literary and museal terrains I examine in this book. I entered the infamous Khiam Detention Center, which had just been emptied of its prison guards, leaving only the dazed and euphoric former prisoners. It was an incredibly visceral experience. The fields of rubble left in the wake of the retreating army, the clothing abandoned by fleeing collaborators, and the ruined outposts exuded an overpowering affect that transfixed my senses. Riveted on the rubble that remained in the wake of the Israeli military withdrawal, I began to view the South as an assemblage of ruins, where "multiple temporalities and shifting assemblages of humans and nonhumans" exist, a "polyphonic assemblage"[56] of resistant remains that refract the multiple narratives of destruction and regeneration.

The South is indeed a borderland and a battlefield, but it is also a place of ongoing resistance, replete with disorderly rubble, not easily barricaded in by borders or ideologies. Resistance here, despite the repressive violence, continues to proliferate and reverberate. On that day in late May 2000, I began to comprehend the centrality of the ruin as a medium through which memories and narratives of wartime violence are refracted to compose memory generative of the South's "separate fate."[57] I wanted to search in "interstices not smothered by the bombastic politics at play nor flattened by the conflicting governmentalities in the region"[58] and to grasp how war remains are claimed, crafted, and versified into nodes of resistance as well as how meaning is made, negotiated, and sustained in precarious times. Ruins were central to my observations in the immediate liberation period from May 2000 up until the July War in 2006. In 2005, Prime Minister Rafīq al-Harīrī was assassinated, leading to the withdrawal of Syrian troops from Lebanon after decades of military occupation and then to a "mini civil war" in May 2008. The aftermath of the devastating July War added a new texture of memory to my research as I turned away from the capital and the reconstruction taking place in the Central District and headed to the heartland of ruination and regeneration. The detention center I had visited on its liberation day in 2000 had been reduced to rubble by its creators (see chapter 3), while (re)construction in other parts of the South unfurled. I followed former detainees turned docents, museum curators, poets, writers, activists, artists, and inhabitants of war as they responded to the rising tides of violence in the South and beyond. I followed them as they reckoned with war and its tenacious aftereffects by turning their observations into generative productions.

This book adopts a multilayered approach to thinking through (and resistance to) ruins. Exploring ruins in a multiplicity of places and across literary and material sites of memory requires an equally multitudinous approach. By entwining close readings of Arabic novels, poetry, and memoirs with extensive fieldwork conducted at memorial sites, I draw from several temporal frames, including ethnographic research conducted from 2000 to 2011 and in 2019–20. Pedaling forward, on August 4, 2020, I was based in Beirut as a visiting professor at the American University of Beirut when the Beirut port exploded in one of the largest nonnuclear explosions in global history. This devastation was preceded by the *ḥirāk*, uprisings, a democratic Lebanese response to the financial crisis in 2019, a crisis that continues into the present.

In the many illuminating moments that I experienced during my fieldwork, one thing stands out methodologically: not only was I forced to think about ruins in textual and material terms, but when the materiality of the ruin was deliberately damaged, I was also confronted with the question of its afterlife (see chapter 3). In thinking of the aftermath of violence, I draw from the geographer Caitlin DeSilvey's compelling ecological perspective into ruinous sites and disturbed landscapes, which asks us to respect the unstoppable process of ruination and to embrace its aftermath.[59] I also draw from Robert Ginsberg's contention that ruins have an uncanny afterlife, for, in his words, "what is not there may cast an uncanny reflection on what is there."[60] I ask how ruins might assist or impede the work of commemoration in lieu of the destroyed prison-cum-museum I examine in chapter 3. Do we need to conceive of memorial ruins differently, depending on whether they commemorate natural decay or catastrophe or various types of governmental and military violence? Could the aesthetic of the ruin help us discern where these structures and practices of violence converge? It seems reasonable to approach these questions, the defining questions of the following chapters, historically. Literary ruins are the most enduring trope in classical Western and Arabic literary traditions alike. From the Latin *ubi sunt* (what remains?) motif to the classical Arabic *aṭlāl* (traces) motif, many a wistful poet's tears have been shed over mounds of rubble. An expansive literature has examined Western practices of ruin contemplation,[61] yet scant attention has been paid to the Arab/ic gaze upon ruins. The latter practice is ancient, though rooted in pre-Islamic oracular Arabia, where the ruins of a defunct campsite symbolized, to the ancient bard observing them, the ultimate erosion of time and memory.

Reinventing Classical Ruins in Modern Arabic Literature and Culture

A central axis of the book is its engagement with a pre-Islamic ruin trope known as the *aṭlāl* motif, often translated as "traces" of an abandoned encampment, which prompts the ancient poet to reflect on his departed beloved and to galivant across the desert toward distraction and, ultimately, catharsis. As a literary topos, the act of "standing by the ruins" (*al-wuqūf ʻalā l-aṭlāl*) can be described as a "lyrical symbiosis of love and grief"[62] that goes back to the amatory prologue (*nasīb*) of the pre-Islamic Arabic ode.[63] Jaroslav Stetkevych paints a vivid picture of the ruins motif as featured in the *nasīb* (amatory prelude) of the originary pre-Islamic Arabic *qaṣīdah* (ode):[64] "In the first section of the *qaṣīdah* the poet halts, stands and remembers. The poet's first . . . image . . . is that of the ruinous remains of habitation, which, as *ṭalla*, a word of implicitly archaizing overtones, presents a frame of time of the utmost remoteness, where there is only an evanescence of objects. As such it is coupled with the psychological frame of some great personal loss."[65]

A nomad-poet halts at an abandoned desert campsite and, while sifting the ashes through his fingers, recalls the amorous affairs he once had there. Animal droppings and traces in the sand are imaginatively refigured as abandoned resting places heavily laden with affective powers. Those nonhuman elements are the *ṭulūl* (ruins) that have sparked an engagement with memory. After an elaborate reverie over a lost beloved, the poet's *raḥīl* (journey) commences, involving a dangerous ride through a haunted desert before it ends in the third and final section known as the *fakhr*, or self-praise. The poet embarks upon his journey to alleviate the unbearable weight of yearning in his present life. In the third and final section of the *qaṣīdah*, after the journey has ended, the poem closes with a message of self-assertion and tribal celebration, thereby signifying the poet's reintegration into society. He revives after an emotionally harrowing journey and rides his camel forth into the desert night to seal the wound of memory. This ritualistic standing before ruins engenders forgetfulness in the hopes of renewal. That is, in the oral nomadic culture of pre-Islamic Arabia (Jāhilīya), ruins served as the potentiality of renewal, thereby constituting one of the most enduring and malleable literary devices of Arabic literary history.

I examine how the classical Arabic poetic motif of "standing by the ruins" (*al-wuqūf ʿalā al-aṭlāl*) is reworked into contemporary memorial practices. By turning to the classical-ruins trope as a portal for probing contemporary modalities of resistance, the arguments in each chapter encourage us to think porously of the classical and the modern divide. I view the *aṭlāl* motif as both an afterlife of classical poetics in modern texts and an incarnation of a classical tradition on its own terms. The modalities that premodern poetic tropes and concepts take on in modern texts are both similar to and different from, affectively speaking, the modalities of their premodern counterparts. This discussion disturbs dyads such as classical/modern and traditional/innovative and helps us rethink the relationship between a culture's literary past and its present, especially as that relationship connects to contemporary memorial practices. Rather than resort to stringent binaries, how might we fruitfully incorporate premodern aesthetic thought into contemporary memory poetics?

A growing group of scholars is exploring the nexus between classical Arabic ruins and contemporary memory practices.[66] In *Metapoesis in the Arabic Tradition* (2015), Huda Fakhreddine has highlighted continuities in a metapoetics of modernism between the ʿAbbāsid period and the twentieth century, while critics such as Ken Seigneurie and Hillary Kilpatrick have enabled a metaphorical connection to flow between the *aṭlāl* motif and twentieth-century Arabic prose. In *Conflicted Antiquities* (2007), Elliott Colla observes how the ruins motif converges with nationalist visions in the literary works of Egyptian writers, such as Rifāʿah Rāfiʿ al-Ṭahṭāwī and ʿAlī Mubārak. In *Fictitious Capital* (2017), Elizabeth Holt draws our attention to the significance of the ruins motif for journals published in Beirut in the 1870s, which offered a range of ways of reading the region's ancient ruins. Finally, Tarek El-Ariss's "Return of the Beast" (2016) draws magnificently on the classical Arabic literary tradition to examine the function of cruelty in the exile's transformation and return as an aesthetic device in contemporary theoretical frameworks. My book is conversant with these important studies while attempting to situate the classical-ruins motif as a figure of reflexive resistance in southern Lebanese literary-cultural practices and while considering this figure's ramifications for the Global South. I show how the *aṭlāl* motif lingers as an affective afterlife, or trace, in twentieth- and twenty-first-century Arabic novels, poetry, public sites of memory, and embodied experiences of remembrance, mourning, and rebellion. While partaking of a common and well-established poetic tradition, the southern counterpublics at the center of this book simultaneously break with the past and inaugurate something altogether radically new. My aim is to harness the poetics of ruins at play in Arabic to excavate a narrative of precarity in the present.

Negating Nostalgia in Modern Arabic Ruins

In part one, "Domestic Detritus," I explore the innovative ways in which the *aṭlāl* motif has been reworked into contemporary Arabic prose and poetry by exceeding and even counteracting the classical regard for a nostalgic past. I show how the modern Lebanese wartime poem and novel do not simply adopt the classical wistful gaze upon ruins but, to the contrary, kindle a pathos quite the opposite of nostalgia. If the classical Arabic ruin involves aesthetic reflection and the exquisite melancholy of time passing, here the modern ruin denotes reflexive rebellion. I show how in the wartime poem and novel melancholy morphs into a counterpublic resistance against ruination (*khirāb*), thus turning the classical-ruins motif into warring terrain. In chapter 1, I show how the counterpublic poets suffuse classical ruins with a rebellious pathos by transforming the lexicon of the Arabic ode's amorous opening (*nasīb*)[67] from a site of nostalgic mourning to one rife with rebellious potentialities, which I call "counter*nasībs*." In the wartime novels by Ghādah al-Sammān, Ḥasan Dāwūd, and Ilyās Khūrī, the appropriated classical ruin becomes a device to challenge ruinous discourses of gender, ethnicity, and subalternity that linger during and after wartime. In this regard, Ken Seigneurie's *Standing by the Ruins*, which shows how contemporary novels have repurposed the *aṭlāl* to counter Lebanese wartime sectarian practice, serves as an important reference point. Through their intimate mediations of the impact of violence on the individual's sense of belonging, the three novels I examine in chapter 2—*Beirut Nightmares, The House of Mathilde*, and *Yalo*—develop a unique counterpublic perspective on human survival during times of crisis. All three position marginalized actors not as defenseless participants but rather as active ones in the internecine struggles that encompass a variety of social classes, minorities, and nonnormative gender identities. For example, Ilyās Khūrī's antihero Yālū explains at the beginning of his fictional testimony that he represents an alternative perspective, a counterdiscourse to the testimony heard by the state. Yālū's intervention embodies the hope that power may be reconfigured through love.

Reckoning with Oblivion

By drawing on the *aṭlāl* motif, I show how what was once a crucial device of internalizing loss in classical Arabic poetics becomes in contemporary Lebanese wartime poetry and novels a medium for obliterating memory and reckoning with its remains. The texts and material sites of memory I explore in the book testify in different ways to the power of oblivion. The latter, I show, is both the material and affective erasure of traces of the past from the intellectual and material geographies of the present. I thus turn to memory's understudied counterpart, oblivion, to bring out a nuanced reading of the collapsed wartime home. I posit that the contemporary Arabic novel and poem (re)construct from fictional ruins a deeply unsettling portrait of the fractured domestic domain of wartime and (post)war existence. That is, instead of being reinserted into society, per the closing section of the classical Arabic *qaṣīdah* (ode), which signifies the classical poet's reintegration into society, protagonists in the wartime novel gladly abandon their shackles to the past by embracing forgetfulness (*nisyān*).

I place Marc Augé's notion of "rebeginning," defined as the birth of a new future that can take place only by forgetting what came before,[68] in dialogue with Arabic literature's greatest innovators, the 'Abbāsid poets al-Mutanabbī[69] (d. 965 CE) and Abū Tammām (d. 845 CE). These poets sought to escape conventional strictures that equated ruins with melancholy by reconfiguring the ancient symbolism of the ruin beyond the abandoned dwelling and into the interiority of the fracturing self. I show how ruins in contemporary wartime and postwar Lebanese novels are no longer within the lost *dār*, or house, of classical poetry but veer conceptually closer to the fractious nature of al-Mutanabbī and Abū Tammām's internal ruins and Augé's practice of oblivion.

In parts two and three, I explore the spatiality of oblivion as it manifests through erasure and the reification of certain ruins around one particular moment or actor at the expense of others. This erasure, I argue, can be shaped by spaces of remembrance curated by dominant actors and events. A vast literature has examined how different actors seek to fix memory through selective reification of ruins, but rather than exhaustively examine the wide gamut of war sites in Lebanon, I pay close attention to certain unrecognized remains of war to explore their implications for and limits in mediating public memory. I explore the public disregard of unmarked war relics in South Lebanon and Beirut as a form of "politically evasive turning away."[70] In other words, intentional sites of memory are overtly commemorative, whereas this second category of memory comprises the "unintentional" detritus of war, which silently reminds us of a violent past while quietly receding into the backdrop of everyday life. I compare war relics that have been allowed to "ruinate" as a result of public disregard and memorials that actively direct the public gaze toward ruins displayed as "official" nodes of memory with allegedly more symbolic value than their unmarked counterparts. Here I draw from Adrian Forty's notion that the permanence of an object does not preclude its oblivion. The object's degree of visibility, Forty maintains, depends on the social life of its memory or on the degree of its disregard.[71]

In chapters 3 and 4, I examine how two war memorials (Khiam and Mleeta, respectively) attempt to cast other modalities of resistance into oblivion by turning our attention toward a specifically militant form of resistance memory that is on hegemonic display. I argue that although the two memorials purport to create participatory zones for commemoration, their use of ruins as a memorializing trope reveals gaps in the singular narrative of resistance on display. Chapter 5 places two forgotten war relics in counterpoint to a war museum located in the heart of Beirut to examine their implications for mediating public memory. Chapter 6 turns to recent global uprisings in Lebanon and the Global South, where ruins were again at the center of these insurrections. I pay special attention to the uprisings that erupted simultaneously in Lebanon and Iraq in October 2019 and how the people's reclamation of ruined spaces expresses popular modalities of militating against state-driven corruption. In the conclusion, I return once again to ruminate on a moment of historical destruction set off by the double blasts at the Beirut port on August 4, 2020, and its implications for reckoning with ruins in real time.

Part One

Domestic Detritus

1

Shu'arā' al-Janūb

The Poetics and Politics of South Lebanon's Ruinscapes

In *Zamān al-iḥtilāl* (The Age of Occupation), the Lebanese journalist and author Ilyās Khūrī describes South Lebanon under Israeli occupation (1978–2000) as "the solitary" (*al-waḥīd*) and "the strange" (*al-gharīb*), with its "daily confrontations, isolation, and blocked crossings."[1] Yet, "in spite of it all," Khūrī maintains,

> the South stands on its own and hurtles forward, as if it has already accepted for itself a separate fate. Or as if it has chosen this fate in order to declare a different horizon than these times in which our society is being eaten alive by armed militias. . . . The South is alone and foreign in this Lebanon. . . . Alone, because it faces, on its own, the odds of the present and the future. The rest are drowning in the illusions of the past. . . . The foreignness of the South and its solitude is an extensive summary of our [the rest of Lebanon] foreignness and solitude. . . . The South will not return to Lebanon, for this Lebanon has nothing to offer it.[2]

Turning to the domain of poetry, this chapter centers on how a corpus of South Lebanese poets known as the Shu'arā' al-Janūb—'Abbās Bayḍūn, Shawqī Bizī', Jawdat Fakhr al-Dīn, Muḥammad 'Alī Shams al-Dīn, and Ḥasan 'Abdallāh—crafted a counterpublic poetics by adopting the South as a malleable trope for ruination and silenced memories to draw attention to its "separate fate" from that of the rest of the nation. I show how the Shu'arā' al-Janūb galvanize the South into a dynamic ruinscape in which *arḍ al-Janūb* (the southern earth) stands in for the pre-Islamic *ṭalal*

2. The border between South Lebanon on the left and Israel on the right, 2010. Photograph by the author.

(ruined site), gripping their imagination, and how they conceive of the ruined South as a repository for their personal and collective experiences of occupation. I argue that the Shuʿarāʾ al-Janūb interpolate and refashion the classical Arabic tradition of ruin gazing known as *al-wuqūf ʿalā al-aṭlāl* (standing by or stopping at the ruins) into their laments over Israel's protracted occupation of South Lebanon as well as over their marginalized position within the nation's literary memoryscape.

The Shuʿarāʾ al-Janūb can be seen as southern counterpublics through their creation of a new texture of memory expressive of an understudied swathe of nation that faced occupation and neglect on the literary, national, and humanitarian fronts. In pursuit of a language of memory distinct from Beiruti-centric war narratives, the Shuʿarāʾ al-Janūb suffused the classical Arabic motif of returning to ruins with a critical and political form of witnessing. I examine how this poetic corpus opens up a counterpublic space of memory, challenging public norms of belonging, by bringing into focus important issues such as occupation, state neglect, and literary inattention. In his book *Publics and Counterpublics*, Michael Warner argues: "A counterpublic maintains at some level conscious or not, an awareness of its subordinate status. The cultural horizon against which it marks itself at some level is not just a general or wider public but a dominant one. And the conflict extends not just to conflicts or policy questions but to the speech genres and modes of address that constitute the public or to the hierarchy among the media."[3]

Warner explores the concept of publicness and meditates on modes of publicity without necessarily aligning with subalternity. He emphasizes the agency of culture in forms of art, public speaking, media, and performance and looks at how people can use culture to create a space for themselves in the social world. In other words, Warner does not address the intersection of publics and politics but rather how people express themselves as individuals and groups through participation in alternative subcultures. He claims, however, that the public is not one cohesive entity but instead multiple reflexive counterpublics.

Similarly, I bring together different poetic voices with no intent to homogenize them but rather to emphasize the uniqueness of each voice as it contends with dominant modes of address, which in turn attempt to reduce and undermine southern voices. I argue that the poets addressed here defy the dominant tendency toward silencing southern literary output by offering an alternative platform from which to view the diversity of wartime experiences while sharing a set of differences as well as commonalities. In the poetry of the Shu'arā' al-Janūb, the South has been dominated not only by occupation and state neglect, as I noted in the introduction, but also by a paralyzing silence as lamentations have been directed solely toward the ruined capital city, Beirut. By appropriating a cornucopia of motifs such as landscape, memory, myth, and, most importantly, pre-Islamic ruins into their lamentations over their ruined homeland, the Shu'arā' al-Janūb craft a counterpublic poetics that contends with the dominant tendency to neglect southern ruins. To this end, I inventory the diverse modalities of remembrance and resistance inherent in the poetry of the Shuʿarāʾ al-Janūb. According to Warner, counterpublics entail "risked estrangement" and entry into "spaces of circulation in which it is hoped that the poesis of scene making will be transformative."[4] In the Shuʿarāʾ al-Janūb's articulation of counterpublics, both dominant public space and stigmatized identities undergo transformation. This chapter shows how, following the Israeli invasions of Lebanon in 1978 and 1982, the Shuʿarāʾ al-Janūb began to craft a new "poesis of scene making" that sought to level the literary terrain to include southern voices in their new world-making cultural imaginary through a unique metapoesis of memory. Part of the larger project of this movement of poetry, then, was an attempt to carve out a space of belonging in which the South would inhabit a central instead of liminal position within the nation's cultural memory. I argue that the Shuʿarāʾ al-Janūb counter the South's silencing by transforming the lexicon of the classical Arabic ode's amorous opening (*nasīb*) from a site of nostalgic mourning to one rife with resistant potentialities.

Southern "Acts of Literature"

Critics have already argued that a new space of representation opened up as a result of the Lebanese Civil War, allowing female authors to break into a predominantly male literary sphere.[5] One of the few productive outcomes of the Civil War, according to Sune Haugbølle, was an altered public representation in Lebanon, which made way for other voices to express and represent themselves apart from the *zuʿamāʾ* (traditional political elites) in the political and cultural realm.[6] Less studied, however, are the literature and poetics that emerged from Lebanon's southern borderland, especially from the "security zone" established after Israel's second invasion of Lebanon in 1982, during which South Lebanon existed in a state of exception, all the while reverberating with muted memories. The question of silence occupies and frames the metapoesis of memory in the work of the Shuʿarāʾ al-Janūb. Building on the root of the Arabic word *mašhad*[7] (scene) as derivative of the root *shāhid* (to witness), *arḍ al-Janūb* (the southern earth) becomes the all-consuming *mašhad* in the poetry of the Shuʿarāʾ al-Janūb.

At the start of the Lebanese Civil War, the capital Beirut became the quintessential trope of the ruined nation, while the South, even as battlefront, was relegated to the dark shadows of literary neglect. Poets from around the Arab world gathered to eulogize the Lebanese capital; from Maḥmūd Darwīsh (d. 2008) to the Syrian poet, essayist, and translator Adūnīs[8] (b. 1930), Beirut became a new cipher for Arab tragedy.[9] Among the slew of poets and writers, Nizār Qabbānī (b. 1923) bemoaned Beirut's descent into war with his famous elegy "Bayrūt sitt al-dunyā" (Beirut the Woman of the Universe) in his *dīwān* (collected works) *Ilā Bayrūt al-unthā . . . ma' ḥubbī* (To Beirut, the Woman . . . with My Love, 1981).[10] Adūnīs's collection of sixteen poems on the Israeli invasion of Beirut, *Kitāb al-ḥisār* (Book of the Siege, 1985), viscerally translated the site of destruction into one where

> bombs are mirrored in books
> along with prophecies and ancient wisdom and hidden places.
> Memory is a needle
> It stitches a carpet of words like threads
> Over the face of Beirut.[11]

Novels, plays, and songs began to take stock of Beirut's interminable war years. Although novels such as Ḥasan Dāwūd's *The House of Mathilde*, which I explore in chapter 2, pried open the door to include South Lebanese protagonists, their perceptual filters nonetheless remained oriented toward Beirut, allowing readers only a partial engagement with the South. Tawfīq Yūsuf 'Awwād's prewar novel *Ṭawāḥin Bayrūt* (Death in Beirut, 1972), lauded as a prolegomenon to the violence that tore Lebanon asunder in 1975, offers us a lingering gaze at the conflict brewing in the South as it centers on a southern village girl, Tamīma, while she navigates her way from her fictional village to Beirut, yet it still offers a monochromatic look at the South. 'Awwād's depiction of the South as battlefront displaces previously idealized portrayals of a bucolic life that writers such as Jibrān Khalīl Jibrān (writing from the northern border) were wont to depict. The southern border villages in 'Awwād's novel are reduced to "a nice cozy place—for humiliation and degradation."[12]

Writing from the so-called periphery, the southern poets proposed a radically different re-reading of the southern borderland. As events in the South began heating up, the Shuʿarāʾ al-Janūb would deliberately distance themselves from the dominant idiom of Beirut through an invocation from another side of this dialectic of place: the southern periphery. Although the South Lebanese poets were not, strictly speaking, a "minority," they share with what Gilles Deleuze and Félix Guattari define as a "minor literature" their proposition of literature's revolutionary potential. In Deleuze and Guattari's characterization, minor literature is always political, imbued with a "collective value" and a language "affected by a high co-efficient of deterritorialization." Written from the margins, minor literature deterritorializes the "fragile community from the border to express another possible community and to forge the means for another consciousness and another sensibility."[13] Similarly, the poetry stemming from (and about) the southern borderland finds itself positively charged with the role and function of collective, even revolutionary, enunciation. My understanding of a minor literature in relation to the Poets of the South has some alliances with their role as southern counterpublics insofar as their poetry marks a political temper and critical space of reckoning different from the dominant forms focusing on Beirut. Here, I suggest that the poetic space carved out by this corpus attends to "structures of feeling"[14] at the margins of the state. For example, this poetic space animates and is brought to bear on perspectives directed both outward against occupation and inward toward an internal critique of the state that historically marginalized the Shīʿites of the South and its poetic interlocutors.[15]

The first and second Israeli invasions in 1978 and 1982 brought the plight of the South to print. Voices long eclipsed by the intense focus on the capital city started hesitantly to grace the pages of periodicals, newspapers, and poetry concerned with new "acts of literature"[16] from hitherto unknown interlocutors. The Poets of the South are a case in point: although they had been publishing books since the early 1970s, it was only in the aftermath of the Israeli invasion that their poetry started to gain traction. The year 1979 was a gateway for publicizing the southern poets, some of whom were featured in a special issue of the Lebanese literary-cultural journal *Mawāqif* (Positions). Published by Adūnīs in fits and starts between 1968 and 1994 in Beirut, *Mawāqif* was burnished in the flames of 1967 and became known for its open support of the Palestinian resistance and the New Arab Left.[17] In the foreword to the journal's pilot issue, Adūnīs minced no words about its raison d'être: "*Mawāqif* . . . is an act of permanent confrontation. It overcomes all oppression and authority with a view to scrutinizing Arab history and culture and fundamentally reinvigorating Arab thinking. . . . *Mawāqif* is culture—revolution."[18] Although *Mawāqif* ceased publication briefly with the onset of civil war, it resumed in 1978 with an even more purposeful drive to capture the trials and tribulations of the writer-intellectual confronting violent warfare. As war returned to the South, attention began to pivot toward its literary representatives.

In its relaunch issues in 1979, *Mawāqif* attempted to carve out a place for young and largely unknown poets. On the heels of the overthrow of the Iranian monarchy under Reza Shah Pahlavi by the Shī'ite cleric Ayatollah Ruhollah Khomeini, *Mawāqif* released not one but two important issues (numbers 34 and 35). According to Yvonne Albers, issue 34 "brought together a Shiite poetry movement and a Shiite revolution in one issue. Reading the two movements jointly sheds light on how 1979 affected a decades-spanning inquiry into the question of modernity, the role of literature, and the mandate of the intellectual."[19] What interests me in particular about issue 34 is the young 'Abbās Bayḍūn's introductory article, "Al-Ḥadātha al-ān: Baḥth fi-l-ḥarakāt al-shu'arā' al-shābbān al-lubnāniyīn" (Modernity Now: Research on the Movement of Young Lebanese Poets), which examines the poetics of a contemporary generation of young Shī'ite poets from South Lebanon, among whom are Ḥasan 'Abdallāh, Muḥammad 'Alī Shams al-Dīn, and Shawqī Bizī'. Bayḍūn questions the "role of the Shī'ite southern intellectuals and their increasing influence in Lebanese cultural life that they were hitherto excluded from" during a time when "the problem of the South of Lebanon was introduced forcefully in the recent period." In Bayḍūn's words, his study attempts to "trace the common thread that organizes them [the young southern poets] into a comprehensive phenomenon." The article parses the poetic trends of the "movement of young poets" from southern Lebanon who are agitating for public visibility and a critical reckoning with the very term *southern poetry.*[20] Bayḍūn attempts to de-essentialize the term *southern poetry* not as a return to

إن الشعر الجنوبي ليس عودة إلى الثقافة الزراعية الجنوبية أو لغة الفلاحين، بل
يقوم على خرابها ودمارها وقل إنه نسيانها التامهو بالأحرى[21]

> a southern agricultural idyll or originary peasant language, but rather as that which is based on its very ruination and complete oblivion.

Bayḍūn here alludes to the tobacco planters' strike of 1973, in which thousands of tobacco planters from the South occupied the offices of the Régie co-intéressée libanaise des tabacs et tombacs in Nabatiyeh, a private franchise-holding company since 1935, "which held the exclusive right to export Lebanese-produced tobacco, import cigarettes and produce local cigarettes."[22] The planters' basic demands for a hike in the purchase price of their products was quelled by intense army fire. Bayḍūn angrily quips, "The state is a claim to unify society, or an illusion of unification, but it is based on playing on the lines of separation and their intersection."[23]

Bayḍūn's article in *Mawāqif* testifies that the Shīʿites, once the most marginalized of Lebanese sects, had finally entered the literary scene of the 1980s. *Shaʿbī* (of the people) musicians such as Marcel Khalīfeh and Fayrūz serenaded the South in mellifluous verse. Take, for example, Khalīfeh's rendition of the South Lebanese poet Ḥasan ʿAbdallāh's poem "Ajmal al umahāt" (The Most Beautiful of Mothers) into a song conveying a mother's interminable anticipation of the return of her murdered son, killed during the occupation, and the urgency of continual resistance. Much has already been written about the popular playwright and critic Ziyād al-Raḥbānī's satirical plays,[24] but noteworthy is his play exposing the emergence of the South in popular culture. *Shī fāshil* (A Failure, 1983) depicts a "typical" folkloric setting replete with villagers, a *mukhtār* (mayor), and young women swathed in traditional attire. The oblivious villagers enjoy a brief period of tranquility before disaster manifests in the form of a missing jug, implying foreign intervention. The play's driving conceit is summarized in the line "Oh South, Oh South . . . Oh wound of the little (no, big) nation. Oh, you who stand alone in the middle of the heart."

"We're in 1983 for God's sake," rants one of the characters. "Why do you still place overused words after *layālī* [nights]? Have you ever thought of using *mallāli* [troop carrier] instead?"[25] Once again, the conceit of a South that stands alone marks this play's satirical pulse.

Literary journals began publishing numerous pieces on the devastating effects of the Israeli invasion, compiled mostly in *Al-Muqāwamah fī al-ta'bīr al-adabī* (Resistance in Literary Expression, 1985),[26] a collection of writings published by the Cultural Council of South Lebanon[27] to mark the third anniversary of the creation of the Lebanese National Resistance Front.[28] Included in *Al-Muqāwamah,* Adūnīs's article "Janūb al-kitābah: 'Arāyis al rūḥ wa-'arāyis al-jasad'" (South of the Writing: Brides of the Soul and Brides of the Body) rebuts accusations of "Shī'ī terrorism" by drawing attention to the "slaughtered villages of the South."[29] *Al-Muqāwamah*'s introduction, however, offers a simplistic picture of resistance by positing a seamless continuity between creative writing and national resistance, as exemplified by the introductory statement written by the council chair, Ḥabīb Ṣādiq, in which he claims that "each successful work of art is also a resistance operation."[30] This statement arguably suppresses the robust shades of the contributors' poetic and affective engagement with occupation, which draws relationships between far more than art and resistance. Although the book featured most of the Poets of the South, which indeed helped shed light on their work, it also steeped their poetics in nationalist overtones, thus eclipsing their critical poetic nuances.

Al-Muqāwamah was not the only forum for the expression of "literary resistance"; other journals entertained similar resistant "acts of literature,"[31] such as the Lebanese Majallat *al-Ādāb* (Literary Journal),[32] which devoted a special issue in 1983 to the Israeli invasion and occupation of South Lebanon.[33] Known to embrace politically dissenting voices, *Al-Ādāb* famously inaugurated its first issue in 1952 with a treatise on literary commitment (*al-adab al-multazim*), stating that "in order that literature may be truthful it is essential that it should not be isolated from the society in which it exists. . . . The kind of literature which this Review calls for and encourages is the literature of commitment [*iltizām*], which issues from Arab society and pours back into it."[34] I do not suggest that one should classify the poetry of the Shu'arā' al-Janūb as *shi'ir waqi'ī* (realistic poetry) or as *adab al-multazim*,[35] for it occupies a murky space between these two movements that neither anticipates a peaceful future devoid of war nor provides a realistic documentation of the scale of war in the South. In fact, the radical reduction of resistance to *iltizām* prompted the Shu'arā' al-Janūb to imbue the meaning of "resistance" with a critical edge. The politics of memory embedded in their poetry complicates the rather flat picture of "resistance literature" offered by *Al-Muqāwamah fī al-ta'bīr al-adabī* and *Al-Ādāb*. Rather, the Shu'arā' al-Janūb's poetics of memory resonates more with Adūnīs's apt hope that "perhaps what is happening in the South can serve as a wake-up call and generate new meanings and a new kind of discourse."[36]

While the Poets of the South critiqued occupation in their poetry, they also wrote polemical ripostes to the state. Ḥasan 'Abdallāh, one of the key members of the Poets of the South, is a case in point. 'Abdallāh published an article titled "Al-Tasalul ilal-waṭan al-asīr" (Infiltration into the Captive Homeland) for the leftist Lebanese Arabic newspaper *As-Safīr* on June 12, 1993.[37] Written in epistolary form, the article points to "the failure of the state to reach out to its own embattled citizens in the occupied territories."[38] The following excerpt from the article testifies to 'Abdallāh's view of the South's forgotten status in relation to the capital:

> في بيروت تحولت المنطقة المحتلة، في الخطاب السياسي الرسمي وما "ينفجر" من خطابات وبيانات ومطولات أخرى الى مجرد رقم "٤٢٥" فهنا في هذه العاصمة لم تعد الذاكرة تعمل إلا عندما تنفجر المعارك في الجنوب ويتساقط "القتلى وتهدم المنازل . . . وهكذا تحولت المنطقة المحتلة الى "خبر أمني تتناقله الالسن والصحف والاجتماعات السياسية.
> وكما يقول أحد الصامدون في المنطقة المحتلة فإن "بيروت" . . . بعيدة عنّا"،
> وكما يقول نواب "متخلية ومتجهلة"
> هنا، وعلى حلقات تنشر " السفي هذا الملف الوثيقة لعله ينفع في تنشيط الذاكرة وفي الاستعداد لاستعادة هذا الجزء المنسي من الوطن وأهله.[39]

> To Beirut, the occupied area in the official political discourse . . . has become a mere resolution "425." Here in this capital, memory only works when the fighting in the south "explodes," and the dead fall, and houses are destroyed. And this is how the occupied territory becomes "security news" transmitted by tongues and newspapers and political meetings.

> As one of the steadfast citizens in the occupied area says, "Beirut . . . is far from us," and . . . ministers say it [the occupied area] is "abandoned and ignorant."
>
> Here, in the episodes published by *As-Safīr*, this document file may be useful to activate memory and to restore this forgotten part of the homeland and its people.

'Abdallāh highlights the precarity of the South and how it always already emerges in counterpoint to Beirut as a rural warzone that "ignites the interests and passion of the capital in sporadic fits . . . when the fighting in the South explodes."[40] It is precisely this kind of exclusionary discourse that reduced the South to a place of distant war, which the southern poets ardently militated against in their poetry.

Negating Nostalgia: Crafting *Arḍ al-Janūb* as Counter*nasīb*

If we agree with Ralph Waldo Emerson (1803–82) that "landscape has no owner except the poet who can integrate its parts,"[41] then a study of the "parts" that the Shu'arā' al-Janūb integrate into their poetic landscapes reveal a world far from the pastoral idylls of the classical *qaṣīdah* and from the *locus amoenus* (place of delight) of the romantic imaginary. An examination of their poetry reveals a panorama of the ruinous southern landscape, contestation and struggle indelibly inscribed on it, and at the same time introduces the reader to a unique form of resistance born out of a poetic encounter with ruins.

Through the act of contemplating the ruined southern landscape, the Shu'arā' al-Janūb critique forced migration owing to Israeli occupation and, crucially, to neglect by the state. Standing before ruined southern villages, cities, and absent loved ones, the poets craft a sense of loss predicated on a reworking of the classical Arabic *qaṣīdat al-aṭlāl* (ruins poetry) motif but turn the motif into something quite other than its original role as a nostalgic marker. A common theme underpinning this poetry is its configuration of the ruined southern landscape as both a reconstruction of a personal sense of belonging and a poetics of the communal that is topographically and politically *janūbī* (southern). The once verdant geography of the southern landscape before occupation perforated it—the rolling land, the lush tobacco fields, and the vegetation—figure into the poetry of ʻAbbās Bayḍūn, Jawdat Fakhr al-Dīn, Shawqī Bizīʻ, Muḥammad ʻAlī Shams al-Dīn, and Ḥasan ʻAbdallāh.

Through a reworking of the classical Arabic *aṭlāl* motif, the poets highlight the precarity of the South by locating it on an edge oscillating between silence and resilience. How to fully grasp the commemorative poetics of the *aṭlāl*? In pre-Islamic poetry, the *aṭlāl* scene suggests at once permanence and ephemerality, destruction and renewal. For example, what is noteworthy in the pre-Islamic poet Imru' al-Qays's (c. 550 CE) *muʻallaqah*[42] is that at the outset the ancient bard paints a picture of opposing forces of oblivion and remembrance. Having returned to the deserted encampment where he and his beloved used to tryst, the poet reminisces about their love in a landscape where nature has not fully reasserted itself, turning the location into a half-ruin. The blurring or erasure of memory's outlines in the *aṭlāl* motif is what provokes the poet's riposte, which consists of both a visceral recollection of sexual conquests and a chivalrous account of love. Loss and reminiscence are planted in the nomadic poet's seasonal migrations, yet one cannot help wondering whether the *aṭlāl* motif does not also express a larger, more complex vision of memory and its inevitable erasure.

Standing before the ruins of modern warfare, the Poets of the South project a similar set of polarized countermemories. In their poetry, the appropriated *aṭlāl* serves as the memory trace of liminal moments suspended between gain and loss, displacement and return. It is precisely in this cadence of the modern *aṭlāl* that the Poets of the South position the occupied South. It follows, then, that the *aṭlāl* motif should perhaps be read not only in terms of personal loss but as a kind of communal memory text, a reminder of the ever-present dangers of diminishment, fragmentation, and dissolution. By directing their gaze beyond the bucolic repose of the South to its ruinous underbelly, the southern poets would agree with Mitch Rose and John Wylie that "the cogency of landscape lies exactly in the creative tensions it threads between apparent irreconcilables. Central to this [are] the tensions of presence/absence, and of performing, creating and perceiving presence. The nature of presence (as a horizon, a marking, a dwelling, a construction), and the issue of how presence and absence emerge and entwine (produced, embodied, perceived, affected), is [*sic*] the problem of landscape."[43]

This merging of presence and absence is an especially poignant trope in the poetry of 'Abbās Bayḍūn,[44] which is inextricably tied to the poetics and politics of the poet's hometown, Ṣūr (Tyre), a South Lebanese port town, as it is occupied by Israel and promptly forgotten by the Lebanese state.

'Abbās Bayḍūn's Poetics of Ruinscapes

'Abbās Bayḍūn's poetry bespeaks a commitment to politics reflected in his involvement in the Lebanese communist movement, which landed him in prison twice: first in 1968 for agitating against the Lebanese army on the heels of its inaction following Israel's commando operation at Beirut Airport that resulted in the burning of an entire civilian airliner fleet and then in 1982, when he was detained in an Israeli prison, where he composed his meditations on the Civil War that he eventually titled *Al-Waqt bi-jur'ātin kabīrah* (Time in Big Mouthfuls). Shortly after his release from prison, he completed his epic poem "Ṣūr," which marked a new phase in his poetic development: an experimentation with the Arabic prose poem. In "Ṣūr," Bayḍūn eulogizes the southern port city Tyre as a commemorative ruinscape that interrogates issues pertaining to the memory of the South as it was simultaneously eclipsed not only by occupation but also by state neglect.

Bayḍūn depicts the prose poem as a sovereign space where protest can thrive by enabling imagery to ebb and flow according to the tide and wont of the poet's imagination. In his article "Al-Shi'ir lam yabda'" (The Poem Has Not Started Yet, 2013), Bayḍūn extends Deleuze's notion of "becoming minor" to the prose poem, which he insists "was born a minority of a minority"[45] through its "antipoetic"[46] challenge to prosody, the strictures of rhythm and categorization common to classical Arabic poetry. Bayḍūn even likens the prose poem to a "hermaphrodite" through its resistance to categorization and democratization of expression. In fact, he claims he began to "wrestle with language" at the start of the war:

> With the start of the war, I stopped writing because I had a huge problem with the practice of writing. The war made the entire intellectual and political project that I had meaningless. It disappeared. . . . I had imagined that one could speak in the name of something, history, that one could possess a whole, complete sense of time and of the place one lived, and this declamatory, songlike, celebratory language we used to use; with the war, all of that became meaningless. The world was reduced to rubble, fragments, and torn pieces. The community crumbled to pieces. And the place that was Lebanon also crumbled, in the abstract and in the material sense: you could no longer move around the country. It seemed that any idea of Lebanese history had been a delusion. One could no longer venture a language that went beyond small and intimate things. It was no longer possible to talk about the world other than through a new form of poetics.[47]

What initially began as a rhapsody about the sea when Bayḍūn started writing it in 1974, his tripartite poem "Ṣūr" eventually took on the colors of the political climate in which it was finally published. The Israeli invasion in 1982 and occupation of the poet's hometown transformed the tone, tempo, and language of the poem to reflect the stripping down of language that Bayḍūn alludes to in "Al-Shiʻir lam yabda'." The occupation of Tyre added a belated tumultuousness to the epic poem, which begins serenely with a bountiful description of the port city of the poet's childhood, titled "The Sea," then gives a description of a much-transformed occupied city in the second movement, "Ṣūr," and focuses on its final release in "Exodus," the third movement of the tripartite poem.

"Ṣūr" bears witness to a new form of poetics in its incorporation of traditional Arabic frames of contemplating ruins within a modernist idiom crafted out of a lexicon of war. "Ṣūr" opens with a deluge of natural imagery in the first section, "The Sea."[48] Although the poem mimics the *qaṣīdah*'s tripartite structure, its unique admixture of prose and free verse disturbs the *qaṣīdah*'s melodic flow, reflecting the stripping down of language that war imposed on the poet's sensibility. In this poem, Bayḍūn merely gestures to the classical tradition of contemplating ruins before completely refashioning its poesis of scene making to mimic that of a contemporary war-ravaged city. If the language of the classical *nasīb* "is the language of what is tangible, the language of things,"[49] the language of this new prose *nasīb* is macabre and surreal. Whereas Bayḍūn's prewar poetry embraced ornate diction, as reflected in the first half of "Ṣūr," which he began writing before the occupation of his hometown, the latter half of the poem evokes the sea change to his new stylistic sensibility after occupation.

The opening section, "The Sea," recalls a childhood awash with the bounties of the sea, from which "the city raised its head." The sea nourishes its people with "sun, salt, and live fish" and a thirst for knowledge that results with the learning of "new words and thoughts every day":

من انا حتى أدلكم على الأحجار التي ولدنا عليها كالسحالي،
حين كانت المدينة ترفع رأسها من البحر. تغذينا بالشمس والملح، وأكلنا على
الراحات اسماكاً حية. وكانت المياه تناولنا من على صخورنا ونحن نتعلم الكلمات
والأفكار كل يوم. كنا رمليين حين اوينا الى الشطوط وتركنا أنفسنا لغسالي الرمل
فحفونا بالزبد الذي اختمر في نسيم الليل، وخرجنا من بيوضنا تحت موجة.[50]

Who am I, to guide you, to show you the stones upon which we were born like reptiles, at the moment when the city raised its head from the sea? She fed us with sun and salt, and in the palm of our hands we ate live fish. The waters lifted us above the stone, while we learned new words and thoughts every day. We were covered with sand when we took refuge on the shores. We abandoned ourselves to sand-washing, which surrounded us with foam, matured by the nocturnal breeze; and under a wave we came out of our shells.

In this verse, the wistful persona depicts an intoxicating reverie of fonder days spent imbibing the fruits of the sea before it "brings the conquerors."[51] The opening lines of "The Sea" also elaborate with poetic efflorescence the grandeur of the port city's natural splendor:

مرت علينا ليلة في مجرى العبير البحري، وليلة في ناحية السرو واكواز الصنوبر تحت
اوراق الزعفران حيث تمتد مراعي البحر، ثم شربنا من دم كبد الفجر ودم قلب
الليل، فاعتكرت اعيننا ونحن في نقيع الماء الاخضر، وخرجنا نلمع من بيضة فصح
البحر وفضة الاسماك، ثم نجم علينا الرمل، وترقرقت جلودنا كأوراق الذهب[52]

We spent one night, immersed in a stream of sea perfumes, and another night near cypresses and pines, under the foliage of the saffron trees, where the prairies of the sea stretch. Then we drank from the blood of the liver of dawn and the heart of the night, our eyes were foggy, while we were under the green waters. We came out, sparkling, from the sea and the silver fish. The sand gleamed on us; our skin glistened like golden leaves.

Still using the florid lyrical diction of the *nasīb* to describe the nurturing qualities of the city's seascape, Bayḍūn composes a picture of a natural idyll infused with the scent of cypress trees, saffron leaves, pinecones, and love:

تمددنا على أحجار طويلة كالأخشاب ملفوفين بالأشرعة، في حجر حاضن نمنا متعانقين وتعلمنا الحب، وعلى طبق صواني جاءنا الحظ وتناولنا فاكهتنا القليلة،[53]

We stretched ourselves on stones as long as the wood, wrapped in sails. Among the welcoming stones, we embraced and learned love; on a plateau of clay, luck came to us, and we ate its humble fruits.

But this idyllic picture is quickly perforated as the war tide literally swells in the second section, "Ṣūr," displacing the sea's loamy underbelly with blackened sands, knowledge with ignorance, language with muteness, dreams with nightmares. A previously nurturing sea becomes a harbinger of war and death:

تتمرمر مياهه في الليل . . . ولا يبقى منه بعد ان يغطس سوى صرير بحريي يملأ الرحب . . . اذ ذلك تجف اسرتنا وتجف نفوسنا كالسواحل. . . . . . تبقى المدينة بلا أحضان وتتقوس عظامها المغبرة، بينما تصطلك مباينها الداخلية كبيوت الخلد، ويرتفع الهواء عن الغرف.[54]

The waters of the sea are tormented in the night, and the wood is torn, the sea slips, and a serpent under the hearths and the stone. The sea rises around our houses and streams our clothes; it remains, after it has plunged into its abyss, only a creaking sea, filling the horizon. Our beds and our souls then dry up like the shores. . . . And the city remains deprived of its lap; its dusty bones curl up while the frames of the houses stagger like molehills and the air emerges from the rooms.

In this verse, there is a tonal shift in descriptive words: "sparkling," "love," "embrace," "stretch," and "immerse" become "tormented," "torn," "abyss," and "deprive" as the poetic "I" is reoriented to the first-person plural. In the third (closing) section, "Exodus," stones are welcoming in one moment and then serpentine the next:

بين الحجر والماء ترقرقنا كفولاذ متبلور . . .
وكنا نرى دائماً أحلامنا التي لا ننكرها تقتل
ونبكي على الضفاف
بقلب حجر حقيقي[55]

Between rocks and water, we flow like molten iron. . . . And we always saw our dreams, which we cannot disregard, assassinated.
And we weep on the shores with the heart of true stone.

The new "we" is engulfed by the sea, even emerging "like molten iron" and taking on its fluvial movements. Rather than on the *qaṣīdah*'s deserted campsite, the new "we" weeps on the banks of Ṣūr's seashore, while the city, now ruined, stands in for the lost idyll of the pre-Islamic ode. Although nostalgia for the ruined city is kindled in the first movement of the poem, its presence in the second is as ephemeral as the *aṭlāl* that stirred this pathos.

In the second movement of the tripartite poem, titled "Ṣūr," nostalgia is evacuated and replaced by a war-ravaged present and the impossibility of ever returning to the opening section's southern idyll. A sense of panic takes over the poetic persona as soldiers overrun the city's once bustling markets, while the learned, the imams, and the leaders are quite literally occupied:

يمر عليك الجنود الفارون من نوافذك
يطلقون على الناس في الأسواق
هكذا من علماؤك وقضاتك ورؤساؤك
تحت السلاح

بينما فقراؤك يثقبون الأسماك الميتة
بحثاً عن ملح المائدة

أنت صور التي سقطت
من جيب التاريخ
كيف تبقين على الرمال
كالعلبة الضائعة
من يدفعك ثانية الى البحر
من يحمل شجرة الى شوارعك المسقوفة[56]

Soldiers fleeing your windows pass you by,
Firing on people in the markets
Thusly from your learned, your judges, and your leaders
Under arms
While your poor dig the dead fish
In search of table salt

You are Tyre that fell
From the pocket of history
how do you remain on the sand?
like a lost box
who will push you back to the sea?
who carries a tree to your roofed streets?

In this elegiac prelude, the poetic voice addresses the "lost box" of a city that "fell / From the pocket of history" instead of the lost beloved as the locus of memory. The rhetorical questions at the end of the stanza intimate a sense of loss predicated on a loss of memory, begging the questions: Who will mourn the lost city? Who can find the lost box buried in the sand? Instead of a recounting of memories of fonder days, as in the first section, a counter*nasīb* of the city in the throes of occupation ensues:

هكذا كنا في أسواقك نرقص بين الطلقات
نمشي وعيوننا في الأرض
كأنها تبحث من زر ضائع ورأس إبرة
هكذا بتنا بقلوب خصبة

ووجوه كالنعال
نخشى أن نبتعد فيك
الى الحدّ الذي تصل إليه جوفان الليل
تنكر أصوات البرق والريح والمطر
لنتعلم كل يوم
لهجة سرطان البحر
المتعفن في المياه[57]

We scurried in your markets amid a sea of crazed bullets,
Walked with eyes transfixed to the ground
As if searching for a lost button and a needle head
And so it went—
We ended up with eunuchs' hearts
Faces numb as the soles of shoes
Fear of heading where the night's rats go
We denied the sound of your thunder and rain
And were doomed to learn each day
The language of the crabs
that fester in the sea.

The background of war in this verse recedes behind the occupied "we" in the domain of absolute alterity, even outside the realm of the human, whereby the "we" are doomed to "learn the language of the crabs that fester in the sea." Consigning the human to the domain of creaturely life can be read as their reduction to those who have the right neither to speak nor to remain silent—those who, in Hannah Arendt's famous words, do not have "the right to have rights."[58] The place of language here, then, is the site of the inhuman. Reflecting Bayḍūn's "stripping down of language" with the onset of civil war, his diction focuses on fleeting moments that separate life from death: the men scurrying in the markets with "eyes transfixed to the ground," stripped of humanity even further by being likened to crabs. The nervous energy and movement emanating from this verse are in stark juxtaposition to the lackadaisical lovers pictured in the opening section. Soon, the "language of love" is exchanged for "the language of crabs / that fester in the sea" as incomprehensibility overtakes the city in the latter half of the poem.

A description of the frozen ruins of time follows the war scene:

تبقى الأواني على الرفوف، والساعات الكبيرة معلقة على الجدران، المطابخ
على نيرانها[59]

Pots remain on the shelves, large clocks hang on the walls, stews on the fire.

Rather than evoking nostalgia, this homely picture warps into a hastily evacuated scene of abandonment: the once resplendent city becomes a haggard mother. In this second wave[60] of the poem, the city metamorphoses into a space rife with blood, fear, gunpowder, and invading rats:

رأسك بين كفتيك وأكتافك تنحني
ولن تستطيع النسوة المنتظرات تحت الأدراج
وفي الغرف العالية
قدوم الأبناء والأزواج المتخلفين في الحانات
لن تستطيع الكلاب الجائعة
ولا أرضك التي تلغي بالفئران
أن تمنع طرقك من السقوط في الخنادق
ودورات المياه[61]

Your head is between the palms of your hands and your shoulders are hunched
Neither will the women waiting beneath the staircase
And in the upper rooms enable
The return of their sons and their spouses lingering in the taverns
Nor the hungry dogs
Nor your land overrun with rats
Can prevent your paths from getting bogged down in pits and puddles
Or getting lost in the undergrowth

The use of the word *lost* signals the voided memory of the city as it falls from "the pocket of history" into oblivion. Thereafter, as the poem's persona reflects on the ruins of the city, s/he is no longer weighed down by a burdensome longing for a lost past but is preoccupied with an alienating present. The poem further departs from the classical Arabic ode in its evocation of nature. In *The Mute Immortals Speak*, Suzanne Stetkevych explains how the pre-Islamic poet Labīd ibn Rabī'a (c. 560–661 CE) raises the issue of the culture/nature dialectic, arguing that "essential to this dialectic is the ephemeral and transitory quality of all that is cultural or cultivated—that is, human—as opposed to the permanence and perpetuity of the natural."[62] The desolation of the campsite in Labīd's poetry evokes a brief yet intoxicating countermemory of earthly paradises carpeted by exquisite flowers during the short spring. In the following scene set forth in a series of vignettes of plenitude, the return of an Edenic idyll is contrasted with the barren traces of ruin:

عَفَتِ الديارُ مَحَلُّها فَمُقامُها
بِمَنىً تَأَبَّدَ غَولُها فَرِجامُها
فَمَدافِعُ الرَيّانِ عُرِّيَ رَسمُها
خَلَقاً كَما ضَمِنَ الوُحِيَّ سِلامُها
دِمَنٌ تَجَرَّمَ بَعدَ عَهدِ أَنيسِها
حِجَجٌ خَلَونَ حَلالُها وَحَرامُها
رُزِقَت مَرابيعَ النُجومِ وَصابَها
وَدقُ الرَواعِدِ جَودُها فَرِهامُها
مِن كُلِّ سارِيَةٍ وَغادٍ مُدجِنٍ
وَعَشِيَّةٍ مُتَجاوِبٍ إِرزامُها
فَعَلا فُروعُ الأَيهُقانِ وَأَطفَلَت
بِالجَهلَتَينِ ظِباؤُها وَنَعامُها
وَالعَينُ ساكِنَةٌ عَلى أَطلائِها[63]

Effaced are the abodes,
brief encampments and long settled ones;
At Minā the wilderness has claimed Mount Ghawl and Mount Rijām
And the torrent channels of Wādī Rayyān

Their grounds are now dung-darkened patches
over which, since they were peopled,
Years have elapsed, the profane and sacred months
all passed away
They were watered by the rain

the spring stars bring:
Upon them rained the thunderclouds,
downpour and drizzle
And every night-faring cloud,
each early morning horizon-darkener,
And evening cloud
with resounding rumble
The ayhuqan thrust up its shoots and
on the two sides of the valley
Gazelles and ostriches
have borne their young.
Wide-eyed oryx cows, newly-calved,
stand above their newborns, motionless,
While on the plain the yearlings,
in clusters, caper[64]

In Bayḍūn's reworking of the trope, however, the natural world has completely morphed with the onslaught of war, which has ripped through the repose of the opening scene, exposing the nightmarish undercurrent that floods the port city thereafter. The sea spits out petrified fish from its stagnant waters, while people subsist off its dead offerings, rats overrun the markets, and migrating birds redirect their course in fear of the city's billowing clouds. "No ample stars," laments the poetic voice, "no glistening moon hung from your firmament," while the sea brings the conquerors:

كنت جزيرة وحصناً
وخاناً للمسافرين
لا يتسع نهارك للبناء
ولا يكفي ليلك للأحلام
لم تكن نجومك كبيرة
ولا قمرك لامعاً
لذا كان بحارتك يسقطون على السلالم
وجنودك يجفون في الأبراج[65]

You were an island and a rampart
An inn for travelers
Your day does not accommodate construction

And your nights are not enough for dreams
No ample stars
No glistening moon hung from your firmament
Your sailors were falling on the staircase
And your soldiers are dying in the towers[66]

Occupied Ṣūr's disconnection from the rest of the nation transforms it from "an island and a rampart / an inn for travelers" into an uninviting space "at the edge of the world."

لن يكلمك أحد فمن يحدس أنك تتكلمين
وسط نسمتك المتعثرة
وسط مصابيح السيارات المسلطة على حدودك
من يحدس ان حرفاً أصغر من جناح ذبابة
ينزل مغبراً بالبارود
وسط الرصاص الذي يدرز نوافذك
ويصمت في الدم الذي يلطخ الأبواب
من يحدس ان فمك الذي ضاع في جوفك
كخاتم في بئر
ينطق في عاصفة رعدية
وموجة ترفع السواحل
لم يكلمك أحد
ولن تتبدل مياهك بعد الآن
ستكونين في طرف العالم
وسيرجع الجميع قبلك
الحدائق التي ترافق البحر
لن تجرؤ على اقتحام أحجارك السود
والطيور المهاجرة تخشى أن تعتقل
في غيومك المدخنة
سحابة أزهار الليمون التي تصحب المسافرين
ستهبط على تخومك القريبة
ولن يصل المسافرون
ولن تتبدل سماؤك[67]

No one will address you because who can guess that you speak
In the middle of your hesitant breeze
In the middle of the lighthouses of cars imposing on your borders

Who can guess that a letter, as miniscule as a fly wing
Goes down with the bullet powder
Which rains upon your gates?
Who can guess that your mouth, buried in your heart
Like a ring in a well
Speaks through a storm of thunder
and a wave that raises the shore?
No one will talk to you
Your waters will no longer change
You will be at the edge of the world
And all will return before you
Gardens, companions of the sea
Will not dare penetrate your black stones
Migratory birds fear the prison of your billowing clouds
The cloud of orange blossoms that accompanies travelers
Will collapse on your nearby border
And the voyagers will not arrive
And your sky will not change

A sense of overwhelming stagnation emanates from these two verses. Soon enough, Tyre becomes an "island" disconnected from the rest of Lebanon. These verses express the poem's more poignantly politicized references to the eclipsing of the South by occupation. As the poetic voice decries,

No one will address you because who can guess that you speak
. . .
Who can guess that your mouth, buried in your heart
Like a ring in a well
Speaks through a storm of thunder?

Hereafter, the city that had once taught its people new words and thoughts loses its tongue, literally and metaphorically, as a paralyzing muteness takes over in tandem with its collapse into ruin.

يا صور، حين نزلنا اليك انتزعت من حناجرنا الوتر الفلاحي، وهنا نحن
بالكلمات اتي تعلمناه منك لا نستطيع ان نصفك.

لا نصفك لأنك ما زلت تبحثين في جلدك عن فمك المندل
ولأنك تنطقين بزفير ساخن
على وجوه مخاطبيك القليلين
لأنك بلا صوت تحكين يابستك ورملك
وتلقين بلا تحية يدك على شمال البحر
هذا هو جسدك يضيع ولا مصباح على جلدك يقرع فوق طرقك الهاربة
ستتآكلين وستتجمع حجارتك كل عام بعد ان تهبط اوتادك ستصبح لك كل
عام جثة حجرية
ستقعين عند البحر
بينما تلمع مطابخك من بعيد
كلن النوافذ التي تفتح في رمتك لا تدعو المتنزهين ولا التلاميذ[68]

Tyre, when we came to you, you pulled the peasant fiber out of our larynx, and now with the words we learned from you, we cannot describe you.
We cannot describe you, for you are still looking in your skin for your sealed mouth
And because you exhale a warm breath
On the face of your few interlocutors
Because you are mute, you scratch your hard earth and your sand and your hand falls, without greeting, on the north of the sea.
Behold, your body is fading and there is no torch on your skin that would illuminate your fugitive paths
You will be eroded, and your stones will accumulate over the years, as your pillars collapse, each year there will be a corpse of stone for you
You will sink into the sea
While your ovens will shine in the distance
But the windows that open in the middle of your ruins invite neither the stroller nor the schoolboy.

Occupied Tyre is metonymic of South Lebanon, and its silencing throughout the rest of the poem mimics its shrouded existence as it recedes into the margins of memory, becoming "a fading body without a torch to illuminate it" as its "corpses of stone"[69] "sink into the sea." The word *mute* signals a form of discursive violence, be it censorship, trauma, neglect, discrimination, or even forgetting. Thereafter, Bayḍūn creates a feeling of muteness whereby silence interrupts the noise of the reading process, creating breaks and pauses in the movement of the poem and descriptive language. We now enter a zone of muteness in which we continue to be engaged with the poem even though we are no longer inhabiting a strictly verbal universe. We enter a poetic world where memory is muted like the blank spaces and stripped-down language of the prose poem that stands in stark contradistinction to its lyrical opening:

هل تهمسين بكلمة . . . هل تحطمت فمك صدفة؟[70]

Do you whisper a word . . . Has a shell broken over your mouth?

This silence becomes embodied in the text, forcing poet and reader to confront it within themselves even as they confront words muted on a page. The muteness of the text as an asemantic space or a site of speechlessness is a critique of the violence of silencing. Muteness signifies a privation, which is brought to the fore when the poetic voice becomes spectral, emanating from the corpse of the fallen city's "putrid carcass":

نحن الذين نتكلم من جثتك
نفتح نوافذنا من رمتك المتخصرة
نرى الدماء تنزل من العصي
والسكاكين
وورق العب
لكن نبقى الى ان يصل التيار
الى ان يلامس قلبك

لا نفارقك كأمر البحر
ولا طيور اليابسة
فنحن لسنا شيئاً سوى قناطرك
وصخورك واسماكك
وانت مركبتنا ندفعك للجبل والبحر
لكن نسقط تحت عجلاتك
في نهاية اليوم[71]

We who speak from your corpse
We open our windows in your putrid carcass

We see the blood flowing from the windows,
knives
And game cards
To remain until the arrival of the flow
Until he touches your heart
Do not give up like the princes of the sea

Or the birds of the earth
Because we are nothing but your gateways
Your stones
And your fish
You are our cart
That we push toward the mountain and toward the sea
But we fall under your wheels
At the end of the day

In place of the poetic "I," "we" once again becomes the preferred pronoun of use. The poet and literary critic Adūnīs argues that the *nasīb* also depends on a transition from the personal to the collective sphere of commemoration. In his description of the *mu'allaqah* of Imru' al-Qays, he writes: "Imru' al-Qays announces his presence by talking of an absence—i.e., through weeping-memory. And the weeping happens upon a stage where he asks his friends to share in his sorrow. And while the poem ostensibly evokes only two people, it embraces all who empathize with the poet in his experience and all who have experienced something similar."[72]

As Adūnīs suggests, the classical tradition of interpolating the poet's companions is a gesture of transition from private memory to a collective one. In Bayḍūn's poem "Ṣūr," personal memory is shared both with a textual other and by extension with a greater audience when the poetic voice implores the city to "not give up like the princes of the sea / Or the birds of the earth / Because we are nothing but your gateways" and "you are our cart."[73]

"Ṣūr" ends as it begins: in the ruins of the present. In a final flourish of resistance, the poetic persona places the city in opposition to its ruins:

ولن تموتي
ستحلقين أيتها الأم على جسورك
ستحلقين
بينما تهبط جسورك الى الأودية[74]

You will not die.
You will fly oh mother upon your bridges.
You will fly.
Meanwhile your bridges fall into the valleys

If, in contemplating Ṣūr's ruinscape, Bayḍūn seemingly ends his poem with a promising discourse of resurrection in which the ruined city literally "flies,"[75] the next lines reverse course once again. The temporal marker "meanwhile" denotes resistance to destruction: the city's futile but heroic uprising. The ambivalences and shifts of this discourse draw attention to that which is not quite spoken but nevertheless haunts the poem. The city, even in its destruction, is not entirely effaced, for although there is "not much to see" because there are no "people," no "city and nation" to revive it,[76] the city persists, but in a spectral way, for "ruins," as Jay Winter writes, "attract words, even when the stones are silent."[77]

Memory in Bayḍūn's poem functions like the palimpsestic traces of the natural world in the classical poet Labīd's poem; it is as ineffaceable as the ruins of Labīd's Rayyān riverbed, which is renewed time and again despite the floods, revivifying a past that remains insistently present. In line 8 of his *mu'allaqah*, Labīd draws an analogy between *aṭlāl* and writing, fixing in place the traces of a past where natural forces have not succeeded in effacing it: "The floods uncovered the ruins as if they were writings whose texts their pens renew."[78] As Suzanne Stetkevych aptly notes, "The passage of time and ravages of nature have only rendered the message all the more permanent."[79] Bayḍūn similarly reinscribes a difference within the forms of destruction consuming the city. The only thing that remains in the final and third section of the poem, "Exodus," is the mark of memory, writing as inscription and, in the case of "Ṣūr," writing as commemorative practice. Bayḍūn literally ends his tripartite poem with words strewn on the ground as a memory trace.

كان البحر مزيّحا بزوايا شموس مكسورة، بزوايا رجال لم تتحطم
كان الرجال مزيّحين بالكلام
كان الكلام باقيا على الأرض الكبيرة كمدينة معظمة
كان البحر، كان الرجال، كان الكلام[80]

The sea was streaked with broken suns and whole men
The men were striated by the word
The word rose upon the great earth, a glorious city
The sea was, the men were, the words were.

Yet, unlike the weeping Jāhilī predecessors, the modern poetic voice in Bayḍūn's poem concludes the lament for the fallen city without cathartic resolution, thus departing from the ethos of committed literature (*adab al-multazim*).[81] The ruins topos has opened up an alternative space of resistance that posits ruins neither as transformative agents of positive change nor as disenchantment. Resistance is situated in an in-between space whereby mourning without resolution is the new ethos that resonates from this modern poetic appropriation of the *aṭlāl* motif.

Rural Ruinscapes: Jawdat Fakhr al-Dīn's Alternate *Aṭlāl*

Jawdat Fakhr al-Dīn was born in 1953 in a small village in South Lebanon and has published more than ten collections of poetry, yet recognition of him came belatedly, as it did for Bayḍūn, when Fakhr al-Dīn was finally awarded the prestigious Sheikh Zayd Book Award in 2014.[82] As in Bayḍūn's case, the occupation of South Lebanon influenced Fakhr al-Dīn's early poetic output. His poem "Ayyām fī qaryatī-al-mahjūrah" (Days in My Deserted Village, 1979) traces an unknown narrator's return to a once intensely familiar space, but the sense of effacement and alienation is palpable through the space's transformed topography; abandoned schoolyards, village squares, and prayer places—all evince life in a southern village at the edge of nation, memory, and history. In the aftermath of one of the first waves of mass exodus from the South following the first Israeli invasion in 1978, the poetic persona's act of return to the freshly abandoned *diyār* (dwellings) of a fictitious southern village is beset by desolation and abandonment. As Bayḍūn does in his poem "Ṣūr," Fakhr al-Dīn makes a great effort to displace tranquil images of the South. The poem proceeds to paint an elaborate picture of the besieged village square, where there is nothing "save the cold remains of empty shadows"[83] as silence, once again, becomes a source of tension with which the poetic persona must learn to contend. The futurity of the poem is thus oriented to the addressee's reply, which inevitably entails a return to memory and loss. Written one year after South Lebanon's occupation, the poem turns to a painful realization: "I forget that I am the only one who hears me"[84] comes the resounding echo we previously encountered in Bayḍūn's poem as the besieged port city lost its tongue and no interlocutors remained to bear witness.

Fakhr al-Dīn's poem then moves into the past and records a series of accusations, betrayals, and painful scenes. It also expresses the unfinished grief that accompanies them. In this way, the poem becomes an archive in which traces of pain are materialized and recorded. The only living entity in the poem is the lone visitor, puncturing the desolation of time and space. In the absence of other human interlocutors, the occupied southern villagescape takes on a mythic presence:

خاسئة كنباحٍ مخنوق، تلتفُّ بأسمالِ شتاءٍ بالٍ،
ونتوء بحشرجَةِ الصخرِ المتهالك، هذي القريةُ تذوي،
تتآكلُ، لا يسمعُ وقعَ هزائمها أَحدٌ
أرَقٌ مَنْسِيٌ، تتماثلُ للموتِ، فينقرها مطرٌ مشبوٌه، إنْ هي إلا
تستلقي خائرةً، وتئنُّ
أنا بعضٌ مما تتوهمُ،
آتيها،
فتهزُلي العطْفَ مَهيضاً،
آتيها منتراً كغبار الذكرى.[85]

Strangled like a stifled bark, shrouded in drenched clothing
A bump in the shabby rock, the village withers,
It erodes, nobody hears the impact of her defeats,
For she is but forgotten insomnia akin to death, a suspicious rain goads
her fields
She lies down and groans

I am that which she desires
I approach her
Compassion fuels me again
I approach her as a hunter like the dust of memory.

Drawing on nature, the poem invokes rain, but it is neither the rain of Qur'ānic retribution, "sā'a maṭaru al-mundharīn"[86] (woe to the rain of the warned), nor the baptismal closing storm of Imru' al-Qays's *mu'allaqah*. Instead, rain pummels the southern village, robbing it of sustenance and prolonging its suffering. The silenced South is likened to "forgotten insomnia akin to death" as it writhes and groans, with only the lone unknown interlocutor as "her" sole witness.[87] The writhing, withering village, battered by the elements and left to fend for itself amid its ruins, is the first image that greets the visitor gingerly entering the village turf. Nevertheless, "compassion fuels" the visitor, who slowly approaches. Memory begins to unfold like tapestry as the poetic voice encounters various other ruins; from former dilapidated dwellings and abandoned village squares to forlorn trees, these points of memory offer the persona little in the way of solace. The interlocutor's bodily estrangement and affective distancing from the village are made palpable as, confession-like, "I approach her as a hunter like the dust of memory."

By contemplating these remnants of ruination, or what Yael Navaro-Yashin refers to as "the material remains or artifacts of destruction and violation, but also . . . the subjectivities and residual affects that linger, like a hangover, in the aftermath of war or violence,"[88] the poet sutures a dark narrative of occupation into the act of bearing witness.

And so the poetic and the political become intimately intertwined. As in "Ṣūr," human and nonhuman ruins bleed into one in "Days in My Deserted Village," creating a filial bond that binds landscape to human memory. As the narrator enters his abandoned *dār* (dwelling), he espies a flickering lantern and wonders at its ability to sustain its luminosity in the absence of human inhabitants. After approaching the curiously lit lantern, the poet feels as though it is about to whisper its secrets, which it eventually does. The poem then unfurls into a series of days mimicking the structure of a personal diary, but rather than belonging to a person, the diary belongs to the southern earth. If the landscape could speak, it would bewail the forced evacuation of its inhabitants and especially the abandoned schoolyard that once teemed with vibrant youth:

في مدرسةٍ — كالثكلى —
ما زالت تتوجس أبناء لها
تختطفهم من بعض قرانا . . .
يحتملون فروض الخوف،
ويجنون علامات الغربة[89]

At school—as usual—
Her sons are still apprehensive
They are abducted from some villages . . .
They endure assignments of fear,
And earn grades of alienation

Fakhr al-Dīn's poem closes with an image of the lone village returnee sitting in his abandoned *dār* as he ruminates on the silence slowly caving in on him. His reverie has ended, and he is left alone to wonder "if anybody else is around to eavesdrop on the night."[90] Although the poetic persona has performed an act of return to his occupied village, he does not feel he has returned and likens his presence to a "hollow echo that bounces back off its source."[91] After the persona's failed effort to connect corporeal presence with affective and emotional return, he resorts to contemplating the very act of return via poetry.

Because the abandoned *manāzil*, houses, offer the wistful returnee no solace in Fakhr al-Dīn's "Days in My Deserted Village," the poet conjures up an alternate homeland out of a play on the *bayt*, or house, of the *qaṣīdah*, even as its real referent is being torn asunder. In a later poem by Fakhr al-Dīn, "Al-Qaṣīdah nafsuha" (The Qaṣīdah Itself), published in 1985, South Lebanon is displaced onto a poetic terrain, where it is continuously constructed and reconstructed out of the remains of language. Invoking the *qaṣīdah* as poetic refuge, the poet writes:

نعود الى القصيدة نفسها
(كتبت علينا)
نستحم بنارها
نطل من أبياتها المتشابهات
كأنها بنيت ملاجئ كي تقينا وهج أنفسنا[92]

We return to the *qaṣīdah* itself
It was written on us
We bathe in its fire
We look out from its similar verses
As if they were shelters to protect us from the illumination of ourselves.

The exiled voice in Fakhr al-Dīn's poem seeks in these verses refuge from his own feelings of estrangement, "as if they were shelters to protect us from the illumination of ourselves." Indeed, Fakhr al-Dīn personalizes and adapts the spirit of the poem to the conditions of his own life, one of forced migration. We might venture that he translates the formal classical tradition of ruin gazing into an informal private confession, using language that eschews solipsism and self-reflection. The result is an intimate self-inventory of his own living and dwelling space. Take, for example, a verse in which Fakhr al-Dīn performs a double return, both temporal and figurative:

نعود الى القصيدة نفسها
بطل على فراغ ليس يملؤه سواه
. . .
يأتي الجنوب كما اتى من قبل جندياً وحيداً
حربه الحرب الوحيدة
حوله خطب قد اختفت حديثاً
وانتصارات هوت في الأسر
يأتي وحده متماوجاً في أسره
. . .
بدم القصيدة نفسها
يأتي الجنوب كما أتى من قبل مفتوناً وحيداً
. . .

نفيسها القصيدة من الجنوب يأتي
. . .
نعود الى القصيدة نفسها
ونبقى مثلها، غرباء
نرجع كلما رجعت
ونفنى في هواها كلما غابت
ونبقى مثلها، شهداء[93]

We return to the poem itself
We write it day by day in the South
. . .
The South approaches as before, a lone soldier
His war is a solitary war
Around him speeches have recently disappeared
The victories plunged into captivity
He comes alone fidgeting in its siege
. . .
With the blood of the *qaṣīdah* itself
The South emerges as it has before, enchanted and solitary
. . .
The South emerges from the *qaṣīdah* itself
. . .
We return to the *qaṣīdah* itself
And we remain like it, strangers
We return whenever it returns
And we perish in its passion each time it perishes
And we remain like it, martyrs

The first return is to the classical *qaṣīdah*, and the second is to the act of writing as a form of bearing witness and in the process a form of resistance to the effacement of memory.

Jawdat Fakhr al-Dīn, rather than leveling his criticism at an external "other," wages his criticism at Beirut for ignoring the plight of the southerners, who are reduced to "hostile bodies" and forced into a sort of eternal Nietzschean migration. His poem "Iḥḏarū mawtanā fī al-janūb" (Beware of Our Death in the South, 1982) deplores the prejudices of "the Beirutis who fear our village customs" and who perceive the southern refugees as "*kharā'ib* [ruins] approaching the city gate."[94] The poetic persona weeps for the human ruins, decrying the absence of Arab support:

انظروا باتجاه الجنوب،
ترَوْا زمناً مستميتاً تسلّل من دمنا
في الجنوب تقول الحرائقُ:
أين سيتجه الزمن العربيّ؟
أو الزمن الحجريّ؟ . . .
نواصل هجرتنا كل يوم
الجهات عدائية، والدّروبُ
غير أنّا نعاكس كلّ الجهات وكلّ الدروب،
وإذ نتشرّد نحو المدينة تنأى بناياتها
تتساءل في سرّها:
من يحاصرُني في السكون؟
من القادمون الى جهة البحر مثل الخراب؟[95]

Look in the direction of the South
You will see a desperate time infiltrate our blood
In the South say the fires:
Where will the Arab Age go?
Or the Stone Age? . . .
We continue to migrate everyday
Hostile bodies, and routes
We do not reflect all sides and all routes
As we move toward the city, its buildings are distanced
She wonders secretly
Who surrounds me in silence?
Who come to the seaside like ruins?

Fakhr al-Dīn redirects our gaze to the negligent capital that ignores the wounded southerners, who are forced from village to capital in their attempt to flee the violence in southern Lebanon, only to be questioned and cordoned off at the capital's gates. The southerners' unwelcome migration to Beirut becomes another form of internal exile, where the capital's "buildings are distanced," and the fleeing southerners are met by "hostile bodies." Recollection, here, becomes a textual imposition on an otherwise blank page.

Resistant Ruins in the Poetry of Shawqī Bizī'

In *The Space of Literature* (1983), Maurice Blanchot speaks of an "essential solitude" that accompanies writing. This solitude is not the solitude supposedly necessary for creative composition. Instead, it is the shadow of infinite thought that encloses the writer. It is also the writer's permanent estrangement from thought once it has been transfigured as words on a page. The writer's solitude adheres to the work, demanding that "whoever reads it enter into an affirmation of the work's solitude, just as he who writes it belongs to the risk of this solitude."[96] Similarly, in the poem "Al-Shā'ir" (The Poet), published in 1995, Shawqī Bizī' performs a sort of auto-exegesis on his own work of bearing witness and writing in solitude during the occupation of South Lebanon: "The poet always follows an elusive arrow and a river whose source is unknown" only to "obscure meaning with every intention to clarify."[97]

Whereas Bayḍūn's and Fakhr al-Dīn's poetry situates itself in the interstice between resistance and contemplation, the poetry of Shawqī Bizī' bespeaks a more forthright language by galvanizing ruins into a defiant poetics of resistance. Yet his poem "Al-'Ā'id" (He Who Returns), in spite of its hopeful title, centers on yet another play on the duality of the meaning "to return": the impossible return of the war dead and the impossible return to an idyllic village life before occupation. On a metapoetic level, like Fakhr al-Dīn, Bizī' is in fact performing his own return to the classical poetic heritage. In the first instance of "return," the poet imbricates *aṭlāl* motifs with Shī'ite commemorative practices. The poem's dedicatory preface, "In Memory of 'Alī Bizī', Friend and Martyr," already establishes its poetic tone as a lamentation over human remains and the remains of memory. Ruins once again figure as an important medium for the excavation of memory and its dialectal relationship to absence. The dismemberment of the poetic identity in "Al-'Ā'id" is reconstructed in ties of solidarity with the ruined land:

يمشي جنوبيون خلف النعش
كوفياتهم مصبوغة بجبينه المثلوم . . .
تتبعهم يدا امرأة . . .

هو الجنوبي الشهيد،
مروض القمح العنيد
يعود نحو الأرض
ملفوفاً بكيس الرمل والعلم الممزق[98]

The southerners walk behind the coffin
Their kaffiyehs stained by his split forehead . . .
A woman's hands follow them . . .
He is the southern martyr
. . .
The tamer of wild wheat
He returns to the earth,
Sheathed in a sandbag and torn flag

Through funereal scenes of southerners weeping for the memory of Karbala before the waters of the Līṭānī River as they follow in somber step behind a fallen "martyr's" coffin, Bizī' conveys a sense of loss tempered by a strong call for retribution. He even ascribes a spectral voice to his martyred persona, who chastises his/her fellow southerners for delaying their own martyrdom. The poem ends with the spectral voice of 'Alī announcing the need to continue to resist occupation:

لماذا تسقطون
وتتركون دمي وحيداً كي يجف كوردة
من سنتين لم تبصركم عيناي
. . .
فلسوف تنهض من عظامك سكة
وتشق هذا الانهيار بنصلها الأجمل
وتقاوم المحتل
وتقاوم المحتل
بيروت، آذار- أيار 1984[99]

Why do you give up?
Why do you leave my blood to wither like a rose in summer?
. . .
For two years, my eyes have not viewed you
A road will emerge from your bones

To carve a path with a beautiful spear
And to resist the occupier
And to resist the occupier.
Beirut, May 1984

The poem ends by circling back to its opening scene, the southerners' funereal march. The spectral voice at the poem's end evokes a visceral "path" to resistance carved out of human "bones" that quite literally emerge from the South's blood-drenched soil.

Ruins, Silence, Love: Ḥasan 'Abdallāh

The question of silence, which has thus far framed the cartography of remembrance in the poetics of the southern poets, resonates the loudest in Ḥasan 'Abdallāh's (b. 1945) poetic corpus. He, too, completed his higher education in Beirut, where he taught at one of the city's secondary schools, a decisive shift in his life that put him in contact with the intellectual circles of *Shi'r* (Poetry) magazine (1957–70) and with European prose and poetry, though he remained under the influence of the Iraqi poet Badr Shākib al-Sayyāb. His first collection, *Adhkuru annanī aḥbabtu* (I Remember That I Loved), published in 1972, aligns with the modernist movement of poetry in Lebanon through its innovative use of imagery and free-flowing poetic structures but also revives classical signposts, such as ruin reminiscence. Like the other poets of the Shu'arā' al-Janūb, Ḥasan 'Abdallāh, who hails from the southern village of Khiam (which is central to chapter 3), wrote passionately in defense of the rights of the downtrodden southerners and other minority groups living in Lebanon. Marcel Khalīfeh selected and popularized into song two of 'Abdallāh's early poems—"Ajmal al umahāt" (The Most Beautiful of Mothers) and "Min ayna adkhulu al-watan?" (Where Do I Enter the Homeland?)—from his collection *Adhkuru annanī aḥbabtu*.

Written in 1972, Ḥasan 'Abdallāh's poem "Where Do I Enter the Homeland?" critiques the place of home from the perspective of displaced southerners seeking refuge in Beirut as home is torn asunder, which leads the poetic voice to decry "this city [that] does not see me," for "she denies me and I deny her, I am the ghost of ruins," while "I carry my apologies and papers and go."[100] The poem continues:

قصيدة "من أين أدخل الوطن" (لحنها وغناها أيضاً مارسيل خليفة)
بين الخرائب والحرائق نحوها
هذه المدينة لا تراني
انها تهوي على صدري ويخنقها دخاني
ثم لا تدري ولا أدري
اصواتاً تبيع وتشتري موتاً
من اين ادخل؟
تنكرني وأنكرها انا شبح الخرائب
أقرأ واجهات تعرض الاصدقاء
اصواتاً تبيع وتشتري موتاً
. . .
من اين ادخل في الوطن؟
أتيت ممتلئتاً دخان
ودخلت في بيروت
من بوابة النار الوحيدة شاهراً حبي
ففرَّ الحاجز الرمليّ
وانقشعت تضاريس الوطن
— من أين أدخل في الوطن؟
— من بابه. من شرفة الفقراء
أحمل اعتذاراتي وأوراقي وأذهب[101]

Among the ruins and the fires unleashed on it
This city does not see me
As it falls on my chest and my smoke stifles it
Then I do not know and she does not know
The sounds that transact death
Where do I enter?
This Beirut is half-asleep
The other half writhes under blood
She denies me and I deny her, I am the ghost of ruins
Voices sell and buy death
Winds slumbering beneath rain
. . .
Where do I enter the homeland?

Where do I enter the homeland?
I came full of smoke
And I entered Beirut
From the forlorn fire gate bewailing my love
The sandy border dispersed,
And the terrain of the homeland dissipated
Where do I enter the homeland?
—From its door. From the balcony of the poor
I carry my apologies and papers
And go.

The poem ends with a hollow rhetorical question, "Where do I enter the homeland? . . . From the balcony of the poor," an implicit attack against the homogenizing discourse that often brands the South as "poor" and "primitive." Unlike Bizī', who issues a call to arms, 'Abdallāh continues to advocate love as resistance to occupation in another poem, titled "Adhkuru annanī aḥbabtu" (I Remember That I Loved), nurturing images of "stroking with words the place of longing" and "loving until I became love."[102] In this poem, the poetic persona proclaims "in silence, everything happens,"[103] evoking Maurice Blanchot's observation in *The Writing of the Disaster* (1995) that "to be silent is still to speak."[104] For Blanchot, the risk of solitude is not the separation of the writer from the other but of the self from the self. Like Bayḍūn's poetic voice decrying the city's muteness in "Ṣūr," 'Abdallāh laments the silencing of Ṣaydā, a port town in South Lebanon, in "Adhkuru annanī aḥbabtu":

لا يسمعونَ
لأنهم
يسمعون لا
وأنتِ صمتٌ واقفٌ
وأنا دويٌّ قادمٌ
لا نلتقي
إلا لينبُتَ بيننا شجرُ الجُنونْ.[105]

They do not hear
Because
They do not listen

And you are an erect silence
I am approaching thunder
We meet only for the trees of madness to sprout between us.

Silence emerges as a contending force rather than a defeated one as the poem develops into an elegy for the fallen city coupled with an amorous conclusion:

وإني: لا اراك . . .
لا أرى إلا انهياراتي امام عناق الممنوع
. . .
هل تسمعين صدى احتراقي في الكتابة؟
. . .
لا تسمعي هذا الكلام اللغة المحال لأقول شيئاً لا يقالْ
. . .
لا نمشي معاً في الصمت بين قصيدة الرعب يصدع حيث لا صيدا ولا إلقاء
. . .
أين انت؟؟
هل كنت لاهيةً وقلب عالقٌ في الخوف؟
ان الجند يقتحمون أيامي بلا تعب،
رأيت على بنادقهم يماماً ميّتاً
وصنوبريات من حنين دمي مكان واضح
. . .
سترتدي صيدا وتأتي
لتلمني من بين اعقاب القصائد والسجائر
والنفايات القديمة والجديدة . . .
تأتي دائماً لتبحث أغنيةً على صمت المكان[106]

And I: do not see you
I see only my continuous collapse in the face of your forbidden
entrance
. . .
Do you hear within the echo of my flames as I am writing?
Do not hear these words because this is the impossible language for
the saying of the unsayable
. . .
We do not walk together in silence between one poem and another

Terror gives tongue where there is neither Ṣaydā nor any meeting with you
. . .
Where are you??
Had you forgotten while my heart was suspended in fear?
The soldiers invade my windows without let-up, I saw dead doves on their rifles, I saw like pines my blood yearning for a clear place
. . .
How is it that my martyred body did not sprout a garden higher than the bullets and ignominious helmets?
. . .
She comes I say
She will wear Ṣaydā and come
To pick me up from the shreds of poems and cigarette butts, old and new rubbish . . .
Fatima, who is a neighbor to the destruction of the spirit, always comes to scatter a song over the silence of the place.

Martyrdom, held in such high regard by Shawqī Bizī', becomes the subject of skepticism in 'Abdallāh's verse, where he questions, "How is it that my martyred body did not sprout a garden higher than the bullets and ignominious helmets?" 'Abdallāh instead highlights the precarious lives of southerners in their state of "endless migration" because of Beirut's "forbidden entrance."

Ruins, Tradition, Dialogue: Muḥammad 'Alī Shams al-Dīn

Muḥammad 'Alī Shams al-Dīn's corpus complicates the chorus of southern voices that funneled their critique of the nation through the trope of the ruin. The persona of Muḥammad 'Alī Shams al-Dīn's poem "Fatiha lil-nār fī kharā'ib al-jasad" (Open Fire in the Ruins of the Body) inhabits the guise of the ancient poet-king Imru' al-Qays, thus resonating with Jawdat Fakhr al-Dīn's and Ḥasan 'Abdallāh's growing disenchantment with the lack of state support for the South in the face of the ongoing war(s) waged there. Instead of engaging in a contemporary dialogue with the state, Shams al-Dīn's poetry takes us back to the pre-Islamic era of sixth-century Arabia. In his verses, the modern persona of the doomed poet-king is made to wander a spectral landscape punctuated by signposts of modern occupation; checkpoints, curfews, and blocked crossings evince a landscape of war reminiscent of South Lebanon. As Suzanne Stetkevych explains, in the classical Arabic poetic tradition narratives were woven around and about famous poems and poets (*akhbār*), and the extant narratives about Imru' al-Qays bespeak a tragic figure. Imru' al-Qays's father, the last king of the Kinda tribe, was murdered by the Banu Asad tribe, and Imru' al-Qays vowed to avenge his father and repossess the kingdom. He is said to have wandered the Arabian Peninsula in vain, seeking refuge and assistance from various tribal lords and brigands—hence, his sobriquet "al-Malik al-Ḍalīl" (the Vagabond, Wandering King). In the end, he was compelled to seek the aid of the Byzantine emperor Justinian in Constantinople. Accompanied by another poet, 'Amr b. Qamī'ah (d. 538), Imru' al-Qays traveled to court, where he was lavished with royal treatment. On his return from Constantinople, however, he received a letter from Emperor Justinian (527–565 CE), along with an embroidered robe laced with gold and poison. After he donned the robe, the poison seeped into his skin, killing him—hence, his other sobriquet, "Dhū al Qurūḥ" (the One with the Wounds). According to Suzanne Stetkevych, Imru' al-Qays's search for his lost kingdom, after being let down by his people and his supposed allies, left the ill-fated poet "politically naked and defenseless."[107] This sentiment and predicament are similar to those of the persona in Shams al-Dīn's poem "Open Fire in the Ruins of the Body."

Wandering the tortured landscape of South Lebanon, where dead fish fill the sea and nature is made to writhe and plead for succor, the persona of "Open Fire in the Ruins of the Body" somberly declares, "I am riding a wave that never crests. I am al-Malik al-Ḍalīl. I die in war and oblivion."[108] The poetic voice splices the conceit of Imru' al-Qays with a narrative of dispossession culled from the revolutionary rhetoric of the Shīʿite cleric Mūsa al-Ṣadr, who represented the "rallying symbol" of the cause of the disinherited.[109] But the contemporary poetic voice adds its own spin to Ṣadr's poetics of disinheritance, clipping the wings of hopeful resolution and offering a reversal poetics of disenchantment: "I am the disinherited of the earth," laments the modern poetic persona; "I raise my voice in protest but nobody hears my cry except one undulating echo after undulating echo . . . undulating . . . and a sky that shuts its holy book."[110] The wandering persona of the modern poem reinforces his state of dispossession by embracing the poet-king's failed search for retribution: "I am the wretched wandering aimlessly behind his mistress and father."[111] By entwining a medley of mythic, religious, pastoral, and pre-Islamic tropes, Shams al-Dīn's poem transmogrifies the familiar rural southern landscape into a site of tension where dashed dreams, limited sovereignty, and oppression reign in an era of occupation.

The fertility and vegetation that normally permeate the classical Arabic odes become sites of aridity and death in this poem: "I crash into corpses forgotten by oblivion," the persona exclaims upon encountering "wailing horses, the faces of crying stones, retreating stars and tribes that never emerge from their alienation."[112] Where humanity and the nation at large seem to have forsaken this southern strip of nation, nature steps in to act as *shāhid*, or witness, to its suffering. In another poem by Shams al-Dīn, "Mūshaḥ ila a'midat al-rīḥ al-janūbīya" (Ode to the Pillars of the Southern Wind), the southern earth is portrayed as a site of mixed portents, as both poison and remedy; it is a "site of murder and an alternate site for the dreams of the murdered."[113] In what Muhsin al-Musawi describes as "a poetic of transference,"[114] whereby the beloved of the traditional prelude is replaced by the homeland, South Lebanon transmutes into the poet's coy mistress, whose unrequited love makes him ask, "Why is our history a cycle of violence?"[115] In a creative reinvention of the *qaṣīdah*'s archetypal journey, or *raḥīl*, Shams al-Dīn's narrator metapoetically re-enters the very poem he has been composing for the reader: "In the twilight of the night after the empty moon sets, I re-enter my poem after the angels have descended, and I begin to wander the land thronged by infirmities."[116] Where a majestic hunt typically ensues after the *raḥīl* commences, the modern Malik al-Ḍalīl of this poem encounters guardsmen, who impede his passage with a slew of belligerent questions:

يتقدم جندي ويسر بأذن مرافقه: هذا بطل وهمي من
أبطال القصص الشعبية)
-: من أين أتيت؟
-: من أفواه بنادقكم

-: لكن بنادقنا مختومة
-: بين الزناد وبين أصابعكم
ماذا خبأت بجلدك؟
-: أمراضي
وهوى الوطن الجارح
-: هل تضحك أحياناً في السر؟
-: أبكي
-: لكنك ممنوع أن تضحك أو تبكي
-: ممنوع أن تتجول.
سجل:
بلغت
(ختم التحقيق)
لكن أتجول في الوطن الممنوع[117]

(The soldier approaches his comrade and whispers:
this is the phantom hero from folk stories)
Whence did you emerge?
From the barrels of your guns
But our guns are sealed. From where did you emerge?
Between your triggers and between your fingers.
What have you hidden in your skin?
My infirmities.
. . . And the air of the injured nation.
Do you sometimes laugh in secret?
I cry.
But it is forbidden for you to laugh or to cry.
It is forbidden for you to wander.
Record:
He has been informed.
(End of interrogation)
However, I still roam in the forbidden homeland

South Lebanon is no longer isolated or silenced. It has become the "air of the injured nation" that cries in secret and acts in defiance as the interrogated persona attempts to reclaim his/her sovereignty, proclaiming, "I still roam in a homeland that forbids roaming." What follows is a poetic image encapsulating the fragmentation of the nation, which is displaced onto the persona's dismembered body: "The people swarm around my body and divide its flesh."[118]

In the final act of the poem, the elegy for the occupied South turns into an elegy for the self that has been dismembered, just as the South has been segregated from the rest of the nation. The narrator's body bears the traces of amputation, but the mind still cannot comprehend "who is killing whom." In its isolation, the South, concludes the poetic voice, "is a crippled tower."[119] Yet the poetic voice resists the signs of occupation in a less polemical fashion than Bizī''s forthright revolutionary poetics. The stark scenes in this poem offer no consolation, and the speaker feels forlorn and insecure. The present is a continuum of recurrent death and desolation with no utopian alternative offered.

Conclusion

In a historical period overrun by the anxieties of war, a metastasizing Israeli occupation, and periodic bombardment, the Poets of the South forged a counterpublic poetics of memory delicately balanced between traditional lamentations born out of ruinous contemplation and a more defiant language of resistance and critical self-examination. Whereas Shawqī Bizī' and Jawdat Fakhr al-Dīn imbricate resistance ideology into the fabric of their poetry, 'Abbās Bayḍūn and Ḥasan 'Abdallāh allow the ongoing war and its lack of closure to betray the silencing of the desolate southern landscape and the greater silencing of its memory under occupation. The sometimes spectral, sometimes enchanted, and sometimes scarred poetic landscapes of the Shu'arā' al-Janūb suture together a discourse that galvanizes nature, memory, myth, and pre-Islamic motifs into a southern counterpublic discourse that troubles common conceptions of the South as monochromatic. Rather, the cacophony of poetic voices from the South presents a critical form of ruin contemplation that rejects the siren call of a utopian past and victorious future through its own unique method. In the poetry of the Shu'arā' al-Janūb, the poem sits in an uneasy tension with the historical context of war and occupation in which it was conceived; its language incises the page, wounding it with testimonial presence, and the poem itself is the experience and the memory.

2

Haunted by Home in Wartime and Postwar Lebanese Fiction

Remembering is a malady, for which forgetting is the cure.
—Georges Perec, "Think/Classify"
(trans. John Sturrock)

Although the topic of memory has garnered a vast literature since the 1980s, very little has been written about its counterpart: forgetting. In his fable "Funes, His Memory," Jorge Luis Borges creatively illustrates what happens when an individual is afflicted with a surfeit of memory. Ireneo Funes's perfect recall creates a chaos of unwanted memories that burden his existence. "The problem is, sir," Ireneo complains to the narrator, "my memory, sir, is like a garbage heap."[1] Marc Augé posits in his essay *Oblivion* (originally published as *Les formes de l'oubli* in 1998) the three forms of oblivion he locates in literature: the first is the return to an ancient past by forgetting the present or recent past; the second is a suspension of time that cuts off the present moment from both the past and the future; and the third, the form most central to this chapter, is what Augé calls the "re-beginning," or starting over, which he describes as a radical inauguration, a birth of a new future that can take place only by the forgetting of what came before.[2]

This chapter examines the modalities of oblivion in three Arabic novels deeply imbricated in the Lebanese Civil War and its persistent aftermath: Ghādah al-Sammān's wartime novel *Kawābīs Bayrūt* (*Beirut Nightmares*), published in 1976; Ḥasan Dāwūd's *Bināyat Mātīld* (*The House of Mathilde*), published in 1983; and Ilyās Khūrī's postwar novel *Yālū* (*Yalo*), published almost two decades later, in 2002. In a departure from the previous chapter, where we saw those trapped by memory, whether individual or collective, left to reckon with war's remains, here we see oblivion enabling legibility and survival for the protagonists. If we agree with Augé that remembrances, or traces of what *remains*, are the product of erosion caused by oblivion, such that "oblivion is the life force of memory and remembrance is its product," then what remains in the mind is not a memory "but the traces, the signs of absence."[3] Oblivion simply casts these signs of absence into relief, allowing them to emerge as nodes of resistance. In this chapter, I trace these "signs of absence" that manifest as the remains, respectively, in *Beirut Nightmares, The House of Mathilde,* and *Yalo,* of a haunted lover, an abandoned apartment building, and a war veteran's memories. Such remains emerge from the dark corners of the texts to unsettle the protagonists' lives by forcing them to renegotiate their sense of being and belonging as they dwell in both the vortex and the aftermath of violence. The Palestinian poet Maḥmūd Darwīsh serves as an integral interlocutor in both *Kawābīs Bayrūt* and *Yālū*, and his haunted voice echoes the distressed voice of the protagonists trying to make sense of their wartime existence. As all three protagonists are entangled in (and produced by) the violence of the war machine, they struggle to integrate into their respective realities. I follow the three narrators as they sift through the ruins of their wartime experiences and as they carefully select what to expunge and what to preserve as self-narrative in an effort to acclimate to their transformed environs.

How does this dynamic of remembering and forgetting create a productive tension surrounding the impulse to belong to the wartime and postwar nation? By interrogating the remains of their experiences and memories, the narrators illustrate a process by which memory gets ruptured and is buried for the purpose of self-renewal. Common to the deliberate acts of forgetting carried out by all three narrators is the sense, even the insistence, that such acts are part and parcel of a larger project of belonging. Augé erodes negative notions of forgetting by animating its positive contours when he writes, "Memories are crafted by oblivion as the outlines of the shore are created by the sea."[4] Similarly, oblivion works by slowly eroding the protagonists' personal entanglements and memories, turning those ruinous relations into what I call "domestic detritus."

Ghādah al-Sammān, writing about and during the opening phase of the Civil War in the 1970s, emphasizes sheer survival by determining which remnants of her protagonist's prewar past to anathematize into oblivion. Told from a southern perspective, Ḥasan Dāwūd's *Bināyat Mātīld* uses the trope of the ruined building to examine discriminatory Beiruti practices against southern refugees. And Ilyās Khūrī's postwar novel *Yālū* introduces his readers to war's persistent aftermath: the forgotten war veteran cordoned off from society, family, and even the self. In all three novels, the desire to forget produces individuals alienated not only from society but also from the family and the self.

Becoming a Southern Counterpublic

In the introduction, I noted the nexus between the *aṭlāl* motif and contemporary Arabic fiction. Although the classical Arabic literary topos of "stopping at ruins" helps ignite the contemporary novel's aesthetic exploration of memory, the Lebanese war novel does not simply adopt the classical gaze upon ruins. Far from inert objects, the ruins encountered in the Lebanese war novel kindle a pathos quite the opposite of nostalgia. Instead of embracing ruins as nostalgic markers, as the classical bards of pre-Islamic Arabia did, contemporary Arabic novelists (re)construct out of fictional ruins a deeply unsettling portrait of the fractured domestic landscape of their wartime and (post)war existence. I explore how their literary mediations of the domestic dimension of war lead to the development of a new conception of belonging. The thread that ties the three novels together is not so much the war itself but rather an intimate focus on the domestic domain of war and its violent traces in the protagonists' personal lives. All three novels portray the Arab citizen, his/her subjectivity, as an alienated product of wartime hegemony. By means of such narration, the novelists develop a unique counterpublic perspective on the human condition during times of crisis. Well-educated, middle-class, and secular, Ghādah al-Sammān, Ḥasan Dāwūd, and Ilyās Khūrī find themselves, as Felix Lang rightly posits, "in a position of marginality in their refusal to partake of sectarian narratives."[5] This is evident in their leftist journalistic and literary writing, their depiction of violence, and the importance of marginal figures in their novels. Deleuze and Guattari's concept of "becoming-minor" can be extended to "becoming-counterpublic" for the purposes of this chapter as all three protagonists trace their own resistance to concepts such as "memory," "home," and "belonging." The result is a nuanced perspective that celebrates rootlessness and oblivion rather than belonging through memory. All three authors not only position their protagonists as active participants in national struggles but also encompass in their writing a variety of social classes, minorities, and nonnormative gender and sexual identities. The ruin trope in their novels is more than a medium to convey a sense of nostalgic loss; it is a platform to interrupt dominant discourses of gender, ethnicity, and subalternity burnished by the violence of the wartime and postwar state.

The Lebanese war novel both emerges from the ruins of a cataclysmic civil war and embraces those ruins as nodes of consciousness. Khūrī contends that "the Lebanese novel was only born during the war," materializing from the "dismantlement of the Lebanese state and the collapse of the middle class."[6] The novel, of course, had been present in Lebanon since the Nahḍā, the Arab "Awakening" at the turn of the twentieth century. But as Khūrī suggests, compared with poetry, the novel remained at the margins of literature until the outbreak of war placed it at the epicenter. It is undeniable that literary creativity did indeed thrive during the Civil War, as scholars have already pointed out. A generation of "Civil War novelists"[7] emerged from this period as a new aesthetic sensibility grew in tandem with the war in Lebanon, leading writers to seek new modalities of writing and, I argue, of remembering in order to forget. Responding to questions of gender and sexuality within and across Arab states, a new generation of Arab women writers—including Nawāl El-Sa'dāwī, Laylā 'Usayrān, Emily Nasrallāh, Sahar Khalīfeh, Ghādah al-Sammān, Hanān al-Shāykh, Liyānah Badr, and Hudā Barakāt, among others—sought to situate Arab literary feminism within the wider political realm. Considering how individual and national liberation intersect, Hanna Kifah shows in *Feminism and Avante Garde Aesthetics in the Levantine Novel* (2016) how national crises impinge on women's lives as individuals and citizens and how traditional and social structures are upended by such upheavals. As a result, Kifah argues, a new feminine discourse emerges emboldened from the ruins of dominant tropes of masculinity to foster survival in the absence of men.[8] In the Lebanese war novels, there is no space for the otherwise omnipresent heroes and martyrs that shape nationalist agendas. Writers such as Ghādah al-Sammān, Ḥassan Dāwūd, and Ilyās Khūrī, who were caught up in the web of war, engaged directly with writing and even rewriting the urgency of remembering it. All three authors question what it means for memory to persist, whether in a state of war or in its ghostly aftermath.

Regenerative Ruination in *Kawābīs Bayrūt*

> Because you woke me up when you stirred in my belly, I knew I was in your coffin. To be born is to die. Memory is for forgetfulness.
>
> —Maḥmūd Darwīsh, *Dhākirah lil-nisyān* (Memory for Forgetfulness)

Ghādah al-Sammān (b. 1942) was one of the first writers to respond to the Civil War in novelistic form, writing two novels within the first two years of the war (*Bayrūt '75*[9] and *Kawābīs Bayrūt*). In fact, war broke out on April 13, 1975, and al-Sammān started writing *Kawābīs* on the night of November 13, 1975. She completed it on February 27, 1976; it was first serialized in a Lebanese journal from the beginning of 1976 until August of that year before it was published as a complete novel in October 1976.[10] This means that al-Sammān would have been working under dire constraints, as evidenced by the novel's dedication dated February 9, 1976, and selflessly addressed "to the printing press workers, who are in this moment typesetting its letters, despite the whirlwind of rockets and bombs, knowing that this book will not carry their names."[11]

We first meet the unnamed female narrator of *Kawābīs* in the ruins of modern warfare and in search of a definition of belonging far from the wistful classical poet's nostalgic gaze. Although the novel was written during the birth pangs of the Civil War and in the very shadow of its most infamous ruin (the Holiday Inn in Beirut), al-Sammān's protagonist refuses to weep for the city's fall but celebrates ruination as the sign of a renewed future delineated by the remains of an imploding and decaying world order. The novel argues that intersectarian tension, economic disparity, and desiccated perceptions of women had eroded any sense of community. In *Kawābīs*, al-Sammān builds on her earlier critiques of patriarchy and encompasses a wider range of social and political injustices related to the crisis of the Civil War through her negotiation of domestic ruination, where the wartime home does not endure in either material or social terms.

Located at the edge of the Green Line (Khūtūt al-Tammās, or "Line of Fire"), the Holiday Inn, facing the protagonist's building, fell into the hands of competing militias in October 1975. The hotel's proximity to the front line made it part of an urban battle as one of the first significant physical manifestations of the conflict. The hotel's strategic location also cemented the sectarian divide of the city between the Christian East and the Muslim West. A short time later, the demarcation line bifurcating the city was pushed farther east to the old city center, where it fossilized into the infamous Green Line. The violence was triggered by what is called the "Bus Incident" on April 13, 1975. That morning, Pierre Gemayel, founder of the Lebanese Phalange (Kataeb),[12] a hard-edged Lebanese nationalist party modeled after the Spanish and Italian Fascist parties, attended the consecration of a new church in Beirut's poor Christian suburb 'Ayn al-Rummana. Four Phalangist militiamen, including one of Gemayel's bodyguards, died in the shots exchanged between them and the armed occupants of two passing cars. That same morning, Palestinian refugees were returning to the camp Tel al-Za'atar, which lay on the eastern, Christian side of town. They had to pass through 'Ayn al-Rummana to get there, and as they did so, Phalangist gunmen ambushed the bus in which they were traveling and shot dead twenty-seven unarmed passengers, including women and children. The incident ignited street fighting and shelling, kidnappings, and sectarian massacres across the religious divide. What followed during the next year was a raging battle to occupy the Holiday Inn, waged between the right-wing Christian Phalangists and the United Forces, a group of pan-Arab militias seeking to defend the Palestinian position in Lebanon. Both groups were fighting to claim the highest building in the Hotel District, which had a panoptic view of the city. This zone and the city center were the locations of the battles named "Ḥarb al-Otelet," the War of the Hotels. The two sides took turns occupying the

Holiday Inn, periodically interrupted by the national army, which took control of and lost the district a number of times. Many hotels, including the Phoenicia Hotel, the Hilton, the Normandy, and the St. George, were the scenes of vicious battles. However, the so-called spark of the Civil War remains subject to debate and contestation to this day as interpretations continue to be funneled through what Sune Haugbølle calls "different memory cultures."[13]

Kawābīs Bayrūt is presented as 197 "nightmares" (151 in the English translation), punctuated by a final dream (omitted in the English translation), that chronicle the protagonist's thoughts and activities as she is trapped indoors with three men: her insufferable cousin, her uncle, and their Sudanese cook. Meanwhile, the neighborhood is overrun by characters who sell their souls for a pittance. The novel follows the form of a metafictional personal journal penned by a nameless female narrator during a two-week incarceration in her apartment block located in the Hotel District. As the narrator awaits her eventual rescue by armored tank, reveries morph into nightmares, which in turn morph into mundane logs as she records her encounter with the variegated ruins of the city in a daily journal not incidentally titled "Kawābīs Bayrūt." The reader follows the protagonist's emotional transformation: she initially cowers in fear of the sniper perched atop the Holiday Inn, but her growing disenchantment with the absence of human camaraderie transmutes fear into brash actions for survival and, finally, into an outright rejection of all forms of nostalgia associated with ruined Beirut.

As the city implodes, the narrator accordingly begins sifting through fragments of her experience of survival, selectively preserving and discarding aspects of it that resonate with her new discourse of what Haugbølle calls "Civil War Schooling,"[14] and in the process she raises the question of whether literature can be an instrument of amnesia rather than a source of remembrance. Throughout her quest to rid herself of the burdensome aspects of memory, al-Sammān's narrator confronts elements of her past that bring her to a visceral reckoning with her shifting sense of being and belonging. Three instances of her encounter with ruins express these valences: the bodily remains of her dead uncle, the remains of her burning bookshelf, and the remains of her slain boyfriend turned apparition.

Ruination Old and New: From al-Mutanabbī to Wartime Beirut

In line with Ann Laura Stoler's proposal that "to think with ruins . . . is to attend to their appropriations and strategic and active positioning within the politics of the present,"[15] to think with ruins in the context of *Kawābīs Bayrūt* entails a double form of working through ruins: as sites that animate both despair and possibility. While logging the destruction of her city as it descends into ruin, the narrator of *Kawābīs* finds herself in the midst of "rubble strewn everywhere, as far as the eye could see; shards of splintered glass, the fragmented remains of doors, ruins that had once been homes and the tattered remains of cherished memories." As one character in the novel observes, "Sacrificed Lebanon transforms into a ghost trapped between ruins and rubble."[16] The narrator likens herself to the Prisoner of Zenda and the Count of Monte Cristo as he rapped haplessly on his dungeon walls, and her sense of feeling "at home" becomes the first casualty of her wartime experience:

> The Civil War came along, making it apparent that I'd built my house in the maelstrom of an earthquake. Was it mere coincidence that on the day I decided to assemble my library and hold on to it to my dying day, the war broke out in my very own house, with the first bullet coming to rest, out of all places—in one of my bookshelves? Was it a coincidence or did fate want to remind me of a lesson I'd nearly forgotten, namely that the basic human condition is one of homelessness, alienation, and non-belonging? As for stability, it's nothing more than a kind of waystation, made possible by fleeting experiences of familiarity and intimacy. Not only that but stability is an impossibility in an unstable homeland.[17]

Instead of embracing ruin as nostalgic marker, the way the classical bards of pre-Islamic Arabia did, the narrator of *Kawābīs* conjures up one of Arabic literature's greatest innovators, the 'Abbāsid poet al-Mutanabbī (d. 965 CE), to whose radical reinvention of ruins she adds a visceral rejection of everything infused with nostalgia. The practice of ruminating on ruins crystalized over the centuries, turning the *aṭlāl* (ruins) motif into both a stable framework and a flexible trope for innovators, such as the

'Abbāsid poets Abū Tammām (805–45) and al-Mutanabbī, who sought to escape traditional strictures that equated ruins with melancholy. Thus, the narrator of *Kawābīs* invokes al-Mutanabbī as a form of protective and poetic incantation from her unhomely surroundings in the hopes of locating in his verses what she lacks in her intimate surroundings. She seeks refuge in his poetic *bayt* (home or house) in the following statement: "Here I am living in a battlefield and defending my body by reciting verses from al-Mutanabbī as if they were some kind of incantation that would shield me from harm!"[18] Apart from her play on the metaphorical refuge of home via the house, or *bayt*, of al-Mutanabbī's poetry,[19] there is also a deliberate engagement with al-Mutanabbī's construal of ruins. Recollection and the preservation of memories are at the center of al-Mutanabbī's poetic oeuvre, especially in the following verse:

لَكِ يا مَنازِلُ في القُلوبِ مَنازِلُ
أَقفَرتِ أَنتِ وَهُنَّ مِنكِ أَواهِلُ[20]

O dwellings, in our hearts you dwell
Though you stand deserted,
You still people them

The poetic image of the ruined premodern *dār*, or dwelling, changes across literary space and time, as with the reinvented *diyār* (dwellings) of this verse; the literal dwelling has been transformed by metaphor into a place of memory in the heart, inhabited and alive when the physical sites are effaced. But whereas al-Mutanabbī's dwellings enclose memory in space and time through the familiarity of habitation, it is the *unhomeliness* of the narrator's environment that increases her resolve to selectively cleanse her memory. Experiencing a profound sense of dispossession, the narrator suddenly feels that the flat in which she is trapped does "not look like home; but it looked like something—possibly a story."[21] The ambiguous language here helps intimate the ruinous interiority, for home acquires a claustrophobic, estranging nature, reflected in her description of her few remaining possessions, which she slowly comes to view as the burdensome clutter of domestic life that weighs down on her evolving sense of self. This sentiment is no better reflected than in the chasm between her and her insufferable cousin, Amīn, who "didn't notice that times had changed," whereas the narrator "seemed to belong to another species." Amīn's obstinate attachment to his besieged apartment prompts the narrator to remind him of his existential homelessness: "You'll be a homeless refugee," she warns him, "even if you stay here. There's no such thing as stability in a homeland which has itself become homeless."[22]

The generational, affective, and existential gulf between the narrator and both her cousin and especially her uncle is reflected in their diverging literary sensibilities: the uncle turns to classical Arabic poetry for comfort, whereas the narrator invokes its innovator, al-Mutanabbī. According to Huda Fakhreddine, the ʻAbbāsid poets "were aware of their position as inheritors of a towering poetic structure, the qaṣīdah, and at the same time they were haunted by the need to say something new to differ from their predecessors and to reflect a new and very different reality."[23] Whereas the narrator seeks refuge in al-Mutanabbī's verse, Amīn's father, ʻAmm Fu'ād, another desiccating rem(a)inder of a now outmoded bourgeois lifestyle, seeks solace in the *muʻallaqāt* (classical Arabic odes) to protect himself from what he perceives as the inevitable fate of war. He shuts his eyes and recites aloud a verse from one of the classical odes, "Huwa allathī ḥāna waqtahu . . . huwa allathī ḥāna waqtahu" (He whose time has come . . . He whose time has come)[24] until his tongue grows heavy, and he collapses into a deep slumber from which he never awakens.

Humans are not the only creatures of habit who cling obstinately to their comforting yet ruinous modes of survival. The narrator becomes obsessed with a pet store beneath her home, where the animals exhibit a senseless attachment to habitation and familiarity, exemplified by their attempt to escape into their cages despite the wide-open doors. Nostalgia for "home," the narrator argues, in line with Stoler, is "a futile projection of desire onto an invented world," for it bears within it the futility of return given that "one is already always too late."[25] The narrator does not yearn for a nostalgic return to a prewar past but, as Marianne Hirsch and Nancy Miller would put it, she goes "sideways in search of the 'off,' the chance encounter, the freedom that comes from alternative genealogies,"[26] such as the chance proffered when she stands before the remains of her dead uncle. When ʿAmm Fu'ād ironically dies of natural causes in the midst of violence, the narrator encounters his corpse tidily decked out in Ottoman regalia and surrounded by his beloved objets d'art, "as if waiting for a distinguished visitor." Calmly, she takes a seat before his remains and starts baring her soul to the man whose company in life she had at best "occasionally endured."[27] But in death he becomes the perfect interlocutor, who listens with "serene detachment" to her anxieties as she realizes once and for all the true isolation of the human condition:

> آه كم انت وحيد . . . وكم تقولها لك الحرب الاهلية بفصاحة لا منقطعة النظير، بل (موصولة النظير) أيضاً . . .
> آه كم انت وحيد وكم هي متقنة الصنع المرآة الحرب الاهلية، بحيث ترى فيها بوضوح مدى شفافية جسر المشاركة . . . حبل المشاركة . . . الحرب الاهلية فرصة نادرة للفنان الذي يعاصرها ويخرج منها حياً لأنه يخرج حياً مرتين.[28]

> How alone you are indeed . . . and Civil War will remind you of this fact with unsurpassed eloquence. Like a masterfully crafted mirror, it reveals to those who are to gaze into it the flimsiness of what we call the "bond of human fellowship." . . . Civil War offers a rare opportunity to the artist who goes through it and survives, since he comes out alive not just once but twice![29]

The word *gaze* here is key to understanding this passage; the narrator is at once disenchanted by humanity, a disenchantment that reveals itself through shattering social relations, and relieved at her release from its shackles. Ruins to the narrator are no longer the lost *dār* of classical poetic memory or even the intimate soul of al-Mutanabbī's ruins; they signal something new, something "alive" rather than inert. The narrator's gaze at the ruins here is thus not a melancholic one but a critical look at melancholy. She opts instead for a celebration of survival predicated on the potentiality of a new life forged out of the remains of the old. This choice leads to her second defiant act of bearing witness to the last vestiges of material attachment: she bids farewell to her beloved books.

Literature, Remains

When a stray grenade sets her bookshelf ablaze, the narrator is made to face the greatest challenge: mourning her "loved ones," whom she guarded with the same intimacy and love "as a fighter to his weapons."[30] Paintings by Ghassān Kanafānī, Rāfi'a al-Nāsirī, Farūq al-Bāqīlī, 'Afīf Saydāwi, Na'īm Ismā'īl, and 'Arif al-Rayyis in the books turn into ash. "If only this fire had eyes," she laments, "it would weep at the sight of the works of art being destroyed by its flames, every one of which was once a piece of a human being."[31] By citing the revolutionary potential of these destroyed works of art, Sammān implicitly gestures toward the resistance activity and literature of the Palestinian writer and political activist Ghassān Kanafānī (d. 1972), with whom she had an amatory epistolary relationship before his violent assassination by the Israeli Mossad in 1972. Kanafānī famously articulated a poetics of "resistance" he called "*adab al-muqāwama*"[32] (resistance literature), predicated on the loss of Palestine after the Nakba in 1948 and on the urgent need to battle the ensuant "cultural siege" on Palestinian cultural and intellectual thought.[33] Throughout the 1960s and early 1970s, Kanafānī authored numerous books, worked as an editor for *Al-Hadaf* (Target) magazine, and organized the political platform of the Popular Front for the Liberation of Palestine, all the while fighting for Palestine's freedom with his pen. In a series of "literary letters" published by Sammān and titled *Ghassān Kanafānī's Love Letters to Ghādah al-Sammān*, she writes: "Ghassān had the greatest refuge: awareness of a cause."[34]

In search of a similar refuge, al-Sammān's narrator proceeds to invoke the classical Arabian poet who anoints his forehead with the ashes of a defunct campsite as a gesture to his bygone beloved. What seems like a gesture to the classical poet becomes at once rejection as she stands before her crumbling bookshelf and smudges her face with its ashes, "like a grief-stricken aborigine at a funeral," before washing it all off lest she make a spectacle of herself "in front of the trees and other plants in the garden." "Houses," she concludes, and the materials they enclose "are nothing but debris piled up one on top of another, and planet Earth is at best an ephemeral home in which we're never more than mere visitors, regardless of where we happen to make our dwelling."[35] The only true "home," she concludes, is the one she has inhabited all her life: her body. The narrator even refuses to remember her apartment's last human inhabitant, Amīn, whom she abandons without a trace of regret because their bond is no more meaningful than the bond to "some locust in a nearby field." She even goes so far as to conclude that Amīn's bourgeois lifestyle had helped create the gory present she is now witnessing.[36]

Toward the end of the book, the reader understands that memory itself is a burden the narrator must learn to exorcise through the delicate art of forgetting. "With every word I penned in 'Beirut Nightmares,'" she asks herself, "do you suppose I will survive, and will my words become print? Or will I be burned along with them beneath the ruins of this house?" Feeling "as fragile and isolated as a lone tear on an orphan's cheek," she chooses survival over perishing at home with the remains of her beloved bookshelf because, as she noted earlier in the siege, "the artist's dying like a rat wouldn't do anyone any good."[37] To justify her decision to live, she cites Ernest Hemingway and Lord Byron, failed fighters whose intellectual contributions were crudely and prematurely aborted by their attempted bravery in wartime.

The narrator's writerly dilemma in the face of violence and her treatment of memory are reminiscent of Maḥmūd Darwīsh's views in *Dhākirah li-l-nisyān* (1989; *Memory for Forgetfulness*, 1995),[38] which grew out of his prose meditations on the Israeli invasion of Lebanon in 1982 and originally appeared in 1986 under the title "Al-Zaman, Bayrūt: Al-Makān, yawm min Āb 1982" (The Time, Beirut: The Place, a Day in August 1982) in *Al-Karmel*, the literary quarterly that Darwīsh began editing in 1981. Haunted by a dream that never ends, Darwīsh's persona in *Dhākirah* is torn asunder by an existential dilemma similar to that of al-Sammān's narrator. Memory, as in the titular metaphor, is for the purpose of forgetfulness, for purging the overwhelming emotions triggered by the experience of Israel's besiegement of Beirut in 1982 in its attempt to expel the Palestinian presence from the city. The contingency of life under bombardment is embodied in the words of Darwīsh's persona as he routinely goes about his day: "What am I searching for?" becomes "I open the door several times but find no newspaper. Why am I looking for the newspaper when buildings are falling in all directions? Is writing not enough?"[39]

Kawābīs inverts the title of Darwīsh's book in the narrator's open plea to forget, but for the purpose of remembrance: "If only one of us would forget the other," writes Darwīsh in *Dhākirah*, "so that forgetfulness itself might be stricken with memory."[40] As *Kawābīs*'s narrator forgets, she creates "an insulating wall, increasing each person's awareness of his individuality and isolation, an isolation in which each of us had fallen into his own personal well."[41] Her treatment of memory ultimately bears on Augé's notion of the spume of memory, "crafted by oblivion as the outlines of the shore are created by the sea."

Revenant Ruins

After being liberated from her prison house, the narrator of *Kawābīs* walks defiantly to the sea, poised at the decisive threshold between remembering and forgetting. It is a pivotal moment as she stands before the last and most enduring ruin to which she must bid farewell: the apparition of her beloved boyfriend, Yūsuf. Amid the plethora of ghosts that jostle for recognition on the pages of her daily journal, the greatest form of haunting manifests in Yūsuf's ghostly return. Early in the narrative we learn that their union was marked by ruin at the very outset: a progressive intersectarian couple, they haplessly encountered an identity checkpoint that led to Yūsuf's cold-blooded murder at the hands of his own former students, now a militia. In light of this horror, the memory of Yūsuf manifests into the most relentless nightmare of the narrative, challenging the narrator's mental stability as it compromises her ability to move on. It is against his melancholic remainders that she must defend herself even more than against the real threat of stray shrapnel. But his memory remains, for, as Jacques Derrida reminds us, the ghost is the permanent return of the absent, and this return is spatially pervasive: the ghost "comes from everywhere," states Derrida, proliferating in "a mob of specters to which one can no longer even assign a point of view: they invade all of space."[42] The ruin here encapsulates an intriguing ambiguity in that the narrator's past has not persisted, and yet it has not been eradicated either. It has left a trace, and, like a ghost, Yūsuf manifests as what Derrida calls the "unfamiliar

familiar"[43] that cannot be eliminated, like something disquieting that refuses to die; hence, the ruin and the undead have much in common. In one such nightmarish scene early in the novel, Yūsuf materializes before the narrator as a zombielike apparition drenched in blood and riddled with shards of glass, but she rushes to embrace him nonetheless, impaling herself in the process as she binds with him "in death and pain," and the shards of glass "become bridges, even shared arteries."[44] Drawing on the work of Simone Fullagar, Tim Edensor discusses the porous nature of ruins in terms of the permeable body, noting that the body, when moving through ruined spaces, "is rendered porous; open to the impacts of matter it becomes a threshold or passage, characterized by multiple surfaces open to other surfaces through which strange substances are able to cross the subject's own boundaries."[45] Yūsuf's role as ghost or, better yet, as revenant—literally, he who returns but also he who is simultaneously absent despite his presence, who threatens to return—creates a temporally ambiguous figure who collapses past, present, and future into frozen time. The image of Yūsuf as revenant ruin contributes to the idea of the porous body by eroding the boundary between the living and the dead as the corporeal in the form of the narrator and the spectral in the form of Yūsuf's apparition fuse into one. Trapped in a spectral freeze-frame of embrace, the narrator suddenly feels the urgency to excise Yūsuf from memory. Ruins, Svetlana Boym suggests, "make us think of the past that could have been and the future that never took place, tantalizing us with utopian dreams of escaping the irreversibility of time."[46] Against Boym's perception of ruins, the narrator, instead of being paralyzed by nostalgia for what could have been, begins to view Yūsuf's ghostly return as an impending *kharāb* (ruin), even as she dialogues with him in an attempt to wrest his memory from her mind. In fact, her recurring dialogues with her dead boyfriend evoke another parallel with *Dhākirah,* which also stages a dialogue with a ghost, another slain Palestinian intellectual and activist, ʻIzzedīn al-Qalaq, who was assassinated in cold blood by Israeli secret service agents in 1978. In an exchange between the narrator of *Dhākirah* and his dead friend, the ghost of al-Qalaq correlates his death with the living death of "everyone," referring to those alive during Israel's siege of Beirut:

قلت: يا عز الدين، ماذا تفعل هنا؟ ألم تقتل؟ ألم أكتب فيك رثاء. ألم نمشي في جنازتك في دمشق. هل أنت حيّ أم ميت؟
قال: مثلكم!
قلت: يا عز الدين، لنفرض أنني قلت لم إننا أحياء، فهل أنت ميت؟
قال: مثلكم.
قلت: يا عز الدين، لنفرض أنني قلت إننا موتى، فهل أنت حيّ؟
قال: مثلكم[47]

I ask: "Oh Izzeddine, what are you doing here? Were you not killed? Did I not write your lamentation? Did we not walk in your funeral in Damascus? Are you alive or dead?"
He said: "Like everyone."
I ask: "Oh Izzeddine, suppose I say to you we are alive; does that mean you are dead?"
He said: "Like everyone."
I ask: "Oh Izzeddine, suppose I say to you we are the dead; does that mean you are alive?"
He said: "Like everyone."[48]

In *Kawābīs*, the narrator's assassinated boyfriend is not the only liminal ghostly figure; most of her nightmares are peopled by half-dead humans who overrun the city in search of release from their purgatory. Driving her need to break with her purgatorial home, the narrator defiantly excises from her mind those memories that no longer fit the narrative she crafts, commits to memory, and eventually narrates into novel form. But the excision of her boyfriend from her memory and his elimination from her daily journal in turn enact her biggest act of oblivion. Returning to the sea, she trains the barrel of a gun on his memorabilia—shooting it while repeating her new mantra, "I remembered, then I forgot . . . I remembered, then I forgot,"[49] before dumping it all unceremoniously into the dark waters of the sea. The ruins of her beloved dissipate with the morning mist as the potential for a new narrative quilted from fragments of remembrance unfurls on the horizon before her. This is Augé's third form of oblivion, embraced as a gateway to renewal; the narrator finally cuts her ties to key elements of her prewar life by marking emptiness as her "new beginning."[50] Out of the ruins of her former life emerges a new and emboldened persona confronting an emptied future: "I remembered everything that had been consumed in the fire, the entire lifetime which I'd left behind, all those voices that had gone up in flames: the pictures, the papers, the letters, and the books. All of these things, I'd imbibed, I'd assimilated, I'd taken into my soul, whereas in fact, I should have spat them out long before, since—as had now become apparent—all of them were actually external to myself."[51]

Herein lies the writerly persona's relationship to oblivion: she determines what is humane enough to be salvaged by the novel's end—selecting what to keep and what to let go, what to salvage and what to shred, what to memorialize and what to anathematize. In "A Duty to Forget," Augé reiterates Nietzsche's imperative for oblivion and against the kinds of fixed memory that arrest life, for memory is always a form of reckoning that challenges our being-in-the-world.[52] In this regard, the value of quotidian life and the meaning we ascribe to it are animated by a constant pendulum of remembering and forgetting, a delicate dance between memory and oblivion, each an inverted trace of the other. Al-Sammān's narrator ultimately puts into practice Augé's simile about remembrance as pruning work; memories are like plants, he tells us: "There are those that need to be quickly eliminated in order to help others burgeon, transform, and flower."[53] Yet when faced with the decision whether to discard her revolver, the narrator rationalizes her choice to hold on to it because, "alas, such contraptions become a necessity when one is left with no solutions to the dilemma at hand."[54] This ambiguous statement begs the question of the revolver's utility: Is it for suicide or for murder? As she goes through the purging process, she gains a sense of control and belonging to herself as well as her renegotiated being-in-the-world. Nestling the weapon near her manuscript, the narrator seals the envelope containing both. Symbolically, the narrator marks only the sealed manuscript and gun as remnants marked for preservation, whereas she casts into oblivion the remaining specters of her past, those burdensome memories consisting of outmoded customs, traditions, and burdensome kinships. She emerges triumphant in her oblivion: armed with only manuscript and revolver, she sees her new self as stepping onto a rainbow across the sky, ready to confront an alternative present predicated on her estrangement from all things familiar.

Displaced Memory in Ḥasan Dāwūd's *Bināyat Mātīld*

Ḥasan Dāwūd's (b. 1950) first novel, *Bināyat Mātīld* (*The House of Mathilde*), was published in 1983, shortly after Israel's second invasion of South Lebanon in 1982. This novel, too, focuses on the domestic domain of a fictional apartment building in Beirut, but this time the story is told through the reminiscences of a southern Lebanese refugee whose family squats in the building throughout Lebanon's volatile transition into civil war. Though the apartment building houses a multisectarian collection of tenants, it soon becomes clear that the Beiruti tenants' discriminatory practices against the influx of southerners escaping Israeli bombardment leads to the ultimate ruination of any sense of homeliness. Like al-Sammān, Dāwūd undercuts the nostalgic notion of prewar "coexistence" by revealing the fissures and implosions that bring the concept of "home" crumbling down with the building itself. The novel argues that it is the building's inhabitants rather than the war that compromise the sense of the building's homeliness and render it "no longer habitable."[55]

Aseel Sawalha explains in *Reconstructing Beirut: Memory and Space in a Postwar Arab City* (2011), "It is estimated that half the Lebanese population was temporarily or permanently forced to evacuate their homes during the fifteen years of [civil] war."[56] Sawalha underscores that although a few thousand displaced villagers from South Lebanon had sought refuge in Beirut prior to 1975, their number multiplied greatly during the war and continued in the aftermath of recurrent Israeli attacks on South Lebanon in 1982, 1993, 1996, and 2006. Furthermore, as the Poets of the South made apparent through their poetry, the Israeli occupation of South Lebanon dispossessed the fleeing southern inhabitants of their villages.

This section considers the extent to which Dāwūd's representation of ruined domestic relations exposes the stark deracination of the southerner, who can never truly feel "at home" in the capital. The dilapidated building is the narrator's portal into the past and his gateway to memory, the modern *ṭulūl* (ruins) of a conflicted past. Through the portal of the ruined building, the reader is made privy to the ruined life-worlds it encloses. The novel is divided into three parts that correspond to before, during, and after the outbreak of war. Its opening section takes us to the building in its prewar days and up until the arrival of the narrator's family from the South. After the arrival of the southerners, including the narrator's family, the building's "vanguard" tenants (the al-Kilanis, the Shibanis, Madame Khayyat, and a French family) feel overrun by their new "squatter" neighbors (bakers, a milkman, a watchman), to the extent that some even flee the building. At the outset, the narrator announces that "no one who had left the building ever came back to live in it."[57] As the building is eventually segregated along exclusionary lines, we are introduced to the novel's unhomely refrain: "The apartment was no longer habitable."[58]

With the arrival of the narrator's family in the second part, domestic tectonics shift as living quarters are hastily renegotiated and power relations are reversed in tandem with the family's forced migration to the city. The partitioning of domestic spaces mirrors the actual partitioning of Christian East from Muslim West Beirut so aptly depicted in *Kawābīs Bayrūt*. Dāwūd's novel's namesake, Mathilde, a Beiruti, is a case in point: she would "pretend that her world extended no further than the closed door of her apartment; that her neighbor's apartments were distant, separate houses which had no connection with her." Moreover, the narrator's grandfather, unable to bear his new neighbors' cold reception of him and his family, decides to leave Beirut because, as he declares, "the French were better than all the Arabs." The Beiruti tenants' increasing hostility toward the southern refugees leads to a mounting intolerance for the "other" and an exacerbating sense of *Unheimlichkeit*, uncanniness, as neighbors huddle in their separate rooms, while "the middle of the apartment was empty, and nobody dared cross it."[59] Martin Heidegger defines the uncanny as unsettlement, rootlessness, nothing and nowhere, being not-at-home. *Unheimlichkeit* in the context of the novel becomes a kind of fear, which shatters the very fundamentals of existence and collapses everyday familiarity. Petra Rau acknowledges the pertinence of the uncanny in fiction: "War is uncanny not only because it literally opens up the home to the strange experience of public conflict, but because it reveals the Freudian Unheimlichkeit at the core of this home."[60]

With the gradual infiltration of predominantly Shī'ite southern refugees into the apartment building, the narrator's family circulates throughout the building until "no one had an idea in which room they would end up sleeping," upending borders and imposing communal practices on their hermetic neighbors.[61] They even bring the "aromas of the country"[62] into the building and organize impromptu weddings on the rooftop despite the general tide of disapproval wafting from the Beirutis. With the increasing ferocity of bombardments in the South, more boundaries blur, and doors hastily unlock as refugees enter the building and its longtime tenants flee. As the southern tenants slowly take over the building, the building's namesake, Mathilde, cringes when she passes her neighbor's doorway, which is always ajar. The spatial trope of the half-open bedroom door, while seemingly innocuous, carries ramifications. Situated in a position to partially view a scene unfolding before her, Mathilde catches sight of her neighbor with his "zipper half open,"[63] resulting in her outward disgust but also an inward piquing of curiosity. "The door is an entire cosmos of the half-open," suggests Gaston Bachelard, for it accumulates "desires and temptations: the temptation to open up the ultimate depths of being, and the desire to conquer all reticent beings."[64] But the barely ajar door's liminality prepares Mathilde for a new beginning, like Bachelard's "many doors of hesitation."[65] The most unexpected "door of hesitation" flings open when Mathilde welcomes one of the young southern tenants to share her quarters despite her prejudice that "linked him to the people from the South who entered the building and the street during the war." But she rationalizes her decision because "unlike the rest he was educated; the sort of educated person she had not encountered before." Nevertheless, she subdivides her apartment and their living quarters, even allowing an "empty space between them that neither dared to cross."[66]

In the third and concluding part of the novel, we are brought back to the ruins of the narrative present, where we meet the narrator as he stands in the bowels of his destroyed apartment building, which he likens to the "abandoned suite of an old beach hotel."[67] As he stands there, his memory is not tinged by nostalgia but by an overwhelming feeling of dispossession:

> لم يقف أحدٌ من الساكنين على النوافذ الكبيرة التي تضيء الدرج وتفصل بين الطوابق. لم يفتح أحدٌ بابه، بل وبدا لي أنّ الأبواب مقفلة منذ زمن. كانت صامتة وكبيرة، والأقفال الحديدية الضخمة التي تتدلّى منها أوحت بأنّ عتمةً

تلفّ الأساسات القديمة. ومن يعرف ماتيلد يقدر أن يتخيّلَ الغبار الكثيف
ينتشر على الكنبايات والأسرّة وخشب الطاولات[68]

> There was no one in the building, or so I thought; I felt the emptiness as I stood on my aunt's rear balcony. The other balconies were empty, and the fine white tiles with which Madame Laure had paved her cement balcony looked dusty and old. The wind had piled leaves, dirt and fine sand in its corners and edges. Madame Laure's door was closed. I knew I would not hear the sound of her frying pan suddenly sizzling and then dying down. I would not see her clean kitchen apron. My aunt would not wait patiently for the stream of questions the Armenian woman used to ask her.[69]

The narrator feels a form of "resistant nostalgia," which Marianne Hirsch and Leo Spitzer characterize as "the longing for a home that no longer exists or has never existed."[70] His sense of estrangement increases as he stands before the ruins of his former home, as expressed through the leitmotif "the house was no longer conducive to habitation," thereby evoking a famous verse by the ninth-century 'Abbāsid poet Abū Tammām. Just as al-Mutanabbī's reconfigured the ancient *aṭlāl* motif, Abu Tammām expanded its archetypal symbolism beyond the abandoned dwelling trope to the interiority of the self. Embodying the elegiac stance of premodern Arab poets before the *aṭlāl* of pre-Islamic *diyār* (abodes, deserted habitations, and encampments), in a panegyric to Abū Sa'īd Muḥammad ibn Yūsuf al-Thaghrī l-Ṭā'ī l-Ḥumaydī (d. 851 CE), Abū Tammām writes:

لا أَنــتَ أَنــتَ وَلا الدِيـارُ دِيـارُ
خَــفَّ الهَــوى وَتَــوَلَّتِ الأَوطــارُ
كـانَـت مُـجاوَرَةُ الطُـلولِ وَأَهـلِها
زَمَـنـاً عِـذابَ الوِردِ فَهـيَ بِـحارُ[71]

> You are not you, the abodes are not abodes
> Passion has waned, desires have changed.
> The vicinity of the ruins and of their people
> That long ago was sweet to drink at, now tastes of salt.[72]

Abū Tammām's verse conveys the pathos of returning to a once-familiar place only to find that the waters of sweet melancholy have turned saline and bitter. This pathos reverberates conceptually and affectively in *Bināyat Mātīld*'s protagonist's estrangement from his former dwelling place. The narrator's refrain, "the building was no longer conducive to habitation," dovetails with Abū Tammām's bitter sense-memory of home. More than a temporal window onto past experiences, the ruined building here represents the lost *dār*, symbolizing home. According to Bachelard, home is, in the end, a metaphor for existence as something that is not merely given but must be experienced. Thus, the house as a construct comprises embodied experience and memory; its different nooks and crannies evoke a stream of sensorium, and with every habitual action endless dimensions of our existence and our pasts open up:

> But over and beyond our memories, the house we were born in is physically inscribed in us. It is a group of organic habits. After twenty years, in spite of all of the other anonymous stairways, we would recapture the reflexes of the "first stairway"; we would not stumble on that rather high step. The house's entire being would open up, faithful to our own being. We would push the door that creaks with the same gesture, we would find our way in the dark to the distant attic. The feel of the tiniest latch has remained in our hands.[73]

It is no wonder, then, that as the narrator of *Bināyat Mātīld* explores the nooks and crannies of his former dwelling place at the beginning of the novel, he feels as if he is "opening the doors onto memory as if for the first time after a long absence."[74] But his memory of displacement undercuts his fleeting sense of nostalgia and results in the need to evacuate his own feelings. The narrative suddenly shifts perspective and propels the reader into the final depiction of actual war. In fact, war seeps into the third and conclusive part of the novel only when a barrage of bullets forces the tenants to become uncomfortable bedfellows. From the narrator's solipsism and reminiscence, the narrative suddenly shifts its focus to its namesake: Mathilde. An intense shelling leads Mathilde and her southern tenant to huddle together in a scene reminiscent of the scene in *Kawābīs* when the protagonist is grudgingly forced to share the safest room in the apartment with her hateful cousin Amīn. But the momentary closeness Mathilde feels for her tenant dissipates as fast as the "fleeting, hesitant smile"[75] she flashes him. The young southern tenant capitalizes on this briefest glimpse of intimacy through his increasingly fluid movements around the apartment and disregard of its "public space" when he lounges around her living quarters in his pajamas. Mathilde's perspective of him suddenly shifts from seeing him as a "venerable" (although young) person from the South to perceiving him as a "thin hollowed out elderly man from the South."[76] The novel draws to a sudden close with a passing mention of the murder of Mathilde at the hands of her tenant two hours after an actual bombardment destroyed the building. Mathilde's body is found among the ruins of the apartment block. The reader discovers only at the novel's end that the explosion that destroyed the apartment building was not in fact caused by bombardment or shelling but, as the novel implies, was made to happen by Mathilde's unnamed southern tenant. Reflecting on the Civil War years, the author suggests that all that remains of home are its domestic detritus, those ruinous relations that erode the possibility of belonging because of an irrational fear of the other. The death of Mathilde in her own flat brings the notion of domestic detritus literally and metaphorically "home." Nevertheless, the powerful impulse to narrate the past compels the narrator to remember his ordeal—in order to forget—and his ultimate estrangement, as well as that of his fellow southerners, from any sense of homeliness.

The Ruin That Remains in Ilyās Khūrī's *Yālū*

Set on February 22, 1992, the novel *Yālū* by Ilyās Khūrī (b. 1948) traces the life of a former militia fighter still struggling to eke out a place for himself in postwar Lebanon. Ironically, the eponymous narrator encounters and exhibits more violence during "peacetime" than he ever experienced during the Civil War. *Yālū* thus begins where *Bināyat Mātīld* and *Kawābīs Bayrūt* effectively end—by confronting the question begged by both wartime novels: whether selective oblivion necessarily eases transition into a postwar setting. The Saudi-brokered Ṭā'if Accord of 1990,[77] founded on the quixotic amnesty law "lā ghālib wa lā maghlūb"[78] (no victor, no vanquished), officially "ended" the Civil War, leaving hundreds of thousands wounded and a nation in ruins. According to the law, warlords of yore were pardoned and thus became state-sanctioned political players. Khūrī provides a scathing assessment of the amnesty law in his lecture "The Novel, the Novelist, and the Lebanese Civil War": "The new post-war political class—warlords and war criminals in alliance with oil-enriched capital and military and security apparatuses—was able to impose an amnesia, a complete forgetting, in order to whitewash their innocence. Their victims were silenced."[79] This oppressive climate of state-sanctioned amnesia also permeated the reconstruction of the war-torn center of Beirut. The neoliberal government of the late prime minister Rafīq al-Harīrī (1992–98 and 2000–2004) delegated the delicate process of rebuilding the downtown area to a private shareholding conglomerate, the Lebanese Company for the Development and Reconstruction of Beirut, more commonly known by its French acronym, Solidère (Société libanaise pour le développement et la reconstruction du centre-ville de Beyrouth). Saree Makdisi suggests that by 1993, "as much as 80 percent of all structures in the downtown area were damaged beyond repair, yet only a third of this destruction was war-inflicted."[80] As a consequence, the remnants of debilitating violent struggle have all but been erased and replaced with an empty reference to a more glorious, illustrious, and mythic past. The "post"–Civil War years, however, unfolded like a palimpsest whereby "peacetime" was indelibly marked by the silenced but persistent "bygone" war years. When the physical violence receded, a new form of epistemic violence wreaked havoc on the memory of that physical violence.[81] The greatest casualty of the "let bygones be bygones" law was that there was no critical reckoning with the past in the realm of cultural production as there was in the state-sponsored arena. As Felix Lang argues in *The Lebanese Post–Civil War Novel* (2016), the novels of the early postwar era tackle questions of accountability that the state would have liked to banish from the public domain, and, as such, they present a challenge to the dominant political forces by filling the void of accountability.[82]

Khūrī's novel *Yālū* challenges the post-Ṭā'if doctrine of reconciliation through amnesia by foregrounding an uncomfortable figure effaced by the conciliatory logic of "no victor and no vanquished": the poverty-ridden minority youth who served as cannon fodder for the wartime militias. The eponymous narrator, Yālū, a child of dubious paternity born to Beirut's Assyrian community, joined the fascist Christian Lebanese Forces militia at the age of eighteen. His vague aspirations of becoming a hero for the nation in "defend[ing] Lebanon" are driven by his fear that he would remain a "stranger" in his country whatever he did. The idea of war in defense of the nation, he tells his reader, was "seductive," but real war and its aftermath left him only with a "profound emptiness."[83] It is precisely such dominant national narratives of Lebanese patriotism that Khūrī deconstructs and challenges in his writings. Fearing the war turned him into a being "worse than animals,"[84] Yālū steals a stash of money from the barracks and deserts the Civil War for Paris. Ironically, however, the post-Ṭā'if consensus, powered by reconstruction and economic goals, disavowed these ruined militia men whose youthful vigor had been grist for the war. Khūrī thus presents a challenge to the dominant discourse of forgetting: first, by positing the war as an event that remains to haunt us in the figure of the war veteran, thus recalling a past largely excluded from official political discourse; and, second, by arguing that even greater epistemic violence persisted in the postwar era. Khūrī's novel *Yālū* thus works as a counterpublic narrative by crafting a metanarrative about amnesia precisely to resist the logic of amnesia that governed the state's nondealing with the past.

Memory, Adrift

The novel opens in medias res as the thirty-three-year-old Yālū is being tortured in a dingy prison cell in postwar Beirut as he faces multiple charges of rape, theft, and attempted bombing. Khūrī weaves a plot of criminality and treason into a narrative of personal displacement and betrayal, demonstrating how the wider political arena of the war seeps into the domestic interior and exacerbates the condition of modern postwar homelessness. The eponymous narrator forges a narrative that moves beyond heroic stories of resistance and into a story of lonely vagrancy and homelessness (*tasharrud*) that can be read as a human allegory of the war's most persistent ruin: its human detritus. Recalling the classical Arabic poetic trope of the lover who has lost his beloved and wanders alone in the desert, residing among the ruins of abandoned campsites and remembering his loss, Yālū is constantly on the move, with nowhere to rest, adrift in the city, a "stray dog"[85] exiled to the margins of all forms of belonging: nation, memory, and even kin. He is arguably the war's greatest living ruin, its flesh-and-blood by-product, its domestic detritus.

The narrative traces the protagonist's transformation over the course of the Civil War from gentle calligrapher to militia thug, rapist, extortionist, and arms dealer. Khūrī presents the former fighter as an anxious, fragmented, and homeless subject who is simply unable to belong. After ten years of devastating thug work with the fascist Christian Forces, Yālū's attempts to escape result in further thuggery after the war. Hired to stand guard in the woods with a Kalashnikov rifle to protect the blood money of a Lebanese arms dealer and war profiteer, Yālū takes advantage of his position as guardsman to engage in sexual exploits with his employer's wife and to rape and harass women seeking refuge (from the same law that later arraigns Yālū himself) in the surrounding woods. His growing affection for one of his victims, Shirīn, seals his fate when she frames him for robbery and reports him to the police, ultimately landing him in jail, where we meet him at the novel's start: a transformed "guard dog" turned "stray dog" at the mercy of his new captors and forced to confess to rape and unspecified collaboration with the Israelis. The constant slippage in Yālū's life—he is a night watchman turned vagabond, a militia fighter turned deserter, a provider turned thief, a voyeur turned rapist—traces and mirrors the murky alliances that shaped the war itself, thereby troubling any straightforward notion of culpability.

Yālū's personal history—which cannot be dissociated from his family's history, beginning with his maternal grandfather, an Assyrian who immigrated to Lebanon after his parents disappeared in a forgotten Turkish massacre—traces the tragic trajectory of a lower-class minority's persistently failed inclusion into a Lebanese civic identity. This outcast was raised in the household of a naturalized refugee, and his attempts at attaining the fullness of citizenship renders him a living ruin, effaced by all forms of identification and subjectivity. As Tarek El-Ariss aptly notes, many a protagonist of Lebanese Civil War novels are "violent and violated (mu'annafīn), dehumanized by war and by tribal and sectarian belonging, and forced to inhabit spaces of 'waḥsha' (wilderness) from which they raid and haunt the tribe, the sect or the nation."[86] In other words, it is by embodying violence that these protagonists are able to expose and resist the violence inherent in structures of inclusion and exclusion.

Far from normative accounts of the Civil War and sectarian strife, the account that Khūrī brings to light via his protagonist has remained the longest in the shadows: the figure of the subaltern minority drawn into war but silenced by the same force that drew him in the first place. As Brad Evans and Bracha Ettinger put it, "Breaking with the violent past demands paying intimate attention to often-erased figures."[87] This, then, is the story of the hapless Yālū, effaced on many levels. He is the namesake of a Palestinian village that no longer exists, having been destroyed by Israel in 1967;[88] the grandson of one of the war's most marginal actors—the "Syriac guys who had come from Syria" to join the war so they could attain Lebanese citizenship but lived in fear of the wrong checkpoint because their dialect was not "Lebanese"; and the descendant of "a people whose story had been rubbed out."[89] He thus embodies multiple repressed, obscured, or effaced memories that attempt to find life through his prison confessions.

Yālū's Ruin Hermeneutics: Writing as Ruin

Confronted with a blank piece of paper and the intimidating order "not to write riddles," Yālū suddenly realizes that he does not remember his story in words "but as a sepia photograph." The torturer insists that Yālū tell him the "story of his life." Yālū tries to appease his tormentor but can find nothing that the torturer wants to hear. He laments over and over: "I cannot tell my story."[90] Yālū's story and his relationship to his war memory are eventually constituted through acts of infiltrating, forgetting, filling in the gaps, and gathering the fragments. Writing for Yālū is a form of ruin, remembrance its trace, a process of ruination in and by itself. The traces that go into his confessions are composed of the materiality of lingering narratives of fear and social alterity, signaling a crisis of inclusion. Yālū's story becomes a trace, a palimpsest, of historically embodied margins. Into Yālū's confessions, Khūrī weaves narratives of Lebanese communities whose stories were left by the wayside of history, such as the submerged narrative of Yālū's Syriac/Kurdish/Arab grandfather, Hābīl Jibrā'īl Abyaḍ. Born in 'Ayn Ward near Tūr 'Abidīn[91] in a "country with no name because it was a country of a people who did not exist," the grandfather survives a massacre that "no one remembers." As his grandson, Yālū is not spared the disparaging comments of the interrogators, who scorn his "Syriac signature" and dub him "temporarily Lebanese."[92] Khūrī, in line with Foucault, suggests that historical memory, as in archives, are not "sites of knowledge retrieval" but "the series of rules, which determine in a culture the appearance and disappearance of statements, their retention and their destruction, their paradoxical existence as events and things."[93] Obsessed with finding that unifying "thread" in his narrative that will prevent him from losing his Lebanese citizenship, Yālū muses over the challenge of reconstructing the ruins of his memory:

> "يجب أن أربط القصّة بخيط واحد" فكّر يالو، وارتسم أمامه خيط الدم الذي يمتد من عين
> ورد إلى بيروت، "هذا خيطي قال يالو لنفسه": "أنا بدأت هناك مع جدّي الكوهنو الذي قُتل
> جميع افراد عائلته في المذبحة من يستطيع أن يحاسب مذبوحاً، سوف أكتب أننّ مذبوح انا
> دانيال سليل المذبوحين، جدي ولد في الدم، وصار يشرب الدم نهار الأحد مع كل قدّاس يقيمه،
> وانا اسكرني الدم، انا شو خصني، شو عملت الحرب وحدي[94]

> "I have to tie the story together with a single thread," thought Yālū, and before his eyes appeared a line of blood extending from 'Ayn Ward to Beirut—"That is my thread," he thought. I began there with my grandfather the Cohno, all of whose family members were killed in the massacre. Who could account for a massacre victim? I'll write that I was slaughtered. I am Daniel, scion of the slaughtered. My grandfather was born in blood and began to drink blood on Sunday with every mass he celebrated, and I have been intoxicated by blood. What does that have to do with me? Did I start the war myself?[95]

Yālū has to learn to tell and interpret stories he has heard over and over. Yet they are not simple stories to tell. Instead of simply recording grand narratives, Yālū must use material that is distorted, repetitive, anachronistic, and murky to craft his own story, reminding us that storytelling here is not simply recounting but rather pulling together disparate traces, filling in voids, making sense of the pieces that remain, and making do without the pieces that have been lost or forgotten. Rather than offering a "collective memory"[96] of war, Yālū's multifocal text emerges as a form of "collected memory,"[97] a bricolage of "the many discrete memories that are gathered into common memorial spaces as an aggregate of its members' many, often competing memories."[98] In fact, Yālū is unable to differentiate between his "inherited" memories and his own memories of his wartime experience, a reminder of Marianne Hirsch's notion of postmemory as characterized by the experience of "those who grow up dominated by narratives that preceded their births, whose own belated stories are evacuated by the stories of the previous generation shaped by traumatic events that can neither be understood nor recreated."[99] Yālū even wonders aloud whether he partook of the massacre that his grandfather survived: "I'll write that I was slaughtered. I, Daniel, am the descendant of the victims of the massacre."[100] The violent history of Lebanon itself becomes a "thread of blood"[101] linking the massacre of Assyrian Christians in Yālū's ancestral village in 1860 to the Civil War of modern Lebanon, in which Yālū himself has fought and been brutalized.

If "oblivion is the life force of memory," as Augé puts it, then the memories Yālū ultimately retains are "the product of an erosion."[102] When through a process of erosion Yālū turns memories into remembrance, he does so by telling tales, by giving them a narrative frame by which he understands them and passes them on. Survivors are bearers of untellable memories, an "un-story, that escapes quotation and which memory does not recall," as Maurice Blanchot aptly puts it in *The Writing of the Disaster* (1995). The "[un-story] cannot be forgotten because it has always already fallen outside of memory."[103] Yālū's testimony functions in a similar way. The past returns so forcefully that it literally possesses him in the process of remembrance as his own memories splice with his grandfather's memories, blurring the distinction between them, thus suggesting that, as Andreas Huyssen explains, "every act of memory carries with it a dimension of betrayal, forgetting and absence."[104] The narratives Yālū produces are traces of memory and forgetting that cleave together. The result is a set of interconnected narratives that proceed in neither a linear nor a circular fashion. Like the novel, the memories remain unfinished. Yālū's stories merge with his recalled, received, and fabricated memories, yielding not one truth but many—or possibly many versions of one truth. Yālū does not so much represent as deconstruct the coming-into-being of memory by laying bare the epistemic violence enacted by the very process of writing to remember. Yālū's narrative confessions—whether forced or voluntary, true or laced with self-aggrandizement, redemptive or incriminating—betray a silencing on the part of the individual behind the act of writing. Like Borges's "Funes, His Memory," Yālū feels "he had taken in too many stories and couldn't bear it any longer" as his confessions "transform into a virtual battleground for competing narratives."[105] Unlike al-Sammān's and Dāwūd's narrators, who find solace in chronicling their ordeal, Khūrī's protagonist suffers the excruciating pain of forced confession. In fact, his confessions appear subject to the torque of memory: they are twisted, disfigured, marked by aporia, silences, and slippages, as if the narrator were writhing with remembrance because "the war taught Yalo to believe his own eyes, not the eyes of words."[106] Yālū suffers in the process of turning his wartime experience into recorded memory and views writing as a mode of self-defense. He even likens himself to a cuttlefish using its own ink to forefend potential attacks:

> فهم أن هذا الحيوان البحري كان المكتشف الأول للكتابة، لأنه كان يكتب بحبره نفسه ومقاومته الموت. يضلل أعداءه مطلقا الحبر في وجوههم، فيختفي عن أعينهم في الدغل الأسود الذي يرسمه خبره داخل مياه البحر[107]

> He understood that this sea creature was the first to discover writing because it wrote with its ink in self-defense and to resist death. Its enemies were completely misled by the ink in their faces, and the cuttlefish vanished from their sight in the dense black thicket that the ink painted with the seawater.[108]

In Arabic, the cuttlefish is known as *al-ḥabbār,* or the "ink maker," an apt metaphor for that pivotal moment when Yālū as *al-ḥabbār* defiantly throws his own inked confessions and, with them, years of recovered memories at his interrogators. In a symbolic gesture spilling into oblivion, all that remains of Yālū's narrative is "water, ink, and a bleeding story"[109] as Yālū and his interrogators bear witness to their ruin. Both innocent victim and violent oppressor, Yālū sorts through his murky memories, pitting one possible story against another, omitting incriminating details, then acknowledging their crucial relevance, eventually becoming estranged even from himself in a surreal climax after the rejection of his confession. Following a short judicial summary of his crime and punishment, the novel closes with the last thoughts of the sentenced narrator as he comes to a sobering conclusion: "No one is capable of writing his life,"[110] an affirmative disavowal of the aspirations of the narrators of *Kawābīs* and *Bināyat Mātīld*. As Yālū turns toward the window of his new prison residence, he intimates to the reader: "I try to remember the stories I wrote, but my memory fails me."[111] Unlike for the classical poet, whose conjuring of past joys mediate his integration into a harsh natural world, Yālū's memory literally cordons him off from the rest of society. Emerging as another species at the novel's end, Yālū, like al-Sammān's narrator, embraces "a different ending."[112] He even reinvents himself by taking on a different name. From the relic of "Yālū" emerges "Daniel," with new plans to write a narrative about love (*ḥikāyat gharām*). The novel's epigraph by the Palestinian poet Maḥmūd Darwīsh introduces Yālū as a "Middle Eastern Christ" who "came down from the cross," in Fabio Caiani's interpretation of the epigraph,[113] and the novel closes with a scene of resurrection.

In a world sundered by violence, Yālū finds hope. Augé's notion of oblivion as the necessary counterpart to remembrance can help us read the story that the new "Daniel" tells as part of his resurrection from the remains of Yālū, a story that begins with the following words: "I can assure you, sir, judge, that I have become a new man. I know my story because I wrote it, and I will write it again if you wish, but here in prison, I feel I no longer have any connection to the past."[114] Khūrī's portrayal of a man without a country, a history, or even an identity ends with a hopeful alternative future for that man. For Yālū, adopting a new identity is the only guard against hegemonic practices of belonging in Lebanon, from citizenry to family, as he ultimately trades in his name in the hopes of expanding his cartographies of home.

Conclusion

Ruins in *Kawābīs Bayrūt, Bināyat Mātīld*, and *Yālū* prompt varying meditations on the estranging effects of the Civil War on characters trying to negotiate and reclaim their sense of belonging to both wartime and postwar Beirut. Ghādah al-Sammān, writing about and during the opening phase of the war, emphasizes sheer survival by determining which remnants of her protagonist's prewar past either to salvage as self-narrative or to anathematize as *damnatio memoria*. In other words, the subject caught in the imbroglio of war writes in the hopes of turning her experience into a legible narrative that might ease her mediation into a transmogrified world. Ḥasan Dāwūd's *Bināyat Mātīld* critiques the violence of social discrimination against southerners that took place within Beirut as the nation devolved into internecine war. Narrated from a southern perspective, the narrator's story provides a bleak view of refugees' experience from within. Finally, Khūrī's postwar novel *Yālū* entreats his readers to meditate, along with him, on the persistent curse of memory, as Yālū, condemned to wander postwar Beirut as a feral animal searching for meaning to alleviate his lonely existence, finds himself cordoned off from society for the remainder of life as what Derek Walcott calls the "rot that remains."[115] Ruins in *Yālū* are not the ruins of *Kawābīs Bayrūt* or *Bināyat Mātīld* but rather the forgotten ruins that persist in human form long after war has ended. By placing characters amid the metaphorical and material wreckage of war, all three authors open up important questions about the role of literature in mediating belonging both during and after a cataclysmic event. In this way, all three novels may properly be considered southern counterpublic literature that resists both the violence of war and the hegemonic discourses that have marginalized and continue to devalue women, minorities, veterans, and their contributions to the nation during times of upheaval.

The next chapter explores what happens when the multitudinous voices examined in part one are subsumed under a singular banner of resistance through the creation of two key memorials: Khiam Detention Center and Mleeta Resistance Tourist Landmark.

Part Two

Resistant Ruins

3

Khirbet Khiam

Ruin as Memorial, Memorial as Ruin

In part one, I showed how contemporary Lebanese wartime poetry and novels appropriated classical ruins to resist dominant discourses of gender, ethnicity, and subalternity burnished by civil war, Israeli occupation, and the violence of the wartime state. In part two, I focus on how a nonstate political party draws upon the material detritus of the Israeli occupation (1978–2000) to construct an arguably dominant space of Resistance memory.[1] I show how Hizbullah accomplishes this construction by appropriating individual secular narratives into a homogenous story of Islamic Resistance (al-Muqāwama al-Islāmiya) via two key cultural projects. Chapters 3 and 4 focus on war museums named after the border villages in which they are located in South Lebanon: Khiam Detention Center (Muʻtaqal al-Khīām, hereafter referred to as "Khiam") and Mleeta Resistance Tourist Landmark (Maʻlam Mlīta, hereafter referred to as "Mleeta"), are Hizbullah's latest memory-building enterprises. I examine how a narrative of resistance is cultivated in a sectarian political climate by a militant, parastate organization that seeks to unify memory into a hegemonic strand of political resistance.

This chapter focuses on Khiam, an infamous site where Lebanese resistance fighters and civilians were incarcerated and tortured during the twenty-two-year Israeli occupation of South Lebanon. Once an army barracks during the French Mandate (1923–46), Israel and its proxy militia, the South Lebanon Army, utilized Khiam as Israel's main detention and interrogation center after it invaded South Lebanon. Shortly after

3. Khiam Detention Center in ruins, August 20, 2010. Photograph by Rola Khayyat.

the liberation of the South, Hizbullah converted Khiam into a museum of the Resistance before the site was later reduced to rubble by a targeted bombing. Today, the museum lies in ruins—destroyed by directed bombardment by the Israeli Defense Forces (IDF) in the July War of 2006 between Israel and Hizbullah. This heavily demolished prison-museum unfurls as a palimpsest of resistance narratives that was questionably effaced by its destruction. Chapter 4 focuses on the Mleeta Resistance Tourist Landmark, a craftily curated "natural memory museum" located above Sidon, where Hizbullah fought the Israeli occupation until 2000. I show how Mleeta exhibits the spoils of occupation to enact the history and practice of Hizbullah guerrillas upon *arḍ al-Janūb,* the southern earth, the lyrical landscape that the Poets of the South contemplated but for a vastly different purpose. In Mleeta and Khiam, *arḍ al-Janūb* is transformed into a communal space of political pedagogy and ruin gazing where visitors are invited to contemplate Hizbullah's resistance activities that led to the victorious release of the South from the shackles of occupation. I show how both sites use war spoils to craft an exclusive narrative of resistance in order to claim memory in the collective and to evince a dominant culture of military resistance. If we agree with Susan Stewart that "the ever-present potential for forgetting is what prompts a monument in the first place,"[2] then oblivion underscores both memorials' demand to halt and remember. Chapter 3 explores the underrecognized gendered dimension of resistance. Women, I underscore, are active agents in networks of resistance, warfare, and survival. Yet "resistance" in its heterogeneous forms is co-opted by the singular and male-gendered dimension on display at Khiam. In this regard, I interrogate the label *southern counterpublics* as potentially hegemonic. What emerges from my explorations of war ruins in the context of both memorials is the controlled quality of ruination as distinct from its literary manifestation, described in part one.

Interrogating Southern Counterpublics: Museums of Warring Memories

Whereas the Lebanese state, as chapter 2 makes clear, has imposed a moratorium on the memory of the Civil War, the nonstate actor Hizbullah has been productively amassing a memory archive of its own to mark its victories since its genesis in the early 1980s[3] by way of exhibiting and curating ruins of war. Rather than simply contemplations of the ruins of Israeli occupation, Mleeta and Khiam signify the party's attempts to "govern" memory by combining ruin gazing with ideological pedagogy. Through the participatory element of both memorial sites, the Resistance tries to extract and activate empathy from the increasingly urbanized and youthful generation, who possess a waning memory or even no memory of war. Today, Hizbullah controls one of the most dominant narratives of resistance. Significantly, there are no state-sponsored memorials devoted to the Israeli occupation, which in turn relegates liberation festivities and commemorations to Hizbullah. Khiam and Mleeta represent the first major public displays of resistance history by any group in postliberation Lebanon and are indicative of a wider contestation over representations of memory in Lebanon. The narratives that both sites cobble out of ruins articulate a form of nationalism that clashes with "other" Lebanese nationalisms, such as the Phoenician origins myth espoused by Lebanon's Christian Right and the nationalism based on neoliberal-style economic policies. As Lara Deeb rightly notes, Hizbullah offers an "alternative nationalism" that delineates Lebanon as part of the Global South, with the struggle for Palestine at its forefront, so "it is also vital to keep in mind that Hizbullah's nationalism is articulated in a U.S.-dominated global context where the party has been subsumed under the label 'terrorist.'"[4] Thus, through its exhibitionary ruins, Hizbullah narrates its resistance history as counterpublic archive against dominant perceptions about Hizbullah, which are inextricably bound to the epistemological power of US media.[5]

Hizbullah began to cultivate its resistance-tourism-oriented history of the Israeli occupation in the latter half of the 1990s. With the growth of its institutional apparatus, the party consolidated its cultural production through an affiliated professional organization, the Lebanese Association for the Arts (LAA, al-Jam'iyya al-Lubnāniyya lil-Funūn). The LAA produced a vast array of exhibitions, videos, billboards, and other media narrating its resistance culture. Both Khiam and Mleeta were initiated as LAA-produced projects corroborating the growing importance of such forms of cultural production to the party in terms of its governance of memory discourses in the South.

Appropriating Resistance

Hizbullah is highly attuned to the affective role of its exhibitionary ruins in kindling affects and allegiances. Given that Hizbullah contends within a dominant international political framework, the party relies on "tangible" evidence in the form of exhibitionary ruins to enrich its narrative. Through its museal ruins, Hizbullah crafts its own counterpublic narrative in a transnational public sphere by pegging the war ruin to a "transnational war of memory and history"[6] in which US and Israeli political, discursive, and military power are pitted against a parastatal army that claimed victory against Israel. In this sense, both Khiam and Mleeta serve to counter dominant narratives that cast Hizbullah as a terrorist organization. Moreover, both sites emphasize the Resistance's role in liberating Lebanon as a way to emphasize the indispensable role of the Shīʿites in the establishment of a sovereign South. Hizbullah represents its story of the South as that of the Shīʿites: the downtrodden, historically oppressed, and dispossessed who suffered terribly in Ottoman times and in the early years of Lebanese independence but who rose up as a formidable grassroots resistance through the crucible of the Lebanese Civil War, the wars with Israel, and the Israeli occupation to thwart and repel one of the world's most powerful armies. This history and these wars burnished Shīʿite identity and are what Hizbullah, as the present-day voice of this community, has put on ruinous display in Khiam and Mleeta.

Yet Khiam and Mleeta also shape their ruin narratives through appropriations and glaring elisions. The museums appropriate and streamline individual experiences of resistance into a collective narrative sourced from "other" histories of resistance—including those of the Lebanese Communist Party, the Syrian Socialist Nationalist Party, and the Amal (Hope) movement—under one Resistance banner. In the case of Khiam, Hizbullah's narrative marginalized secular women's narratives and overshadowed gendered acts of resistance. Moreover, the centrality of the military ruin as the medium by which Mleeta inscribes its version of an ascendant memory culture reveals how the party's cultural production appropriates other genealogies and narratives. Mleeta Tourist Landmark draws on heterogeneous (pagan) practices by tapping memory and affect stored in nonhuman remains such as trees, rocks, birds, springs, caves, valleys, and hills and grafting those remains and their memories into a militarized ruinscape. In so doing, Mleeta overwrites pagan traditions to evince an exclusive ideology and practice by drawing on the ruins of the former to authorize the latter: a modern sectarian military present. In this way, Khiam and Mleeta reduce a multisectarian setting into a monolithic display of singular resistance.

Resisting Appropriation

In chapters 3 and 4, I draw a counterpoint between what I term "Resistance ruins" on display in Khiam and Mleeta and "resistant ruins" that subtly but powerfully challenge the dominant framework of memory on singular display by pulsating with stories of overlooked experiences and narratives. I equate Resistance ruins with the heavily politicized war ruin and resistant ruins with the more-than-human, nonsectarian practices, narratives, and modalities of memory. I locate these resistant ruins in stories of solidarity forged between detainees amid the rubble of incarceration in Khiam; in oral memories of former detainees, whose eclectic and often contradictory experiences complicate Resistance ideology; and in my own evolving embodied visits to the sites and interviews with its surviving witnesses. Resistant ruins diffract the monopolization of memory by giving breathing space to modalities of memory devoid of the hegemonic categories "nation" and "religion."

Following a practice-based feminist approach,[7] I show how resistant ruins forge alternative practices for narrating memories of past violence and genealogies that are based on collectivity and solidarity. Throughout my discussion of how the kinds of memories stimulated in resistant ruins might be used to critically assess dominant ways of producing memory, I take recourse to my own visits to Khiam and Mleeta. Approaching the museum experience from an "embodied" perspective allows me to assume an active role: not as a passive recipient of content but as an active participant actor in a multisensory process of communication with my surroundings, in which I am fully immersed. The museum no longer acts primarily as a place for the gathering and communication of knowledge but as a place for the gathering of different forms of experience and encounter. In recognizing that nobody can stand at a Punctum Archimedis, I am careful to acknowledge my own role as interlocutor as I watched ruins morph from inert properties awaiting museal inscriptions to disorderly resistant ruins. It is to these varying and vying ruins of resistance and their palimpsestic potentialities that I now turn.

Genealogy of a Prison Palimpsest: Khiam Detention Center

> Ruins are places from which counter-memories can be articulated, for in spatial terms, ruins are consigned to the margins of urban space, and it is there where we must venture if we are to confront the most densely haunted spaces of the nation, for following the ghosts is about . . . putting life back in where only a vague memory or a bare trace was visible to those who bothered to look.
>
> —Avery Gordon, *Ghostly Matters*

During the July War of 2006, the masterminds of Khiam Detention Center returned to delete their mark of infamy by reducing it to a pile of rubble. During the twenty-three-year French Mandate, Khiam had served as an army barracks. It was converted by Israel and its proxy Lebanese militia, the South Lebanese Army (SLA), into its main detention and interrogation center after it invaded South Lebanon and withdrew to its "security zone" in 1984.[8] That year, Khiam became a site where more than five thousand Lebanese resistance supporters and fighters were imprisoned and tortured by the SLA.[9] After the occupation ended in May 2000, Hizbullah converted Khiam Detention Center into a museum of the Resistance. Then, after being remade into a monument reminder of political and humanitarian atrocity, on July 20, 2006, it was reduced to rubble by directed IDF bombardment, whereby only "fragments of walls, concrete held erect by stubborn rebar, point mute to the sky."[10] In the wake of the prison-museum's destruction, this chapter pays special attention to embodied memories buried beneath the rubble and explores the lingering affective power the ruins have on how memories are preserved and communicated through alternate narratives, archives, and encounters. It also examines the precarity of the trauma memorial as an aesthetic and political category of commemoration. I show how Khiam is a palimpsest of remains, a layering of stories of human suffering that struggled for recognition within the domineering framework of the museum. Palimpsests are layered texts, whether manuscripts, landscapes, or ruins. In Khiam, I explore how such layering nurtured multiple narratives of resistance to create "resistant ruins," which, I argue, continue to pulsate with memories even in the aftermath of the prison-museum's destruction. Thus, I read the afterlife of the prison-cum-memorial in three forms of encounters with its ruins: my own embodied visits and walks through the wreckage; creative acts of solidarity forged between female detainees during their incarceration and embodied by its most famous political prisoner, Suha Bshāra; and oral memories of former detainees turned docents. Rather than silencing the torturous stories that Khiam's carceral walls contained, the destruction of the prison-memorial transformed the spatial order of memory and its affective capacity to haunt the visitor. My return visits to the wreckage of the former prison-memorial demonstrated to me that the wreckage remains uncannily fecund with memory as stories continue to emerge from the void. While excavating the stories hidden beneath the rubble of the hegemonic museum narrative, I am no longer guided by museum placards but by the silence of the ruins. I contend that the afterlife of the ruin often exceeds the bounds of political commemoration. I propose a shift in focus beyond the materiality of the trace to the prison's affective afterlife in the narratives woven around its existence—that is, in the stories that emerge from the ruins.

The town of Khiam perches atop a windswept hill edging the heavily fortified border fence between Lebanon and Israel. Using a French Mandate–era barracks, Israel and its proxy militia established the infamous Khiam Detention Center, where inhabitants of the zone were dragged and imprisoned. In March 1978, following Israel's first large-scale land invasion of Lebanon, named Operation Līṭānī after the much-desired Lebanese river, the IDF achieved two stated goals: to eliminate the Palestinian guerrillas from Lebanon's borderland and to install a proxy militia. In addition to the devastating human losses, the invasion left behind a ruinous landscape strewn with unexploded cluster bombs. After Israel's withdrawal in 1978, the IDF placed army major Sa'ad Haddād in charge of the grotesquely named Free Lebanese Army (FLA), a Lebanese pro-Israeli militia that came to rule what eventually would be known by the euphemisms "the strip," "the security belt," or "the zone." The FLA was the precursor to what became the SLA (1979–2000) under General Antoine Laḥd. The SLA was a predominately Christian right-wing proxy militia created, controlled, and funded by Israel to administer South Lebanon and give a Lebanese facade to the occupation of the South. Ironically, the surname "Laḥd" carries its own set of sinister connotations. According to the Hans Wehr *Dictionary of Modern Written Arabic*, a *laḥd* is a "grave, tomb; (ancient meaning: a charnel vault with a niche for the corpse in the lateral wall)."[11] South Lebanon was similarly entombed under General Laḥd's hegemonic rule. Following Operation Līṭānī,[12] the United Nations Security Council passed Resolution 425, which called "upon Israel to cease its military action against Lebanese territorial integrity and withdraw forthwith its forces from all Lebanese territory."[13] It took twenty-two years for the directive "forthwith" to be honored. The United Nations Interim Forces in Lebanon have remained in "interim" status in the border zone ever since.

The SLA established a buffer state in the South, which expanded after the IDF's invasion of Lebanon in 1982, an invasion that culminated on September 15 when the Phalange (a Maronite militia), the SLA, and the IDF coordinated and carried out a massacre of defenseless Palestinians in the Sabra and Shatila refugee camps in West Beirut. In response to the heinous massacre, leftist groups, including the Lebanese Communist Party, founded the Lebanese National Resistance Front.[14] The SLA fought Palestinians and their allies in the Front at first, then the Shī'ite forces of Amal and Hizbullah until 2000, when Hizbullah finally drove the IDF out of Lebanon.

The occupation zone, cut off from the rest of "free" Lebanon, was, in short, an "economy of terror."[15] The prison existed in a remote periphery of "the strip," a twelve-kilometer-wide sliver of Lebanese land buffering the northern marches of Israel from the rest of Lebanon. More than just a twelve-kilometer–wide "defensive" buffer zone, the "strip" included an active military front that enclosed twelve hundred square kilometers of Lebanese national territory and about 150 small towns. The occupied South was a place of zero legal accountability, where "prisoners in Khiam were negated, buried, conveniently wiped from the world of the living."[16] Khiam's many detentions took place outside any legal framework: there were no judges, trials, lawyers, evidence, arguments, law, or judiciary in

Khiam.[17] In *The Texture of Memory* (1993), James Young aptly describes the double helix of occupation: "It was one thing to be ravished outside one's land," he writes, "another to be occupied and enslaved at home."[18] From 1985 to 1994, at least nine Khiam inmates died from torture and medical neglect while in custody or shortly after their release,[19] and many minors grew up there. Between 1987 and 1995, detainees were not even allowed to see their families. Torture methods reportedly included electric shock, suspension from poles, threats of the rape of wives and female relatives, and confinement in pitch-black, solitary cells for months. The International Red Cross, which prides itself on being able to penetrate the darkest corner of a prisoner's cell, struggled for ten years with the Israeli government and the SLA commander, Antoine Laḥd, himself a native of South Lebanon, to permit its delegation to enter the prison.[20] In a darkly paradoxical fashion, when the Red Cross was finally allowed entry in 1995, it was denied permission to publish its findings.[21] Khiam remained in juridical limbo. The Lebanese media disseminated mute thirty-second clips of prisoners roaming zombielike around their "sunroom," as if to affirm to the public that the epithets by which this prison was known, the "cemetery of the living" and "cradle of heroes," were indeed realistic descriptions of the place.

Suha Bshāra: Khiam's Resistant Ruin

On September 3, 1998, a window into Khiam opened with the release of Suha Bshāra, its most famous Lebanese political prisoner and activist. Born in Beirut to an Eastern Orthodox family, Bshāra hails from the Christian village of Deir Mimas in southern Lebanon, which suffered frequent Israeli attacks in the 1970s before occupation in 1982. Many people within the "security zone" depended economically on the occupation either directly or indirectly. On the eve of 1983, South Lebanon was riven in two: some resisted the Israeli occupation with arms, while others traversed the porous border in pursuit of employment in Israel as money became "the lifeblood of the occupied zone," according to Roberta Arnold in her case study of Khiam and its violations of the laws of war.[22] Bshāra similarly paints an ambivalent picture of resistance with respect to her fellow southerners: "Each looked after his own interests, not worrying about how much compromise or collaboration with the occupying powers this really meant."[23] For Bshāra, however, real resistance to occupation would entail a future act of violence that she would pay for with her freedom. She joined the Lebanese Communist Party (the secular resistance coalition, the Lebanese National Resistance or Lebanese Resistance Front), and on November 7, 1988, in the guise of an exercise instructor she aimed two bullets at the SLA leader General Antoine Laḥd. Her smoking weapon was a gift from George Hawi, secretary of the Lebanese Communist Party, which had been given to him by the Cuban president Fidel Castro.[24] Despite a fleeting moment of hesitation, Bshāra shot Laḥd as he viewed a report on the Intifada. Asked why she only fired twice, she replied that she pegged her two shots to two causes: "The first bullet was a message for the Lebanese people to save their bullets in the Civil War and to use them against Israel's occupation, not against each other. The second was a salute to the children of the Intifada, so I kept my promise by only shooting two bullets."[25] But Laḥd survived, and the SLA immediately captured and "disappeared" Bshāra in the detention center without charges or trial, holding her there for ten years, six of which she spent in an isolation cell (two and a half feet wide by six and a half feet long by eight feet high). In her prison hell, Bshāra would be known among her fellow prison mates as "the woman who sings" because she sang to muffle the sounds of torture.[26] When an interviewer later asked if her gender compromised her mission, Bshāra responded that it had worked in her favor because she was able to infiltrate the IDF and the SLA more easily when the guard at the entrance to General Laḥd's house was unable to see past her gender. In Bshāra's own words, he was "touching the body of a woman, not frisking a militant, even though I had a pistol hidden on my belly."[27]

Rhetorical Ruins

Formerly one of Khiam's "disappeared," Bshāra's unexpected release in 1998 turned her into a "reappeared victim."[28] To the public she became known as "the living martyr." Mothers of "disappeared" children in South Lebanon adorned their walls with pictures of her in the hopes that their children, too, would "reappear." Her name became a metonym for the torture, pain, and suffering at the prison. The epithet used for Bshāra, "the surviving martyr," turned her into a living martyr of resistance, such that, as the documentary film director Jayce Salloum points out, "the [surviving] martyr's narrative was ever-present, an overexposed and overshadowing structure."[29] The individual behind the act became a living martyr to be consumed but then forgotten. This form of "living-martyr" memorialization linked the dead and the living into a single collectivity, with the memorialization's intended audience marked as part of this collectivity, a perspective supported by the way Bshāra's internment and release were claimed first by the Lebanese Communist Party and later by Hizbullah-affiliated media. When her story was taken up by both political parties, she was transformed from a resistant female activist to a symbolic Resistance ruin.

Bshāra, however, resisted being made a female martyr after her attempted assassination of Laḥd and remained committed to a revolutionary praxis during her ten-year imprisonment. Her narrative of her resistance hints at a tension between political attributions of meaning to martyrs and her own private rendition of resistance.[30] She intimates this in her memoir *Resistance: My Life for Lebanon* (2003): "During those few hours of liberty I felt I had been swept into a whirlwind[;] . . . as the weeks passed, I was never left in peace, never able to rediscover my life. My liberation had turned into a kind of national holiday."[31] When her story was circulated by the Resistance after her release, all of its contours were flattened, especially her role as an active leftist female revolutionary. Bshāra's personal story of resistance encapsulates this problematic hitching of individual agony to wholesale political allegory. In an interview conducted one year after her release, Bshāra was asked what she had left behind and what she had retained from the prison, to which she replied: "I left everything, and I left nothing, at the same time. . . . I left martyrs who are still there as corpses. . . . I left them but at the same time I didn't leave them."[32] Bshāra's troubling role as a living ruin of the Resistance functioned to eclipse the reality of her lived experience.

Shortly after Bshāra's capture, posters of her at the forever youthful age of twenty-one began to circulate. Then during her internment, a photograph of her within the confines of the prison was released to the public. Still smiling, the imprisoned Bshāra looks the camera squarely in the eye, but with unmistakably harrowing signs of torture and fatigue now imprinted on her visage. Her prison photograph acts as an eerie continuum of the preprison photograph by unsettling the latter's serenity, especially in that the *same* smile prevails on an almost completely transformed face. Her disheveled hair, oversize T-shirt, and clearly strained expression gesture toward a reality that exceeds the framework of the photograph. Bshāra's youth is still somewhat evident in the prison photograph, but her forced smile betrays a different, haunting reality. The exclusionary function of framing, Judith Butler reminds us, entails a constant "breaking away from context," leading us to different ways of understanding both the frame's "efficacy" and its vulnerability to "reversal, subversion," and even "critical subversion."[33] The prison photograph's almost brutal efficacy in capturing Bshāra's defiant smile serves to subvert the hidden layers of torture, allowing her smile to betray a strong sense of resilience that breaks away from the uncaptured context of suffering and intense torture of her lived everyday reality. In fact, before her attempted assassination of Laḥd, Bshāra allegedly burned photos of herself, which she feared would be used for martyr posters, and rejected the nom de guerre chosen for her: "Flower of the South."[34] What escapes capture in Bshāra's prison photograph, then, is a relative public awareness that there is violence involved in hegemonic representations, in this case political photographs, that is unaccounted for. The prison photograph of a smiling Bshāra glosses over the personal ruptures silenced by such modes of memorialization, even as they are entangled with them.

Bshāra's memoirs take us beyond the limits of the photograph by immersing us in her experience of everyday carceral life and in prison-based antisectarian female solidarity. Bshāra identifies her self-narrative as a self-conscious type of resistance; she was not a nationalist but a specifically independent critical leftist fighter, individual, writer, and daughter who struggled to create an inclusionary space in opposition to Israeli occupation and Lebanese sectarianism. Bshāra conceives of her memoirs as another form of resistance to the moratorium on the recognition of the part that secular fighters, communists, and especially women played in the South's liberation. In a rhetorical statement reminiscent of the spirit of the Poets of the South, Bshāra reinscribes agency away from the political and toward the land as testament to the suffering of the South: "You may wonder why the others didn't recognize us as a part of the resistance. . . . We don't need them to. Ask the soil in the South and it will tell you."[35]

Reengendering Resistance in Khiam: Crafting Detention Detritus

Bshāra's memoir *Resistance: My Life for Lebanon* captures practices of resistance not in terms of military or religious struggle but in terms of the indomitable personal will to survive in its raw and visceral reality. "Those who broke down, or became informers, were those who did not understand the reality of occupation and resistance, those who could not grasp the radicality of freedom," writes Bshāra. "For me, the fact that I was a girl, that I put my family in danger, that I was incarcerated—none of this mattered. To have stopped fighting would have been to turn my back on what it means, for all of us, to be human."[36]

In the previous chapter, we were introduced to the Lebanese novelist Ilyās Khūrī's fictional antihero Yālū, whose confessions while interned betray the immense violence of the postwar state. But Bshāra does not dwell on the horror of prison or the glories of resistance for fear that such rhetoric risks submerging the individual behind the act. She instead focuses on the individual behind the daily bid for survival, the individual that enables her to resist by persisting in impossible conditions. Bshāra emphasizes the mundane modalities of surviving as an important form of resistance. Practices of steadfastness and friendship forged in inhumane conditions are the ultimate form of resistance against the prison's siege on dignity and self-worth. Bshāra decenters the act of resistance across a variety of personal relationships and practices not commonly understood as resistance in religious or political parlance. In other words, she diffracts resistance across a variety of activities that can be considered simply heroic survival. She places the emphasis on resistance activity in prison as a form of kinship making because nationalist rhetoric fails to capture the idiosyncrasies of such connections and exchanges.

Resistance requires creative improvisations to navigate the everyday challenges that incarceration imposes. Resistance, to the detainee, is in and of itself a way of remaining alive. Through Bshāra's self-narrative, we enter Khiam as a place rife with creative acts of solidarity forged amid and despite the ruins of daily torture. "In the camp, deprived of everything," writes Bshāra, "our hands had become scavengers" because "to create was finally to reclaim our freedom of expression, to speak our thoughts when everything around us was telling us to be quiet and forget who we were."[37] She proudly describes how they sculpted olive pits into rosaries, toilet paper into parchment, crumbs of bread into "The Game of Peace" board game; repurposed tattered bedding into artistic fabrics, sweaters, baskets, tapestries, and headscarves; and stealthily exchanged craft work as symbols of solidarity between detainees. They gave these ruinous creations as "gifts" to representatives of international human rights organizations, who, as I mentioned earlier, were not allowed to enter the prison until 1995. These creative acts of resistance, forged from the ruins of carceral life, exuded the human solidarity that Bshāra had exchanged her freedom for. Here I return to Khūrī's protagonist, Yālū, for when he faces his final judgement behind bars, he decides to change his name to Daniel and to write a narrative about love (*ḥikāyat gharām*). Life can quote fiction at times, and in Bshāra's case this resonates loudly in her decision to combat her own internment with a similar antidote: "My poems were not only political. I also described the conditions of life in Khiam, the stories of the female guards, and the friendships that bound me to some of the detainees, my dear *Kifāḥ* among them. Of course, I dedicated a poem to my parents. Lastly, two of my compositions allowed me to describe my vision of love."[38]

In 2011, Bshāra copublished a second memoir, *Ahlumu bi-zinzānah min karaz* (I Dream of a Prison Cell [Made] of Cherries), with former Khiam internee Cosette Ibrahim, who was released on May 22, 2000, when the SLA forces fled Khiam. In the introduction to the memoir, Ibrahim tells her reader that she wrote neither to "glorify heroism" nor to "denounce cowardice," but "because these walls no longer exist" she felt the urgency to mark her words and with them her memories, like scattered

"Post-It notes."[39] In their collective memoir, Bshāra and Ibrahim recount how they and their fellow detainees converted Khiam Detention Center into a counterhegemonic site of sisterly solidarity. Focusing on constant efforts at communication and affective solidarity, they take the reader on a journey of kinship and friendship, the most potent form of resistance against the dehumanizing conditions of their incarceration. In "Antigone Becomes Jocasta" (2015), Jim Holstun aptly refers to the detainees' friendship as an "anti-sectarian collectivity."[40] In *Ahlumu bi-zinzānah min karaz*, the reader is made privy to fellow internees' names and the dates of their internment, release, and death and is given detailed accounts of crafting olive-pit rosaries, embroidery needles out of comb teeth and electric wires, chessboards out of scraps of cloth and string, pens out of cheese cartons, playing cards out of soap, menstrual pads out of sheets of cloth, and bandages out of stockings. Bshāra and Ibrahim recount how they and their fellow detainees passed "gifts" to one another fabricated from a string of scarves they nicknamed "the donkey."[41] They relate how they stitched together an "ordinary world of dreams and quarrels"[42] in the pits of hell. Chapter 13 focuses on Bshāra's kindred spirit and dear friend, Kifāḥ Afīfī,[43] a friendship they fostered for five long years through stealth, passion, and creativity. "On the day they put me and Kifāḥ in the same cell," Bshāra reminisces, "I could not believe that the one in front of me was the same Palestinian girl who was leading a group of fighters to infiltrate Israel through the occupied South. I was dumbfounded at her young age. She was seventeen years old, and her extreme slenderness and smile did not suggest even these seventeen years."[44] On October 24, 1988, galvanized by the loss of her two brothers in the horrific Sabra and Shatila massacre, Kifāḥ Afīfī had led a group of Palestinian and Lebanese to the border in the hopes of capturing Israelis for a hostage exchange. Her mission failed, and she was thrown into Khiam. Although Bshāra and Afīfī were eventually separated into different cells, their friendship would not be muted: they turned the shower into a communication quarters, carving letters to each other onto the soap bar, on which Afīfī drew a heart for Bshāra on the latter's release day, March 8, 1994.

In chapter 15 of Bshāra and Ibrahim's book, we meet another female detainee, Nawal Baidoun, when she surreptitiously slips a perfectly modeled rosary made of out olive pits under Bshāra's cell door. Baidoun would go on to write a memoir of her own, titled *Memoir of a Militant: My Years in the Khiam Women's Prison* (2022), in which she illuminates, much like Bshāra and Ibrahim, how her "personal impulse can only accept to live a life of freedom and dignity."[45] Baidoun was thrown into Khiam on April 1, 1988 (and released on December 1, 1991) for suspicion of involvement in an Islamic resistance plot to assassinate the notorious Israeli collaborator and agent, Huseyn Abdel-Nabi, in occupied South Lebanon. In her memoir, Baidoun intimates that one of the main reasons compelling her to write about her involvement in the Islamic resistance "is to refute the common and prevailing idea and assumption that most of the key players in the Islamic resistance were and are male youth."[46] As for Bshāra, Baidoun's gender worked in her favor when she was plotting her assassination of Abdel-Nabi because "we young women weren't being watched as much, we were able to avoid drawing the attention of the occupation forces."[47] In the introduction to *Memoir of a Militant*, Michelle Hartman and Caline Nasrallah outline that their purpose in translating Baidoun's book was to bring visibility to "women's participation in resistance struggles more generally," adding that "Nawal and her comrades were not miserable and sad. In fact, they defied the misery of prison routines. They remained firm in their hope for victory, throwing off the chains that had oppressed them and defeating their enemy, however long it took."[48] In Bshāra's, Ibrahim's, and Baidoun's memoirs, we enter a counterpublic camp where a resistant alliance is forged from all that remains of hope despite detention. No matter how spectacular it ends up being, resistance for all three former detainees always begins with the simple act of recalcitrance—in the sense of being fiercely defiant against cruelty and predation.

Three decades ago in "The Romance of Resistance" (1990), Lila Abu-Lughod had already inverted the relationship of resistance to power by proposing resistance as a diagnostic of power, thereby shining light on the machinations of subjugation and their relationship to "unlikely forms of resistance."[49] In recent years, scholars have similarly begun to probe sensitively the gender component of resistance and feminist modalities of memory making. In *Waste Siege* (2020), Sophia Stamatopoulou-Robbins shows how "resistance" as an analytical category fails to account for quotidian life under siege, as in the Palestinians' efforts to eke out a living despite the toxicity of the Israeli occupation.[50] Moving beyond questions of silencing and obscured histories, the contributors to the collected volume *Women Mobilizing Memory* (2019) (including the Turkish feminist scholars Ayşe Gül Altınay and Banu Karaca; the Chilean director, performance artist, and theorist María José Contreras; and the American professors Marianne Hirsch, Jean Howard, and Alisa Solomon) illuminate how feminist acts of memory in and of themselves become powerful acts of resistance. *Women Mobilizing Memory* builds on Judith Butler, Zeynep Gambetti, and Leticia Sabsay's thought-provoking anthology *Vulnerability in Resistance* (2016), which proposes that "vulnerability is part of resistance, made manifest by new forms of embodied political interventions and modes of alliance."[51] Furthermore, in "The (Little) Militia Man: Memory and Militarized Masculinity in Lebanon," Sune Haugbølle troubles Lebanese cultural representations of ultramasculine militiamen who are "feminized" by public repentance.[52] Laleh Khalili's *Time in the Shadows* (2012) questions "the transformation of the political process of dissent, of the intimately embodied and therefore—as feminists have taught us—political processes of interrogation into categories without content, technical processes evacuated of political contestation."[53] Finally, Munira Khayyat's *A Landscape of War* (2022) introduces us to "resistant life in impossible worlds" in South Lebanon and especially to the women "who farmed tobacco, tended to their goats, their olives and vines, some grain, their fruit trees and kitchen gardens, unheroically, stoically resisting the vicissitudes of war by staying—like their fruit trees—rooted through rough seasonal war storms."[54]

Ultimately, the forms of resistance that Bshāra illuminates are not connected to the "overthrow of systems" or to "ideologies of emancipation"[55] but rather to shared vulnerabilities and acts of creative countercarceral practice. Bshāra proposes another register of resistance by way of reinscribing obscured events and voices through listening and participating in the transmission of their stories. In the end, she presents herself as an individual with the cathartic need to tell her own story: "Resistance for me is a mission and part of this mission is the talking about it."[56] If we agree with Avery Gordon that "stories release experiences that can be retold by listeners and collectivized through reminiscences," then Bshāra's memories leave us with a "haunting recognition"[57] of what transpired among women of varying genealogies whose internment engendered a unique form of transnational solidarity out of the rubble of carceral life in Khiam.

Encountering Khiam Detention Center

> A site could be threatened not by destruction but by preservation—the ruination of the ruin.[58]
>
> —Caitlin DeSilvey, *Ruin Memories*

Roughly two years after Bshāra's release, on May 21, 2000, in a hasty overnight retreat code-named Operation Morning Twilight, Israeli troops and SLA members began slinking back across the border to Israel, closing out twenty-two years of occupation. As the troops clambered to get across the border, they destroyed fortified positions in their wake and caused panic among SLA prison guards, who in turn fled with keys in hand, leaving behind their 145 detainees still holed up in their dingy cells at Khiam. Hizbullah has, to date, proudly proclaimed the Israeli withdrawal and long-awaited liberation (*taḥrīr*) of the South as its greatest victory.

On the heels of the retreating soldiers, I headed South in an unexpected "return" (for many, like me, born in 1982, it was their first time in the borderland) to visit the prison I had only ever had access to via horror stories and video stills. That day will forever remain imprinted in mind and memory. It was an incredibly surreal experience: a mixture of giddy excitement and nervous anticipation washed over us south-goers as we crossed into what felt like virgin turf. Massive street celebrations, rice throwing, and ululating rippled throughout the long queue of cars—a stark contrast to the angry blare of horns during the usual traffic jams in Beirut. But there was nothing usual about that day. Driving around the southern borderland, we encountered the material remains of the former military occupation at every turn: shredded identification cards, license plates, empty weapon boxes, tattered photographs of Antoine Laḥd, IDF fatigues, helmets, rotting Israeli food packages, abandoned Israeli/SLA

4. Israeli soldiers ferry family mementos back and forth over the Lebanon-Israel border, May 25, 2000. Photograph by the author.

outposts, forbidding warning signs, and glistening unexploded mines. In the village of Dhaira, we spontaneously witnessed the meeting of Palestinian families who had been separated by barbed-wire fencing for more than fifty years. These ecstatic Palestinian families, seeing each other across the span of only a few feet, immediately put the young Israeli soldiers stationed in between the border fence to work ferrying letters and memory to their loved ones (see fig. 4). At once, an impassable divide turned into intimate intersection.

As I continued to navigate my way through the former "security strip," newly liberated village after village came into view, expanding my vision of a country I had always thought I had known to the last rock. I saw SLA clothing hung like effigies over the fortified border fence, immortalizing the SLA's panicked exit. When we finally reached the border, I stopped to gaze at it with gaping jaw. Remembering my visit to the occupied village of Arnūn in 1998, I was in utter disbelief that I was finally within a stone's throw of occupied Palestine.

But my euphoria abruptly ended when I reached Khiam Detention Center, which had just recently been liberated by throngs of jubilant townspeople, who bare-handedly released the remaining prisoners in what was later titled the "Citizens' Liberation." One prisoner described his ordeal: "We got close to the window in our cell to try to hear better as we did not understand what was happening. There was shouting and we heard shooting. Then we saw a boy out of the window. He said, 'where is the door?' We knew then that we were free."[59] The camp was exactly as it had been left: in a state of utmost decrepitude. We were not allowed to stay in the prisoners' "rooms" for more than thirty seconds because of the pungent stench of rotting. Mementoes still adorned their walls, and the hoods that the torturers covered the heads of their victims with before routine beatings lay scattered—big, light-corduroy sacks littered the ground, covered by large angry footprints from the previous night's stampeding crowds. My strongest sense memory remains of the solitary-confinement cells where prisoners were held for months at a time: about five concrete boxes, slightly larger than telephone booths. Each had a brown metal door with a book-size slot that could be opened or closed only from the outside. The doors had been opened only irregularly to allow for a cursory cleaning. I gingerly entered one of the isolation boxes marked CELL NUMBER 7, and after thirty seconds ticked by, I tapped on the door. "Let me out," I asked weakly. Suha Bshāra spent ten years of her life in a cell like that.

Wandering around the prison grounds, I encountered one of the former detainees among us, whom I refer to here as "Ali." An impromptu interview ensued, and he became one of my main interlocutors as I continued to trace the evolution of this prison as it morphed into a museum and eventually into a pile of rubble. As we wandered from room to room, I asked myself, What might happen to the memory of this space if it ceased to exist? In the silence that enraptures one's very being, I thought: *I am witnessing the making of memory.* Diana Taylor begs the question of all site-specific memorials: "How does being there affect what and how

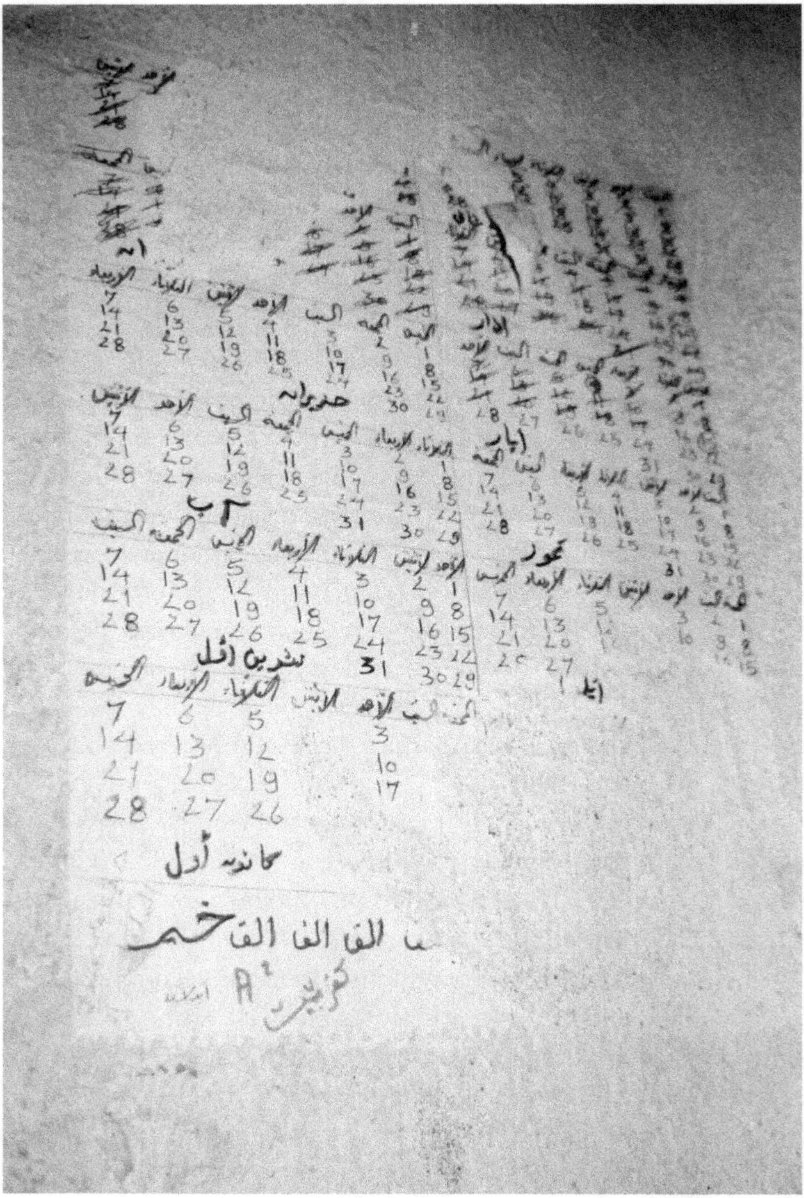

5. A makeshift calendar produced by a Khiam detainee, May 27, 2000. Photograph by the author.

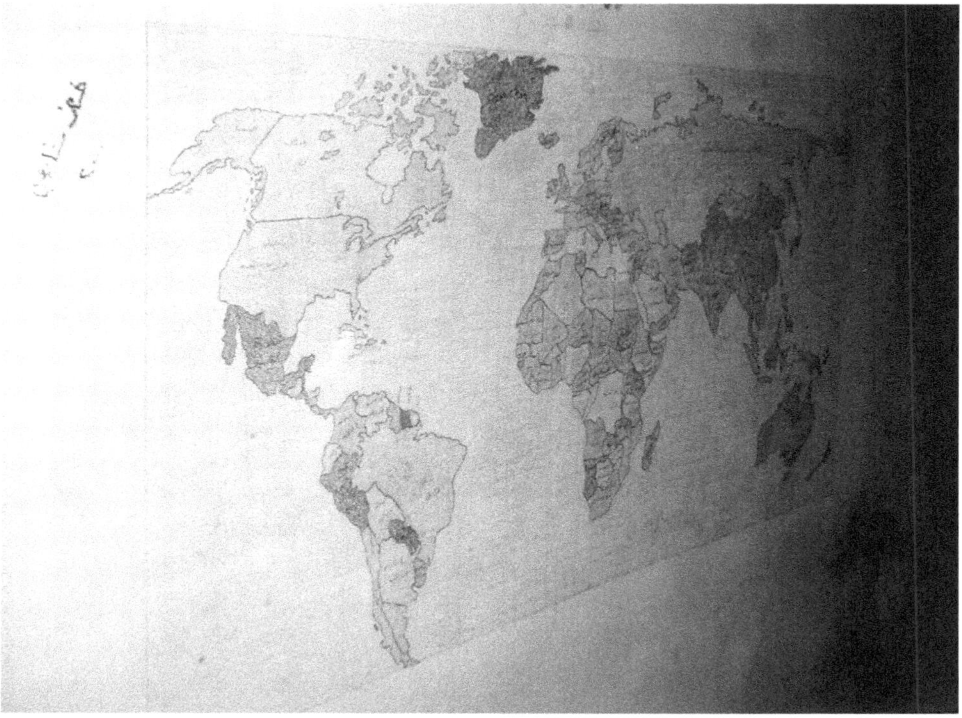

6. Map of the world improvised out of prison rubbish by a Khiam detainee, May 27, 2000. Photograph by author.

we know?"[60]—a question that haunted my return visits to Khiam as it morphed from prison to museum to ruin. I explore this question in greater depth in the following section. As I write, I am reminded of James Young's statement: "How and what we remember in the company of a monument depends very much on who we are, why we care to remember, and how we see."[61] With this in mind, do we activate ruins as we physically walk through them or by sifting them in our hands, as did the classical Arabian bards? Does this activation ebb if the ruin is, say, ruined? Can we encounter memory in Khiam beyond its memorial interface? What differentiates a ruin as memorial from forgotten heaps of rubble, even if they remain sites of trauma?

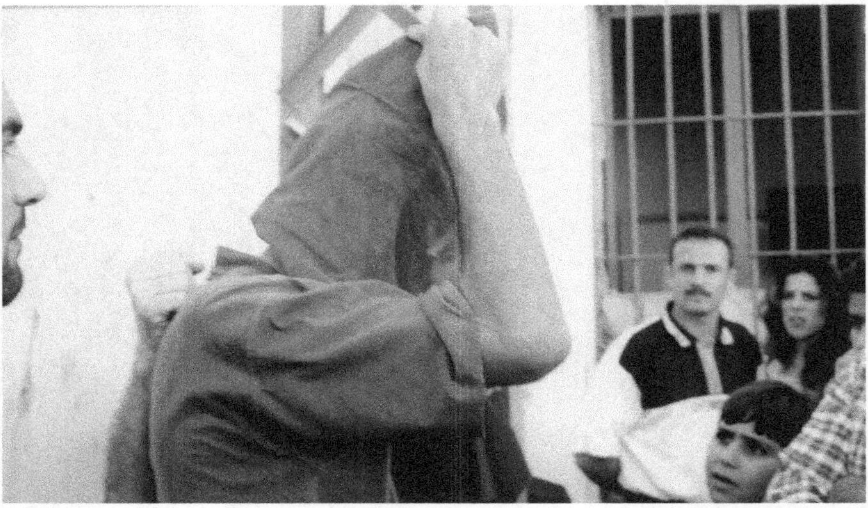

7. A former prisoner gives an impromptu demonstration of one of the torture methods inflicted on him to a crowd of onlookers, May 27, 2000. Photograph by the author.

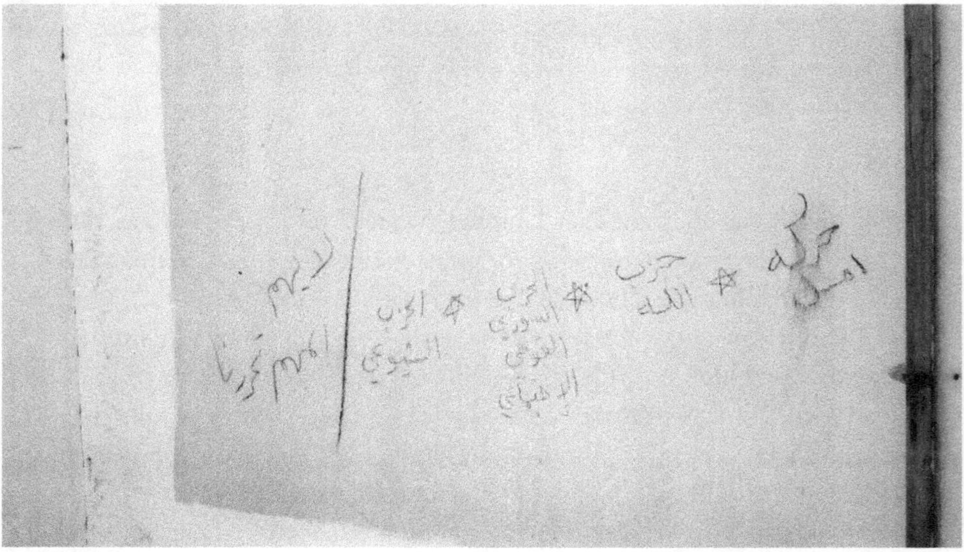

8. "Amal. Hizbullah. Syrian Social Nationalist Party. Does not matter. What matters is we are liberated." Statement written on a wall in Khiam Detention Center, June 1, 2004. Photograph by the author.

Khiam's Forgotten Remains: Detainee Docents

After the euphoria of liberation eventually ebbed, signs of disillusionment started to crackle through the veneer of liberation rhetoric. This is most apparent in the fate of the prisoners, whose liberation was touted as a national feat but who were left by the wayside of history after the cause of the South slowly receded into distant territory. Here, I address the prison's human remains, whose stories following their release unsettle grand nationalist narratives by pointing to their silencing in the act of becoming docent.

Between May 2000 and July 2006, Khiam was turned into a museum of the Resistance, replete with tours by former volunteer detainees, who administered and maintained the site "in loose consultation with Hizbullah" and with the aim of educating citizens and tourists about its role during the occupation.[62] Leaving no room for equivocation, a large sign at the prison gates bore the names of Lebanese who had collaborated in Khiam's dirty work. Once inside the grounds, an annotated path with signage in English and Arabic directed visitors to the harrowing spaces of torture and interrogation that permeated this hellish pit. Beyond the gates, new art installations were added: more than forty-four artists from seventeen countries gathered there in 2003 to create site-specific works to be donated and housed on site. Murals depicting the camp's liberation and effigies of collaborators were among the works on display. The prison courtyard was remade into an open-air museum of abandoned SLA material—troop carriers, Jeeps, ancient howitzers, and Hummers were showcased for anyone to clamber into. Nearby, a canteen with pool tables sold soft drinks.

In 2005, I returned to the prison museum. As soon as I entered the prison-museum grounds, I heard a detainee-docent announce to a crowd of onlookers: "Khiam is a symbol of the Israeli occupation of South Lebanon, and its role is a *mazār* [visiting site] such that you [visitors] can view the state of the occupation and its demise." He then walked us through the camp, reenacted some of the torture methods inflicted on him, narrated the camp's history, and finally waved us in the direction of the camp paraphernalia on sale at the exit. It was in this moment that I began to question the role of the former detainee turned tour guide who revisits his/her site of traumatic memory, day by day, transforming it into a spectacle of torture. In the documentary *Sajīn al-Janūb* (Prisoner of the South, 2000), a former detainee is asked to revisit the prison, and as he looks into the prison wards, his interviewer poses the following question: "When you stand here and look at the prison, what goes through your mind?" Words fail him. Instead, he shakes his head and walks away.[63] In *Regarding the Pain of Others* (2003), Susan Sontag sees a risk in proliferating images of political violence, proposing that everyday familiarity with such images has the potential to anesthetize viewers rather than mobilize them against war and atrocity.[64] Similarly, trauma memorials risk asking visitors to reconcile torture and murder with everyday war tourism. By the same token, though, they also push us to think about trauma as something that happens not only far away but close to home in "familiar" spaces.

I cannot help but wonder if we, as spectators to the prison museum's "packaged" memory in the form of real tortured bodies, risked inhabiting the space of "just watching, a position often associated with voyeurism, even disempowerment."[65] The former detainee is an exemplary figure here as the texture of his memory, with its many inconsistencies, risked being flattened beneath the scripted narrative. I began to wonder if the prison-cum-museum as a node of memory operated by tacitly overwriting the individuals enmeshed within its violent past. My interlocutor, Ali, the former detainee whom I encountered while walking around the prison grounds back in May 2000, had spent a total of eleven years in the detention center until he was released in a prisoner-exchange deal with Israel. During our impromptu conversation in 2000, on the eve of liberation, Ali had walked me to the prison-guard post at Khiam, and as we looked out at the villages he was never allowed to see during his imprisonment, he said, "This place should be kept forever as a witness to our history." But it was not.

I met Ali again in 2005 shortly before the prison memorial's destruction by Israeli bombardment in 2006. This time, Ali was palpably apprehensive about speaking openly until we were distanced from the prison grounds and recording devices were removed. Once he was no longer acting in what was now his role as docent, he was more forthcoming. Suddenly veering off the script with which he routinely conducted his tours, he told me: "Khirbet beītī [My house is ruined]," by which he meant that he was no longer able to support his family on the meager wages doled out to him in his capacity as docent. "We are the forgotten," he lamented as he walked away.

The ruination of the house, Maḥmūd Darwīsh writes, is the first and most lasting casualty of war, such that "in every object there is a being in pain . . . a memory of fingers, of smell, of an image."[66] The house as a placeholder of memories is the perennial casualty in the wars that keep returning to Lebanon, as reflected in the novels, poetry, and personal narratives I have examined so far. In "A Possible Poem on Dahiya," 'Abbās Bayḍūn, using a demolished home as a metaphor for resilience, suggests

9. Into the rubble of memory: Khiam prison-memorial in ruins, July 20, 2010. Photograph by Rola Khayyat.

that though the memories it encloses might never be redeemed, even by the poet, the forgotten survivors it once homed remain steadfast in their resolve to survive.[67] Over the course of this book, the ruined *dār* (home) of pre-Islamic poetry has evolved from an effaced physical site to the symbol in premodern poetry of a place of memory enclosed in the heart. But what happens to the interiority of a home ruined by warfare? The poets and novelists of part one tarried over what I have termed "domestic detritus," the remains of the wartime concept of home or what remains of human empathy during wartime. With reference to Khiam, Ali's declaration, then, bears witness to more than a destroyed home, for it also bears witness to a justice system in ruins.

Spectral Murmurs: Memory between Silence and Erasure

I returned to Khiam to walk with Ali amid the wreckage on July 20, 2010, when he explained his interpolation into the ruination of the now destroyed prison-memorial:

> After the liberation, the Lebanese Army used the prison as a base before Hizbullah decided to convert it into a museum. In 2006, Khiam was destroyed, and since then we have never received any state care; nobody came to the site to ask if we needed anything. Our plight could have been advertised. The Resistance wants to renovate it, but it can only do so partially since it belongs in part to the state now. We, the prisoners, have drowned beneath the rhetoric of resistance, but we, too, live daily lives, and we need to be reintegrated slowly, but nobody seems to think of us in that way. We carry stories, but we also carry personal wounds that run deeper. Those too need to be attended to. We are the forgotten remains.[68]

Carrying his personal memories like a wound in perpetuity, Ali reifies the precarity of the detainee turned docent, who, like the prison-memorial's museal ruins, performs memory in the service of war tourism, only to be obviated in the aftermath of the memorial's destruction as a forgotten human remain(der).

Leaning heavily against the charred interrogation pole he routinely demonstrated as a torture method to tourists, Ali muttered under his breath: "In some ways, Khiam in ruins is a more effective memorial right now than it will ever be again." Through my interlocutor, I enter the role of "co-witness,"[69] carrying his stories and transmitting them to others, who will hear about Khiam only through its narratives of survival and loss. Perhaps, then, the perpetually open wound that is Khiam in ruins indeed encapsulates the traces of human life, loss, and destruction.

Khiam today remains suspended between ruination and restoration. According to Ali, the LAA plans to rebuild the prison as it was in its former state of decrepitude and not after the International Red Cross visited the premises and made cosmetic changes. But these plans have yet to come to fruition. According to Harb and Deeb, "The Lebanese state has not been involved with the site's maintenance and administration due to its refusal to claim the Resistance as a Lebanese national project and a conflict over which ministry (tourism or culture) would be responsible, a conflict related to financial concerns over both costs and any potential

10. Makeshift Khiam Detention Center sign, July 20, 2010. Photograph by the author.

profits."[70] Khiam in ruins is a glaring reminder of the ruinous relations between Hizbullah and the state, which is most profoundly experienced by Khiam's neglected former detainees.

(Dis)locating Memory: Mute Witnessing and the Affective Afterlife of Ruins

Today, locals refer to the prison-museum as a *khirba,* the Arabic noun deriving from the verb *kharaba* (to demolish). Four years after its targeted demolition, I returned to visit "*khirbet* Khiam" (ruined Khiam) to observe how the destruction affects visitors' experiences, including my own. As I made my way up the steep hill to the destroyed prison-memorial, I encountered an elderly man biding his time in a desolate corner shop at the foot of the hill, who told me not to bother because "there is nothing more to see but ruins." But the destroyed prison-cum-memorial struck me as an afterworld of violence that, although neglected in the present, continues to pulsate with stories from amid its ruins. Atop the mountain, the wind howled rhythmically, sweeping its gusts over flattened slabs of concrete as it wove in and out of the wreckage of former interrogation rooms, solitary-confinement cells, prison wards, torture rooms, sunrooms, and administrative offices. I parked my lone car at the gates and stepped inside the transformed premises, taking my cues from the make-shift "open" sign pointing limply in the direction of the rubble—a signifier gesturing toward an absent referent.

Upon entry, I paused to scan the scene and allowed the uncanny silence of the ruins to fill the void. The absent din of tourists, tour guides, and insistent journalists gives this ruinous space a spectral melancholy. I use the word *melancholy* with caution here, particularly when such spaces are the ruins of anthropogenic violence. As I stood in silent contemplation, I wondered inwardly: What sense does it make to feel melancholy at the ruins of a torture center? Surely, these are not the nostalgic *aṭlāl* of pre-Islamic times. To be sure, ruins are implicitly part of all site-specific memorials, but many trauma memorials explicitly embrace ruins as a dominant core element of their exhibition strategy, as did the former

11. The remains of Khiam's solitary-confinement cells, with Suha Bshāra's cell in the forefront, July 20, 2010. Photograph by the author.

Khiam as museum. Standing in the ruins, I wondered whether, as Caitlin DeSilvey maintains, "a site could be threatened not by destruction but by preservation—the ruination of a ruin."[71] Looking around, I noticed that I was in the center of a scene flanked on all sides by rubble. Here is a space where the destroyed materiality of violence disrupts any sense of being unified in place, transforming the former site of trauma into a counter-monument to the layered testimonies, stories, and lives of its former occupants, alive and dead. An aura of haunting emerges from the voids as the "violence congealed"[72] in the rubble comes through as a spectral murmur from among the traces of a past that cannot be easily reconciled by memorial alone.

Writers such as Robert Bevan and Pierre Nora argue that memory is contingent with the materiality of the trace. The destruction of memory, they maintain, is more or less synonymous with the destruction of its architectural house. In *The Destruction of Memory: Architecture at War* (2006), Robert Bevan makes the case that "the link between any physical reminder of a people and its collective memory and the killing of the people themselves is ineluctable," whereby "the destruction of one's environment can mean disorienting exile from the memories they have invoked."[73] With the absence of such tactile touchstones of memory, the ruins risk an "out-of-sight, out-of-mind" futurity. Moreover, the French historian Pierre Nora has argued that such *lieux de mémoire* (sites of memory) have become the cornerstone of modern memory prompts because "living memories" are fast receding in modern culture. He thus proposes a conflation of memory and history whereby "modern memory" relies entirely on the archive—that is, the materiality of the trace, "the immediacy of the recording, the visibility of the image."[74]

Like Gastón Gordillo's reading of the bulldozing of the ruins of Esteco in Argentina to produce a fruit-packaging plant in his book *Rubble: The Affective Life of Destruction* (2014), I contend that although the bombardment in 2006 sought to wipe out the prison, it left behind a new affective field of rubble: the ruin of the ruin of Khiam, a double layering of violence now congealed in the ruined ruin. Instead of standing in metonymically for the bodies of victims, the ruin of the ruin works "affectively" to invoke the "visible residue of violence" atop a former site of trauma.[75] Thus, in spite of its ruinous state, Khiam feels awash with memory. The wreckage of the prison-cum-memorial's solitary-confinement cells, yards, and interrogation rooms now recalls a double-edged memory. First, it recalls the "disappeared" traces of stories buried beneath the rubble of the museum, and, second, it recalls the destroyers' willful attempt to eradicate evidence of their crime. The ruined ruin of Khiam is now a countermemorial both to its multilayered past and to the guilt of the destroyers, and what remains is defined by what is absent.

My walk-through amid the wreckage made memory paths visible in a vastly different light. Tony Bennett proposes that the sequestering of spaces of memory in museums was devised to develop "new norms of public conduct" by miming movements through sequential routes to ensure compliance with "a program of organized walking,"[76] making them what Paul Connerton calls embodied "habit memories."[77] The ruination of the ruins of Khiam opens up alternate forms of memory encounters with the detention center's painful past(s). I experienced this most clearly in the seemingly chaotic entry point to the heaps of rubble that greeted me at the gates, for there was no clear route to follow. In contemplating the mounds of twisted metal and corrugated sheets of concrete, I was reminded of Bshāra's initial feeling of disorientation upon returning to visit her destroyed solitary-confinement cell: "I felt lost," she admitted. "I couldn't find my bearings anymore. It was in ruins. The two women's sections are a heap of rubble. But you can't erase the memory of a place," she asserted. "It goes beyond Lebanon. It's the history of humanity."[78] The destruction creates a vastly different sensory engagement than the one proffered by the scripted museum routes, whereby "things in ruins . . . rebuke the way things are supposed to assume a position in regimented linearity."[79] The rhetoric of walking among the ruins of the former prison-museum site becomes akin to a ruptured narrative in the sense that Michel de Certeau defines "walking": "A kind of 'story,' composed of debris . . . leftovers . . . fragments of scattered semantic places . . . combined with things extra and other which interrupt the accepted framework and order."[80]

This begs the question as to whether the ruins of Khiam were silenced on July 20, 2006. I have argued that rather than being silenced, the ruins of the destroyed prison chart a new terrain for remembrance that could not be accommodated by the memorial but that must be read on its own terms, as must Ali's and Bshāra's narratives. Unencumbered by the encodings of the normative that go hand in hand with the routine practices that contribute to a spatialized order of (memory) production, the wreckage of the prison-cum-memorial reorganizes the spatial experience of memory into an apparently disorderly one. Thus, we experience the ruins of the former prison-museum as the narrative of voids saturated with invisible stories that nonetheless throb with the discarded effects and affects of experiences and memories. The ruin, here, assumes the role of a fragmented narrative that invites the visitor "to fill out the broken form through the active dynamism of the imagination."[81]

The perpetually deferred plans for Khiam's reconstruction have been realized in a massive resistance memorial named Mleeta Tourist Resistance Landmark, the subject of the next chapter. When I met Ali during our walk through the wreckage in early 2010, he asked me whether I had heard of the Mleeta Resistance Tourist Landmark, which had not yet opened its doors to the public. I had not. Nor was I prepared for the gargantuan museum that greeted me upon my visit a few months after I wrote this chapter.

4

Curating Resistance

On the Mleeta Resistance Tourist Landmark

Close to the Lebanon–Israel border, where guerrilla fighters and the Israeli army periodically clash, there lies a defunct front line in the South Lebanese village of Mleeta, which is home to South Lebanon's largest Resistance museum. Reaching deep into the bowels of a steep oak-sheathed mountaintop, where an array of bunkers and intricate tunnel systems funnel memory tourists to and fro, the Mleeta Resistance Tourist Landmark (Ma'lam Mlīta) proudly sits its ground. Once a live outpost for Hizbullah fighters during the occupation, the former military bunker was converted by Hizbullah into a gargantuan memory museum to "narrate the story of its Resistance"[1] by showcasing the length and breadth of its military memorabilia. Iqlīm al-Tuffāh, where Mleeta is located, became a key Resistance stronghold following the withdrawal of the Israeli army in 1985 to its "security strip," where the remains of the Khiam Detention Center are now located. Iqlīm al-Tuffāh was also the site of active warfare during the war between Hizbullah and Israel in 2006. Mleeta narrates and memorializes the military resistance of Hizbullah by utilizing military ruins as a medium.

To be sure, Mleeta is not the first time that Hizbullah put its military ruins on display. It was preceded by Bayt al-'Ankabūt, literally the "Spider's Web House," a metaphor often used by Hizbullah's secretary-general Ḥasan Naṣrallah to describe Israel's ephemeral state of being, which can allegedly, at any moment, be easily destroyed, like a spider's web. This temporary show of arms was installed in the midst of building debris in Ḍāḥiyah al Janūbiya in 2007 and was meant to commemorate the July War of 2006 by showcasing Hizbullah's might through a multifaceted approach.[2] Some of the objects I encountered on display at Bayt al-'Ankabūt are the same ones I encountered in Mleeta: captured Israeli Merkavas; Israeli paraphernalia confiscated from outposts after the Israeli withdrawal; dingy uniforms, bullets, and helmets. An interactive media center featured short highlights of the war, mainly emphasizing Israeli military cowardice through the amplification of Israeli soldiers' weeping and mourning following a guerrilla ambush.

The sheer enormity of Mleeta renders it the first of its kind in Lebanon. It took about seven years of stealthy work before it opened its doors to the public on May 25, 2010, to commemorate the tenth anniversary of the South's liberation.[3] Mleeta is significant as it represents the first major cultural production of a particular history, memory, and legacy of (Hizbullah's) resistance by entwining natural ruins with collected military

12. Bayt al-'Ankabūt (Spider's Web House) exhibition in Ḍāḥiyah al Janūbiya, June 8, 2007. Photograph by the author.

remains. Yet, unlike most sites of memory that commemorate the pastness of an event, this memory museum is fraught with a unique temporal disjuncture: it claims to (re)present a "past" spanning two decades but that in reality thrives in active bunkers only a few kilometers away. The "real" front exists a few kilometers south at the heavily fortified borderland between Lebanon and Israel, where the Khiam Detention Center Museum now lies in ruins. In Mleeta, however, war memory is interrupted, packaged, and showcased as pedagogical cultural experience.

From Pagan Ruins to Military Splendor

Surrounded by rugged mountainscapes, the Mleeta Resistance Tourist Landmark encompasses 5,000 square meters of building grounds and 60,000 square meters of natural reserves at its lofty perch 1,050 meters above sea level. From the terrace of its Martyrs' Hill (Rawḍat al- Šuhadā'),

13. The Mleeta Resistance Tourist Landmark's sprawling grounds, August 10, 2010. Photograph by the author.

one can survey the entire underlying village of Mleeta, the mountaintops of Sujud and Rakab, two former Israeli outposts, and the Lebanon–Israel border a mere twenty-three kilometers away. The namesake of Sujud Hill is a holy man referred to as "Nabī Sujud," whose shrine occasioned a plethora of interreligious encounters. According to Toufoul Abu Hodeib, "The Jewish pilgrims at the shrine concluded with a feast and a bonfire, at which local Christians and Muslims joined the Jewish pilgrims, offering their own sacrifices."[4] Today, Sujud Hill has shed its pagan past and morphed into a Resistance ruin and a targeted site of politically charged remembrance forged through participatory memory building. In doing so, the memorial indexes itself as a singular site worth remembering. The genealogy of Nabī Sujud, from pagan ruin to military splendor, underscores how Mleeta's rhetoric of resistance is aided in part by appropriating such traces of religious practice and tradition and streamlining them to suit its political intent. The museum also enrolls the remains of natural caves in its overarching narrative of victory in an ongoing transnational struggle, transforming these nonhuman ruins into avatars of Resistance ideology. As Mona Harb and Lara Deeb put it, "In Mleeta, the tree, rock, flower, bird, sky, cloud and mountain are each (and all) symbol(s) of Hizbullah's resistance which is equated with (one) history, which is associated with (this) nature, (this) land, which forms (our) culture, and these correspondences are made to be incontestably right, or righteous."[5] One of the powers of Mleeta is its ability to tap such sources of memory and affect—in trees, birds, springs, caves—in order to claim these ruins as testament to a particular history, community, and political-theological trajectory.

A Pedagogical Walk through the Ruins

I first visit the landmark on a sweltering August afternoon a few months after its inauguration on May 25, 2010. As I make my way up the steep hill, I view a succession of giant billboards advertising the museum and repeatedly featuring Sayyed Ḥasan Naṣrallah's famous axiom repeated throughout the July War of 2006: "Law 'udtum 'udna [If you return, so shall we]." This sentence is brought to graphic effect with images of a guerrilla fighter

أقول لكم إن إسرائيل هذه ، التي تملك أسلحة النوويه وأقوى سلاح جو في المنطقة
والله والله هي أوهن من بيت العنكبوت

14. Secretary-General Ḥasan Naṣrallah with a pointed finger, the caption underneath reading, “Wallāh wallāh hiya awhan min bayt al-'ankabūt” (By God, by God, this enemy [Israel] is weaker than a spider's web): placard at Mleeta, August 1, 2010. Photograph by the author.

peeking through the barrel of a Katyusha rocket. Above this image, the fine print reads: "In commemoration of the fifth year since victory" (alluding to the war between Hizbullah and Israel in 2006). Another billboard features the secretary-general with pointed finger, the caption underneath reading, "Wallāh wallāh hiya awhan min bayt al-ʻankabūt [By God, by God, this enemy (Israel) is weaker than a spider's web]." As Jacques Rancière reminds us, "These metaphors of visibility," such as the "sentence-images" of the Resistance billboards, "become the key artistic strategy by which aesthetics and politics can themselves be thought in common again."[6] Driving through the largely Shīʻite hinterland of Sidon and past these signposts, I am being readied for the highly affective and visceral experience that is Mleeta. I finally pull into the supersize parking lot, which already speaks volumes about the landmark's expectations regarding visitors, a stark contrast to the forlorn Khiam. I pay the entry fee of two thousand Lebanese lira (back then a little less than US$1.50), collect my multilingual brochure (Arabic, English, and Farsi), and join the variegated crowds of families, schoolchildren, curious visitors, and researchers before an eager guide absorbs me into his group.

Capturing Ruins: Exhibiting Interrupted Memory

Inside the museum grounds, where the meaning of detritus can be fully controlled, our guide waves to an extended display of broken drywall, bent electrical conduits, the debris of cinderblocks and collapsed shelving—all neatly corralled. This is the Exhibition Hall, featuring IDF spoils of war and a floor-to-ceiling poster exhibiting Hizbullah's "insider knowledge" of the intricate structural divisions and subdivisions of the Israeli army, we are told. I already begin to feel a creeping sense of verisimilitude just by walking through the first intricately crafted chamber: a walk that enjoins the visitor to experience Henri Lefebvre's "absolute spaces"[7] of memory through the prism of an aesthetic education of resistance, defined by the trope of the occupation in ruins.

Next up on my tour is the Multipurpose Hall, where I view a short film that dramatically sets the scene by unfolding the history of the landmark and linking it to the history of the Resistance, which culminated in the "Divine Victory" of the July War of 2006. Secretary-General Ḥasan Naṣrallah appears on the large screen imparting his message of popular resistance, followed by a genealogy of Israeli–Lebanese warfare, starting from the invasion in 1982 and extending to the war in 2006, and Naṣrallah's famous pledge that "the time of defeats is over, and the time of victories has begun." The clip closes with the words of the late secretary-general of the Resistance, Sayyed 'Abbās al-Mūsawī, assassinated by Israel in 1992, as he defiantly turns to face the screen and declares: "Isrā'īl ṣaqaṭat [Israel has fallen]." The room resounds with impassioned seated applause from what Rancière defines as "audiences on whom these speech acts [are] supposed to produce the effects of mobilizing thoughts, emotions, and energies."[8] Adrenaline soaring, our guide then ushers us out into the bright sunshine, where he directs our blinking eyes downward at the Abyss (al-Hāwiya), the site of an Israeli bombing that occurred during the peak of occupation, now strewn with Israeli Merkavas, armored vehicles and tanks, helmets, boots, bombs, and bullets captured between 1982 and 2006. Nestled amid the debris is an IDF helmet encased in cracked glass, which symbolizes the universal proverb "People in glass houses should not throw stones." Designed to be viewed from above, the Abyss is a message of defiant mockery to the Israeli jets and unmanned drones that continue to patrol and control the skies over Lebanon.

In the Abyss, a narrative of a vanquished enemy is woven out of testimonial objects. It is here that the thrum of resistance is at its loudest because the Abyss is intended to graphically represent the political and military morass in which Israel finds itself vis-à-vis Hizbullah. A Merkava Mark 4 lies belly-up, its barrel contorted into comic submission to symbolize its "defeat at the hands of the Resistance," according to the accompanying placard's description.[9] According to the site's description, the dead Merkava tank is an important symbol of defeat because of its transformation from a "mobile land fortress" into a "coffin on caterpillar tracks" after the successful ambush of it by guerrilla fighters. The overarching narrative of defeat is visually encapsulated by the dispersal of the Hebrew acronym TZ-K-l, by which the IDF are identified. Each letter is carved

15. The Abyss, Mleeta: schoolchildren in the background are being ferried around the museum grounds by a guided tour officer, August 10, 2010. Photograph by the author.

out of large concrete blocks that, as our guide explains, can be viewed aerially by Israeli warplanes, an underlying index of future war. The scattered Hebrew letters spell out "the Lebanese Quagmire"[10] around the sunken vehicles to complete the picture for those who read Hebrew and care to crane their necks (and shudder in memory or anticipation). The Abyss, my guide explains, faces westward in a perpetual state of sinking to symbolize the dusk of the Israeli occupation and "the defeat of the Zionist enemy [*al-'adū al-sahyūnī*]" against the intractable will of the Resistance fighters. Gazes lower, and bodies strain over the railings to get a closer look at the scene of carnage on display in the ruins beneath. Pointing victoriously to a captured Israeli rocket in the Abyss, my guide tells me, "We call it 'the dumb rocket [*al-saroukh al-ghabi*]' because it didn't achieve the results it was designed for."

Interpolating Postmemory Moral-Political Subjects

From the Abyss, a circuitous path (*al-masār*) leads us through a densely forested area spanning 250 meters, which eventually leads to a spiraling limestone staircase that laces its way around a steep mountain, where visitors are invited to actively participate in "postmemory" building—a mode of interpolating the waning war generation into the museum's moral-political narrative. Our guide encourages us to pause and pose for photographs alongside effigies of guerrilla fighters and even to step inside the scene and peer into the barrel of an extended AK-47 to the chorus of camera flashes. This path, which visitors tread daily, was an active front used by guerrilla fighters between 1982 and 2000, from which the party lobbed attacks against the occupied zone of the "security strip" just one mountain away. To reanimate this particular history, the Path (al-Masār) is riddled with "points of memory," such as martyrs' artifacts (*āthār al-šuhadā*), that "mediate between a forlorn past and an ever-encroaching present,"[11] painting a picture of life and death on this rugged stretch of earth for the duration of the twenty-two-year occupation. Marianne Hirsch and Leo Spitzer conceive of "points of memory" such as photographs, objects, and remnants from the past as having the power to interpolate the postmemorial subject by linking past and present, memory and postmemory, individual remembrance and cultural recall.[12] Thus, to foster a sense of authenticity for those with no memory or only a waning memory of the historical chapter of occupation being narrated, history is brought "alive." A radio stowed neatly in the brush emits live reports of skirmishes across the "security strip," which waft through in waves as I wind my way down the hill, and somewhere in the distance life-size models of guerrilla fighters in varying poses of combat dot the landscape. One soldier tends to his comrade's wounds, while another soldier carries supplies up the mountain, and others rest in between combat. Martyrs' artifacts mark the spot of fallen guerilla fighters as spectral voices come through in supplications read by the former secretary-general of the Resistance, Sayyed ʿAbbās al-Mūsawī, thus registering memory through both visceral and auditory means. The dense materiality of the artifacts

16. "Combat casualty care" diorama depicting a guerrilla fighter tending to another's wounds, Mleeta, August 10, 2010. Photograph by the author.

on display is intended to help visitors who have little knowledge about the events and their political contexts to connect affectively to this historical chapter. The ruins on display here envisage a form of mourning through which visitors can cathect a past by experiencing their own position and role in the here and now, just as much, if not more, than they do the suffering of those who are remembered. My path finally leads into the belly of the mountain through a 300-meter-long natural tunnel (*al-nafaq*)[13] formerly used as a hideout by guerrilla fighters. Elaborate battlefield maps adorn the walls of the cave (*al-mghāra*) as if they might be consulted at any given moment. The insistence here is on a past war that could become present at any given moment.

Similar bunkers in active use exist throughout the rest of southern Lebanon in secret locations, but this bunker in Mleeta is an open secret on display as part of the museum's elaborate performance of what I term "interrupted memory." As Hatim El-Hibri theorizes in relation to the museum's politics of concealment, Mleeta restages the tactics, infrastructure, and theology of guerrilla warfare—which is to say, the site puts the materiality of concealment on show for a global audience.[14] Structures of feeling emerge in this cramped space, where empathy is pegged to the notion of an implacable ethos of redemptive self-sacrifice writ large on the bunker's walls. Emerging from the cramped tunnel, I am met with a breathtaking panoramic view of the villages reclaimed by the Resistance following the Israeli withdrawal of 1985, and on a clear day even the shoreline of the Mediterranean Sea is visible. This is the Outlook (al-Mattal), where visitors can bear witness to repatriated lands, a visual reminder of a form of redeemed memory. A short tunnel ferries me back to Liberation Square (Sāḥat al-Istiqlāl), the museum's main grounds, yet another site boasting a recent memory of war between the guerrillas and the Israeli army stationed on the neighboring Sujud mountaintop. Liberation Square is essentially an annotated military rocket garden. Variegated weapons glisten amid neatly planted rows of colorful flowers and trees, all carefully manicured to adorn each iconic ruin. Children smile sweetly for pictures in front of the peeping weapons. Mleeta's architectural design has its own logic. According to Harb and Deeb, the landmark was constructed in "a quadrate shape in order to mimic the Muslim's Kiblah, while pointing to four sides: the north and south that represent the journey of the flying birds that seek a warm homeland, the east that points to the sunrise of the resistance and its society, and the west that points to the fading star of the occupation and tyranny."[15]

Spatial politics infiltrate every aspect of the museum, but it is at its peak in the last stop on our tour. At an elevation of 1,050 meters above sea level, Martyrs' Hill the highest point of Mleeta, looks disparagingly down upon its sunken neighbor wallowing in the Abyss. The steps leading to the Hill are daunting, and for this very reason, my guide tells me, it is reserved for the end, where visitors have to try (*juhud*) to climb to this arena reserved for the sacred. The pinnacle exposes the expansive southern landscape formerly occupied by Israel. My tour ends back at Liberation Square, where visitors can enjoy a drink at the canteen and purchase a memento from the gift shop. An amusement park, hotel, picnic area, and cable car connecting the surrounding iconic mountain tops form part of future plans for the sprawling museum grounds, where intermittent breaks between memory gazing and partaking can take place.

17. Panoramic views can be seen from Martyrs' Hill in Mleeta, August 10, 2010. Photograph by the author.

18. Gift shop, Mleeta, August 10, 2010. Photograph by the author.

Appropriating Natural Ruins: Storing Memory

Mleeta's resistance narrative is deeply imbricated in its natural surroundings, whereby memory is literally planted in the soil as a seed out of which a verdant narrative of resistance sprouts. From a distance, the landmark looks contiguous with the mountain save for the iconic yellow Hizbullah flags undulating in the wind among the dense foliage. The museum's buildings are made of *béton brut* (raw, unfinished concrete) to craft a sense of seamless continuity with the surrounding rugged terrain. The staircase spiraling down the steep mountain is skillfully etched out of limestone, and its "points of memory" are discretely nestled into the surrounding environs.

On July 21, 2011, I met one of Mleeta's head architects in his headquarters in Ḍāḥiya, where he discussed the museum's pedagogical and ideological purposes. The architect confirmed the notion of *al-taʿāțuf maʿal-tabīʿa* (cooperation with nature) as the guiding principle behind the museum's design. He explained how he consulted foreign museums (among those he cited were the Ashmolean Museum in Oxford and the

19. The Outlook, Mleeta, August 10, 2010. Photograph by the author.

Holocaust Museum in Berlin) before settling on an "indigenously Lebanese design."[16] In fact, the landmark bears more than a passing resemblance to the Jewish Museum and the Holocaust Memorial in Berlin. The naked and unadorned concrete and metal structures of Mleeta emulate the battlefield architecture but also the materials and forms of the two Jewish memorial structures. "Know thine enemy" is one of the dominant themes running throughout the landmark. As the architect put it, "We saw how *'adūna* [our enemy] uses the museum medium to express its cause, such as the Holocaust. We discovered that we needed to combat the enemy with its own medium." Mleeta's self-claimed feat is that, unlike any other museum in Lebanon, it makes efficient use of its natural surroundings (*min bī'itna*) by harmonizing architecture with land and, thus, maintaining a so-called native connection to memory. "Even Beitteddine [Palace], which is supposed to be representative of traditional Lebanese design," the architect exclaimed, "was conceived by an Italian!" He then explained the rationale behind the choice of the museum's location:

> We could have chosen a location for our museum in Beirut that would have been more easily accessible to the public, but it did not have the stored memory of place [ma 'indūhal dhākira allathi ikhtizinuhal makān]; therefore, the decision was made to locate it in a place that witnessed live resistance activity. And since Mleeta, which is now Israeli free, was once on the front line [*tallit sujud*]—because this valley served as the connection [*fāsilah*] point between Israel and the Resistance—we chose it for its natural beauty; . . . it is one of Lebanon's most beautiful villages, and, second of all, as a landmark it is an important one because its caves were used by resistance fighters up until the 2006 war.

Even the etymology of the landmark's name, "Mleeta," is organically sourced: it is believed to be of Syriac origin, *al-imtīlā'*, which means "repletion," referring to the abundant water sources of this fecund region. Thus, even the Syriac root of the name "Mleeta" is harnessed to political intent, for as the architect explained, "We thought of giving it another name but decided to preserve its historic name in line with the landmark's spirit of preservation." Here, "stored memory" binds people and land into a singular narrative whereby the resistance fighter becomes synonymous with collective self-sacrifice, and the land serves as witness to this symbolic gesture. More than a symbolic ordering of space, the landscape becomes what Tim Ingold calls a "taskscape," composed as a temporal-material document or "testimony" of being: "The landscape tells—or rather is—a story. It enfolds the lives and times of predecessors who, over the generations, have moved around in it and played their part in its formation. To perceive the landscape is therefore to carry out an act of remembrance and remembering is not so much a matter of calling up an internal image, stored in the mind, as of engaging perceptually with an environment that is itself."[17]

This suturing together of place and memory is made manifest by the act of walking in the steps of the guerrilla fighter. The visitor experiences the contours of the landscape underfoot, thereby imbibing what Gaston Bachelard would call "muscular consciousness"[18] of the dire conditions in which the guerrilla fighter safeguarded the land during the occupation. The experience of memory becomes a hypersensory one that involves a corporeal engagement as a way of regimenting the ideology of singular resistance and sacrifice. In the interview, the architect also directly addressed the importance of providing a counternarrative to US and Israeli narratives of the occupation and liberation of Lebanon: "We want the museum to serve as a corrective to Western misinformation about us as terrorists by showing the world the devotion of a people who lived and died by their love for Lebanon."

Local authorities further expanded the affective power of the monument to appropriate the tree, bird,[19] and stone, which are reconstructed along supernatural lines to symbolize the spiritual strength of the Resistance. In fact, the museum's resistance narrative garners its impetus from the remains of the *sindiān*, or oak tree. "No visit is complete," my guide insists at the end of our tour, "without a visit to the tree." Ushering us behind a giant cement structure, he points emphatically to a narrow crevice in the wall where a lone *sindiān* sits forlornly with exposed roots nestled deep into the limestone. "This is the tree that inspired the spiritual concept of this landmark," he proudly declares, "and if you look closely at the roots, you will even decipher the letters of Mleeta [the Arabic letters that spell 'Mleeta']!" The tree had been conveniently "discovered" just a hundred meters from the monoliths, and workers cleared the area of vegetation and turned it into a memorial of sorts to the tree. Thus, the *sindiān* is invested with totemic qualities. Just as the *sindiān* is considered inalienable from the southern landscape, so, too, is the Resistance densely woven into the fabric of the South, which includes its people, its geography, and, by extension, its archive of memory. To better flesh out the totemic quality of the tree's protective spirit, my guide ends our tour with an anecdote that reifies the notion of *altāf al-bahiyya* (nature's graces) by way of the tree's guerrilla-sheltering qualities: "During the occupation, the Israeli military was extremely bothered by the *ḥirsh* [cluster of *sindiān* trees] because it served as a hiding ground for the *muqāwimūn* [resistance fighters], so they attempted to burn it down, but the wind blew the flammable liquid away from the mountain, so the trees were spared, such that the fighters could continue to maintain their posts."

The ruins of Mleeta's natural surroundings are thus enrolled into the dominant matrix of Resistance memory. They are places where, as Pierre Nora has argued, memory oozes, becoming a tangible component of the geography.[20]

Despite its discourse of fixity through the *arḍ,* landscape, Mleeta's memorial aesthetic is premised on a rather precarious future as "ruin" (*kharāb*)—one that construes the war museum as a continuum in an "unfinished war" (with Israel) that could result at any given moment in its "erasure" by directed bombardment. The rhetoric of the Abyss points to this very probability; it is directed outward and upward toward a potential Israeli air force jet—taunting an attack that could reduce the entire site to a pile of rubble. Mleeta even promotes itself as situated in this in-between role: it is that which "carves the memory of a continual stage in the history of Lebanon."[21] Thus, the ruin here has a twofold rather contradictory function: along with the museum's efforts to solidify a narrative of resistance in part mobilized through its appropriation of "natural" and military ruins, it simultaneously posits its futurity as ruin, pointing back to its "interrupted" memory in an as yet unfinished war with Israel. The museum's

20. *Sindiān* (oak) tree with exposed roots supposedly spelling "Mleeta," August 10, 2010. Photograph by author.

potential future as ruin thereby undercuts its attempts to fix memory in a volatile spatiopolitical landscape.

Conclusion

I have argued that the affective capacity of memorials is a product of tensions and negotiations between competing memory forces. Today the main identifying memory that governs the southern borderland is sectarian political identity, but the rubble at Khiam and the eclectic and often contradictory narratives of its detainees, including the resistant sisterhood of Suha Bshāra's memoirs, remain resistant ruins. I have shown how Mleeta is rife with remains that can serve as portals to other worlds. Such places can be encountered when one sensitively probes for hidden memories beneath the rubble, memories that do not entirely fit the tamed topographies of remembrance and their singular political projects, as at Mleeta. These alternative memories evoke stories of resistance amid the wreckage that comes across as a form of quiet but powerful haunting, as silent but resistant ruins.

Part Three

The People's Right to the Ruin

5

Toward an Archive of Unintended Detritus

> What I shall call an archive is neither the totality of texts that a civilization has preserved, nor the ensemble of traces that have been saved . . . but the play of rules that in a culture determine the appearance and disappearance of utterances, their paradoxical existence as events and as things.
>
> —Michel Foucault, *The Archaeology of Knowledge*

Throughout my inquiry into the representation of ruins from varying textual, vernacular, and material sites of memory, I have thus far explored the eclectic memory poetics and politics of ruminating over ruins against the backdrop of Lebanon's understudied South. The reader of this book is left to sift through growing piles of wreckage and to piece together the fragments of a ruinous past that shifts kaleidoscopically. Standing before various ruin traces of war, the writers, poets, activists, and former detainees I feature have mused over war and its various iterations, raising challenging questions about the way memory is mediated, erased, or hitched to greater politico-discursive projects. I have thus far placed the focus on readily apparent literary-cultural forms of commemorating war; in this chapter, I take account of the uncommemorated ruins that fall outside memory-building practices but that nonetheless warrant closer inspection. These ruins are the "unintended" detritus of war that riddle the urban landscape, silently yet persistently haunting the nation.

Over time, most ruins fade back into the landscape and become spectral markers of a troubled past. Lebanon's urban landscape is riddled with such silent reminders—derelict houses, bullet-scarred walls, abandoned sites of trauma: dark presences that embody the ghosts of the past. As modern warfare proliferates, the ceremonial act of standing before its ruins acquires an even greater urgency. This chapter places unmarked relics of war in opposition to a ruin turned memorial, the Beit Beirut Museum and Urban Cultural Center, which has been curated to narrate a particular story. In the two previous chapters, I examined ruins in "intentional" sites of memory in South Lebanon alongside heterogenous countermemories that resist the hegemonic discourse of sectarian memory culture. I showed how two memorials, Khiam and Mleeta, command the public to pause and remember by turning our attention away from other genealogies of resistance and highlighting a specifically militant form of resistance on ruinous display. Intentional ruins are the preferred modality of the state or, in the case of South Lebanon, of the shadow state. In other words, intentional sites of memory are overtly commemorative, whereas the second category of memory that I focus on here comprises the "unintentional" detritus of war, which silently evokes a violent past while quietly receding into the backdrop of everyday life. Adrian Forty insists that objects may be forgotten even as they continue to exist because the life-world of an object depends not on its enduring materiality but on its social currency.[1] In other words, officials and museum curators can induce oblivion even without eradicating traces because the materiality of those objects is not as important as how the objects activate public memory.[2] Yet the haunting potentiality of the ruin is clearly a difficult one to bury or to silence, as the previous chapters have demonstrated. Attending to the spectral afterlife of ruins, Jeanette Bicknell distinguishes ghosts from ruins: "If all that remains of a structure are piles of rubble, perhaps marked by a memorial plaque, then the structure is a ghost rather than a ruin."[3]

I posit that the potential of the ruin to exude affective haunting is due precisely to its uncanny presence as a mound of rubble that refuses to remain invisible. Rather than exhaustively exploring the wide gambit of war sites, I draw a counterpoint among the Burj al-Murr (Murr Tower), the Holiday Inn hotel, and a curated ruin-memorial called "Beit Beirut" (House of Beirut), Lebanon's first intentional Civil War museum. I explore the silencing of the Holiday Inn and Burj Tower through public disregard and the ventriloquizing of Beit Beirut as a form of memory imposition. As Ann

Laura Stoler notes, disregard involves a form of "politically evasive turning away,"[4] a notion that is key to understanding the spatiality of oblivion as well as its implications for and limits in mediating public war memory. As Gordillo rightly notes, war relics may lose their capacity to haunt if the public is encouraged to look elsewhere, to direct our gaze at sites and ruins that are galvanized as significant nodes of memory with allegedly greater affective value.[5] While examining public disregard for Burj al-Murr and the Holiday Inn and the nudging of attention toward Beit Beirut, I engage cultural-artistic practices, virtual and material archives, and fictional forums of memory that attempt to impede the process of oblivion.

Untracing War: Absent-Present Countermemorials

The heart of Beirut is haunted by two iconic ghosts: the Holiday Inn and the Murr Tower, locally known as "Burj al-Murr"—but also known as the "Tower of Bitterness" (Murr Tower)—notorious sites of sniper activity during the Ḥarb al-Otelet (War of the Hotels) in 1975–76. In chapter 2, we encountered the Holiday Inn as a fictional ruin in Ghādah al-Sammān's wartime novel *Beirut Nightmares,* which centers on the burned-out hulk of the edifice as it was occupied in 1975–76 in the opening phase of the fifteen-year Civil War, when armed factions battled for control of the capital at the site of its glamorous nest of luxury hotels. The fictional narrator's entrapment beneath the smoldering fumes of the burning Holiday Inn gives us a sense of the building's impending future as ruin. In line with Adrian Forty's insistence that the permanence of an object does not preclude its oblivion,[6] it is the edifices' quotidian existence that makes them uncomfortable to bear witness to because they are daily reminders that violence once permeated their walls. These buildings are not easy to miss, nor are they peripherally located: they provide panoramic views of Beirut's former *burj* (city center), where traffic weaves its daily course around the buildings' unfinished boundaries. Their invisibility to the public eye call into question their quotidian existence as markers of a civil war, which, like the buildings themselves, remains largely unacknowledged.

The Holiday Inn was built between 1971 and 1974 and opened only fleetingly as a luxury hotel before serving as a strategic military position throughout the war. Beirut's hotel district "was part of the active, daily and contested production of the geopolitical imaginations of the militias," according to the political geographer Sara Fregonese.[7] Rival groups fought ferociously for control of the city, turning the twenty-six-story Holiday Inn into a notorious snipers' nest. On one side were Lebanese right-wing parties, backed by the United States and aiming to expel armed Palestinian groups from Lebanon. On the other were left-wing parties allied with Yasser Arafat's Palestine Liberation Organization and backed by the Soviet Union, who saw the right-wing Christians as an extension of Israeli and American influence. According to Aseel Sawalha, from the initial stages of war the Beirut Central District "became the epicenter of a maelstrom of violence," the streets transformed into "icons of destruction."[8]

For more than forty years, the skeletal remains of the Holiday Inn have spectrally stood ground in central Beirut. Today the hotel is cordoned off by the Lebanese army to keep the pubic out. The other ghost is the Murr Tower, which also faced a thwarted future. The Murr family had envisioned an illustrious future for the tower as the Beirut Trade Center; then the Civil War erupted, and it has remained a massive gray eyesore. The tallest building in Beirut at the time, during the Civil War the Murr Tower became a landmark of morbid strategic importance in the militarized urban geography as it soared over what became the divided city's frontline, exposing surrounding areas. Haunting stories of humans tossed to the ground far below permeate its many identical stories. After the war ended, the Murr Tower was deemed structurally deficient and in violation of numerous zoning laws, yet it was never destroyed because of its density and height. It remained petrified in the postwar landscape, and, like the Holiday Inn, promptly disappeared from everyday view. As Chad Elias underscores in relation to such sites in the postwar period, "Rather than seeking to resolve the contradictions of the [reconstruction] process, these counter-monuments heighten them and thus implicate viewers in mnemonic practices."[9] As uncommemorated sites of trauma, the Murr Tower and the Holiday Inn highlight the politics of nonmourning of war remains in the postwar era. Yet rather than melding into the postwar landscape, these countermonuments stand out like sore thumbs, troubling dominant memorial practices that privilege the transformation of sites of trauma and their associated ruins into fixed memorial spaces. In an attempt to stave off the process of oblivion, several artists have attempted to revivify the Murr Tower through pop-up art installations and animations.

From Burj al-Murr (Tower of Bitterness) to Burj al-Hawa (Tower of Wind)

For two short days in July 2018, the Lebanese architect Jad El-Khoury draped colorful curtains from the prison-size windows of the thirty-four-story Murr Tower, turning the former eyesore into eye candy. Khoury titled his project *Burj al Hawa* (Tower of Wind) to reflect its undulating drapery, and for a fleeting moment, the tower turned heads before Solidère officials forced Khoury to dismantle his installation for so-called security reasons. The idea behind El-Khoury's project was to garner public response to the transformation of the Murr Tower from a morbid monolith to an eye-catching reminder of the Civil War's ruinous persistence despite the officially designated rupture between "war" and "peace." In 2019, another animation by the Lebanese architect Jean-Paul El-Hachem, titled *Coming Back to Life*, transformed the Murr Tower into a phantasmagoric edifice enveloped by a sheer exoskeleton through which we could see grass and trees sprouting, instead of dust mites swirling, in the warm sunlight. In the animation, the Murr Tower even sported a rooftop memorial space, where a halo of light shimmered on rainwater trickling into a circular pool. By turning the building's ruinous entrails into verdant lungs, the animator redefined its traces of war as traces of life and the tower as a living rather than decaying entity. By breathing life into the ruins of the Murr Tower, both artistic engagements reinscribed the dilapidated edifice into the present and future lifeworld of the city's inhabitants. Gastón Gordillo argues that how ruins effect and exude haunting is not by their material presence as objects alone but also by how particular bodies are affected by them.[10] In line with Gordillo's suggestion that the ruin's capacity to haunt the viewer is dependent on its affective haunting, these two artistic interventions attempted to restore the Murr Tower, even if fleetingly, on the mental and emotional map of commuters too accustomed to looking away.

21. Silent ghosts: a building in central Beirut flanked on its right by Burj al-Murr, October 1, 2012. Photograph by the author.

Collecting War

Projects undertaken by nongovernmental organizations (NGOs) also attempt to open up an alternative space for memory work that counters the silence of the Lebanese state on the subject of war memory and foregrounds the forgotten, whether they be the wartime missing or physical markers of violence. Founded in 2004 by the German filmmaker Monika Borgmann and the late Lebanese publisher Lokman Slīm (d. 2021), Umam Documentation & Research presents itself as the cultural bastion of Lebanese war archives, separate from the state and its ongoing policy of public censure and denial: "The collection being built by Umam D&R is destined for Lebanon's public, and . . . is open to everyone without the restrictions imposed by State or academic entities."[11] According to Umam's mission statement, it "aims to preserve, examine and debate the memories" through alternative archival practices.[12] Umam's memorial site is both physical and virtual. The organization's base and material archive are physically located within a traditional Lebanese villa compound in Ḥāret Ḥreik in Beirut's southern suburbs (al-Ḍāḥiya). The organization's "citizen archive" is a ballooning collection of newspapers, journals, and memoirs; workshops; films; public discussions; and exhibitions held in a gallery space called "the Hangar." Umam attempts to counteract state-enforced oblivion through several projects that address the Lebanese disappeared, such as *Missing* (2008) and *What Is to Be Done? Lebanon's War-Loaded Memory* (2008–9), which profiled some of the seventeen thousand persons whose fates have yet to be officially determined, as well as through projects that address war crimes, amnesties, and peace initiatives, such as *Peace Upon You: Revisiting Past Attempts to End Lebanon's Conflicts* (2015–16).[13] Part of Umam's stated objectives is to "inventory" the traces of the Civil War through archival practice; for instance, its virtual database Memory at Work, claims to be a "virtual museum that collects thousands of war-related articles, photographs, films, texts, and testimonies."[14] While claiming to give expression to local voices and interests, Umam nevertheless remains dependent on international donor research agendas and global trends. As some critics caution, that dependence can both depoliticize and distance organizations from their social bases, who become "social groups in need of instruction" rather than "constituencies from which they take their direction and legitimacy."[15] Yet despite Umam's troubling "NGO-ization"[16] and theoretical assumption that archives can be repositories for "truthful" reconciliation, the organization has generated some affective projects for cathecting Lebanon's troubled past.[17]

One year after the July War of 2006, Umam curated the exhibition *Collecting Dahiyya*, which aimed at documenting the history of the southern suburb of Beirut and its rapid transformation caused mainly by the ongoing wars in the region. The ethos of this project resonates with 'Abbās Bayḍūn's poem "A Possible Poem on Dahiya," which recasts Ḍāḥiya's ruins as markers of resistance to the homogenizing discourse that reduces its complex demographic to a monolithic belt of misery. Similarly, *Collecting Dahiyya* sets out to expand the cartographic imaginary of Ḍāḥiya by offering an alternative genealogy of the area through heterogenous memories, affects, histories, oral histories, vernacular memory, and pluralistic pasts. According to Lokman Slīm, "People should know that beneath this generic term [Ḍāḥiya], is concealed a complex and multi-layered world."[18] By means of posters, maps, photographs, interviews with former residents of Ḍāḥiya who have since 2006 migrated to other parts of Beirut, a series of short films captured during the war and called "Dahiyehscope," and an interactive whiteboard map, guests are interpolated into the re-creation of the southern neighborhood. Rather than paying attention only to memory, the exhibition focuses on the futurity of Ḍāḥiya by inviting guests to mark up a "map in progress" and thus to creatively contribute to the construction of the neighborhood. Part of the aim of this project is to disabuse the viewer of the notion of a singular monolithic Ḍāḥiya and, as Craig Larkin put it, "the homogenizing logic of displacement and sectarian ghettoization."[19] The posters trace Ḍāḥiya's origins from provincial Ottoman farmland to depopulated wasteland to evoke the large wave of displacement during the Lebanese Civil War and the violent aftermath of segregation after the war with Israel in 2006.

In 2012, Umam marked the anniversary of the Civil War with the launch of its memory bus tour project, *The Bus Takes the Podium: Voyages into the Memory of Lebanon and Its People*, a yearlong tour of Lebanon's historic conflict sites, or "memory stops," in a bus purposely built for the project. The idea was to gather people and put them in visceral contact with the forgotten detritus of the Civil War. The bus is a simulacrum of the actual bus that infamously sparked the outbreak of the Civil War. After the massacre of thirty Palestinians in a bus in 'Ayn al-Rummana in 1975, the bus was repaired and put back in service for almost a decade, until a rocket exploded next to it, riddling the vehicle with shrapnel. Considering the vehicle a bad omen, its owner finally dumped it, leaving it abandoned for decades in a parking lot before Umam founder Lokman Slīm and his colleagues tracked it down. The contrast between the original bus and its replica strikes at the heart of what the whole project represents. "'Al-Bosta' [colloquial for 'the Bus'] is the principal icon of the Civil War," Slīm asserts. "Everybody agrees that the war started on board it. So, with our new bus, we tried to create a counter-Bosta, whose message is to say no to war."[20]

Shortly after my interview with Slīm in late 2012, a modern version of "the Bus," outfitted with pedagogical tools, began touring the country on its first "memory bus tour." In this modern war ruin, passengers are ferried from one Civil War marker to another as a tour guide annotates each stop in relation to its context within the Civil War. Although I did not partake of said memory tour, in a similar spirit, on a balmy September morning that same year, I managed to defy army orders and enter the Holiday Inn's echo chambers. Inside its hulk, a collection of ruined objects coalesces in the present: light bulbs dangle precariously, tangled wires snake out of walls, smashed-up chairs huddle in corners, and a piano defiantly squats in the middle of a giant "reception hall." Something about being in this unrecognized space of conflict reignites a pathos akin to the spectral haunting I felt in the ruins of the Khiam ruins. A sense of haunting emerges from the void, coaxing the ghosts of the past into spectral conversation with the unexpected visitor. In this hollowed-out space, I cannot help but be reminded of Tim Edensor's notion that ruins generate affective forms of evocation that are usually felt and interpreted through the most universal figure of a haunting: spirits.[21] As Trevor L. Hoag puts it, "Because the struggle to mourn and/or grieve is often blocked, occluded, prohibited, even struck down and put to death[,] there is quite a lot at stake ethico-politically in the morbid 'undertaking' of attending the dead and their desires. Yet one must accept bearing such palls and sorrows if one is to respond to the call for justice that the ghost issues."[22] The Lebanese state's attempts to impede access to the Holiday Inn (and thus the state's wishes for hegemonic memory and/or obliviousness) produces surprising and unintentional effects; more precisely, the ghost at issue here is a rhetorical figure for envisioning the haunting force of memory and its indissoluble link to justice. Thus, to experience haunting in this space is to attend to a countermemorial narrative and its complex rhetorical relations among memory, ghosts, and justice.

The resurrection of the iconic bus was preceded by a spate of artwork dealing with the issue of war and memory, such as the Lebanese artist Hūsām Bukailī's silk-screen interpretation of the 'Ayn al-Rummana bus in his exhibition *A Bus and Its Replicas*, depicting a series of cartoonish figures gesticulating frantically as assailants approach a cheerfully colored bright-red bus. This exhibition was followed by a slew of other artistic productions dealing with the memory of the Civil War. *The Road to Peace: Paintings in Times of War, 1975–1991* is probably the most chilling account of the shards of war that lodge themselves in the viscera of artistic imaginaries. Curated by Sāliḥ Barakāt, hosted by the Beirut Art Center, and named for a book of harrowing, diary-style charcoal drawings by the late artist Aref al-Rayess published in 1979, *The Road to Peace* made public a hitherto unseen body of art produced under duress by twenty artists from the Civil War era. Many of the works were culled from artists' studios, estates, and private collections. Some had never been shown before, and several were never intended for public exhibition. *The Road to Peace* made its debut in 2009, before being withdrawn from the gallery space allegedly because of its reference to the "hostility, brutality, and cruelty" of a "mad environment."[23] Twisted shrapnel contorted into sculptures graced the gallery space as visitors weaved their way around, gazing, touching, and photographing these tactile manifestations of a tormented past suddenly made all too present.

Umam's "fictional" counterpart, the Atlas Group of the Lebanese artist Walīd Ra'ad, conceives of itself as an imaginary foundation of memory whose aim is to research, document, study, and produce audio, visual, and literary artifacts of contemporary Lebanese history, while snubbing its nose at archival "truth."[24] The idea behind the Atlas Group is to push the notion of archiving war memory to its utmost fictional limits. The Atlas Group's archive is populated by imaginary characters to deconstruct the way history becomes documented, made believable, and eventually petrified as hegemonic truth. Many of Ra'ad's projects present what appear to be long-lost visual archives from the Lebanese Civil War, like those collected by Umam. Much has been written about the Atlas Group, yet one project among many stands out: *Hostage: The Bachar Tapes* (2001), a sixteen-minute experimental documentary that renarrates the Western hostage crisis between 1982 and 1992[25] from the perspective of a fictional Arab captive held hostage in 1985. The video introduces "Souheil Bachar," an imaginary character inspired by the real-life Suha Bshāra, whom we encountered in the narrative of Khiam Detention Center in chapter 3. In *Hostage*, Ra'ad draws a counterpoint between the Western hostage crisis, which received much news coverage, and the overlooked hostage crisis—that is, the detention of thousands in Khiam Prison in South Lebanon. Souheil Bachar narrates his time spent in captivity with five American hostages in Beirut during the 1980s and his feeling of being ostracized despite his claustrophobic cohabitation with the other men in a dingy small room. Ra'ad's video probes the fraught relations between the Lebanese detainee and his Western counterparts, especially in the privileging of white-male subjectivity in contemporary hostage narratives. Bachar's account, although told in the first person, is mediated by a female voice in English that mistranslates his words, thereby not only muffling his voice but giving his words new meaning altogether. Even though Bashar speaks openly to the camera, the documentary implies that his voice will remain muted.

Although many of the documents in the Atlas Group Archive[26] are based on genuine historical sources, Ra'ad inserts an alternative story within the grand narrative to trouble the latter's truth value, bringing fictive histories to bear on discourses on terrorism. He ultimately conceives of his fictional documents and archives not as "emblems of fact or scraps of evidence" but "as traces that oscillate between history, memory, and fantasy."[27]

The Atlas Group has also fastidiously collected photographs of bombed automobile engines from the archives of the Lebanese Arabic newspaper

An-Nahār (The Day), printed throughout the Civil War, to create an alternative archive of supposedly meaningless rubble. By systematically archiving what is deemed worthless by society and considered to have no memorial value, Ra'ad asks for a radical shift in perspective that reshapes worthless debris into affectively charged matter. At the same time, Ra'ad mocks the seemingly random choices about what enters or exists in the archive of memory in line with what Foucault describes as a "play of rules which in a culture determine the appearance and the disappearance of utterances, their paradoxical existence as events and as things."[28] In a statement reminiscent of Khūrī's fictional character Yālū, Ra'ad posits war as an event that remains beyond the experience of the witness or survivor. Rather, it is only belatedly, in the deep viscera of the survivor, that this event leaves its mark. Accordingly, the archival project that Ra'ad has undertaken in the name of the Atlas Group seeks not to bear witness but to question archival truth. In *Posthumous Images* (2018), Chad Elias argues that this alternate archive gives form to affective dimensions of lived experience that counter militant forms of resistance. Elias shows how, like *Hostage*, Akram Zaatari's experimental video documentary *All Is Well on the Border* (1997) and Rabih Mroué's video *Three Posters* (2000) problematize the representation of subjects whose stories have been excised from the official narratives of Lebanese history. Elias argues that rather than ventriloquizing the resistance fighters of the Lebanese Left, both works challenge the possibility of representation in the artistic and the political sense.

Like the novels examined in chapter 2, Ra'ad's work addresses the mute subjects, but instead of speaking for them, he asks how fiction can function as a critical alternative to both the state's silence on the question of war memory and the equally detrimental homogenizing effects of a collective memory. By focusing on images that are normally shunted from the archive, such as images of bombed cars, the Atlas Group points to ways in which quotidian memory gets lost in the dominant archive's cracks. Whether consciously or not, these archival practices by the Atlas Group and Umam attempt to encode alternative ways of collecting war memories that are often eclipsed by domineering narratives of martyrdom[29] or by its counterpart, total oblivion.

Whereas Umam pegs a moral imperative to its memory work, Walīd Raʿad's approach to archival practice asks us to undo our received notions of history, memory, fiction, and, above all, morality. What Raʿad's work is meant to foreground is not so much the question of what constitutes a genuine history but the construction of narratives out of the textual tools that we often deem "fictitious," such as the novels and poetry examined in part one. Raʿad's fabrication of history, together with his use of multiple and often contradictory authorial positions, undoubtedly serves to undermine the stability of archival truth seeking.

So, what differentiates a memory site from a fictional work? Is it the framework that deems one and not the other credible? The achievement of Raʿad's work is that it pushes us to consider the fraught nature of trying to "house" a certain version of memory within one discursive framework. In that vein, I close this chapter by invoking a museum problematically designated as Beirut's first intended house of memory. If Ḥasan Dāwūd's *Bināyat Mātīld* were to traverse the realm of fiction into reality, Beit Beirut, in its originary guise before it turned into a museum, would be the embodiment of that house.

Standing before the Ruins of a Great House

On August 28, 2018, the sound of Yo-Yo Ma's cello could be heard gently wafting out of the dilapidated remains of a ruined yellow building at the corner of Damascus Street and Independence Avenue on Beirut's former Green Line. This was a special pop-up performance by Ma, the Syrian clarinetist Kinan Azmeh, the Lebanese vocalist Oumaima al-Khalil, and the oud player Ziād al-Ahmadieh to celebrate "culture's ability to connect at the intersection of Lebanon's divided past and inclusive future,"[30] perhaps best encapsulated by the melancholic sound waves' ability to seamlessly cross the formerly uncrossable divide. The choice to house the concert in the ruined yellow house has everything to do with the house's genealogy. It is supposed to be a symbol of remembrance and reconciliation first conceived of as Mathaf li-Dhākirah Beirut (Museum for the Memory of Beirut) and eventually renamed Beit Beirut (House of Beirut).[31] As Sophie

22. Cross-sectional view of Beit Beirut as seen from the ground, September 9, 2017. Photograph by the author.

Brones points out, the museum's unique challenge is its purported goal to "incorporate local collective memories and stories and to build part of the museum discourses on the various interpretations of the public spheres."[32] The so-called Barakāt Building, named after its former owners, or the "Yellow House," as it is more colloquially known, is both an architectural landmark and a historical symbol of life in wartime Beirut. Built in the 1920s, the building is a French-era residence, and, like the Holiday Inn and Burj Tower, it played a strategic role during the Lebanese Civil War as a favored snipers' nest because of its location on the former Green Line. Physically (pock)marked by its history, the building, Beit Beirut, is now a museum of the history of the city of Beirut and an urban cultural center. It was, however, under constant threat of demolition before it became the property of the municipality of Beirut, its destruction suspended by sheer activism. Mona Ḥallāk, the leading activist behind the eleven-year conservation campaign, pitched the building as an important testament to the war: "As a monument produced by the war, it should stay as such."[33] In 1997, the Barakāt family had asked for the demolition of the building in exchange for monetary compensation, but the Beirut Heritage Preservation Activists, among whom Ḥallāk is a key member, began to fight for its preservation.

Starting in 1997, Ḥallāk organized public actions around the building (press articles, internet sites, TV coverage, lectures, public tours of the building) and an exhibition there of all the objects and artifacts she had collected in the dentist's clinic on the building's third floor. Among the exhibition attendees was the novelist Ilyās Khūrī. Ḥallāk dreamed up a project of inventorying collection practices in which everyday visitors would be interpolated into the stories of complete strangers. Her hope was that this memory game, which she named *The Photo Mario Project*, would be added to the museum's permanent collection. People would be invited to identify one of the nameless photographs of the Yellow House's former inhabitants in Ḥallāk's collection and trace the hitherto unidentified person back to his/her family and thus in the process to cathect to the missing person's genealogy and prewar lifeworld. Through the practice of collecting wartime photographs, an archive of the imagination would be generated via photographic appropriation by visitors. In turn, stories of birth, love, family, friendship, reunion, pain, fragmentation, diaspora, death, survival, and resilience as well as of the many transformations of the city and its people over the past fifty years could be brought to light. Ḥallāk believed her memory project would finally be brought to fruition in 2003, when Beirut's municipality permitted the transformation of the Barakāt Building into a memory museum after it expropriated the building to turn it into a "public-interest space." The Beirut City Council released the following mission statement:

> The city of Beirut shall expropriate lot 1237—Achrafieh—and turn the Barakāt Building into a museum, a civic cultural centre focusing on the history of urban development of the City of Beirut, offering people a place for interaction and debate in the heart of their city, a place for meeting and reconciliation, a space for memory so as not to be swept up by amnesia. This project is a unique opportunity to have a living museum dedicated to our urban history and collective memory, a witness to the rebirth of pre-war successful endeavors, an effort to which every citizen is invited to contribute.[34]

In this statement, the museum is described as a counterpublic space—first to counter amnesia and second to counter its own demolition. Yet, despite this counterpublic mission statement, the building in its museum guise began to catalyze certain forms of oblivion as the curatorial process papered over many significant memory triggers, as I explore later in this chapter. But before I do so, it is important to provide a genealogy of the Yellow House as it morphed from a sniper's nest to a museum of memory.

From Yellow House to Sniper's Nest

In 1924, the affluent Barakāt family commissioned the construction of the sandstone building, which was taken up by the architect Youssef Aftimos (1866–1952). The "Yellow House" still exudes Ottoman elegance with its high arches and elevated terraces overlooking a district of generic, eyesore tower blocks. Many of the mansions built during that period evoke central Beirut's fast-vanishing charm: arched pillars, floor-to-ceiling windows, red roofs, balconies draped over the Mediterranean, and generous salons where richly colored tiles basked beneath the warm sunshine. Aftimos conjured up a mansion of ochre sandstone decorated with carvings made from another harder local stone known in Arabic as *furne*. In 1932, Fouad Kozah, another famous Lebanese architect, designed the second and third floors of the building. It is essentially two houses spliced together, each with several apartments, adjoined by an unusual central hall straddling a corner that allows light to infiltrate almost every single room. The Barakāts occupied the second floor with its view of the Mediterranean and rented out the other apartments. A Palestinian Christian family lived opposite a Maronite dentist—thus, supposedly opposing factions were coexisting peacefully when war broke out. In time, according to Ḥallāk, the Barakāt Building allegedly became a welcoming space for the followers of all religions alike, their faces immortalized in the negatives found in a destroyed photo studio on the first floor of the building, which Ḥallāk now has in her possession. The photo studio is the basis for Ḥallāk's memory project. "And they [the building inhabitants] lived in harmony until 1975," Ḥallāk told me and a group of students during a tour in 2017.[35] The Barakāt family fled to safer ground as soon as the war began, and militias swiftly occupied their evacuated house. The streams of light strategically infiltrating the building enabled sniper "optics," offering ideal peepholes for target practice. When snipers made the building their home, they proceeded to demolish elegant staircases to enlarge snipe lines and barricaded themselves behind the two-meter-thick walls, aiming through wooden slats across the building's interior and out the other side, without ever risking exposure. Meanwhile, decoy silhouettes painted on walls absorbed spent bullets.

Peering through the slits in the wall, I had a perfect view of sticklike figures going about their daily routines. It was a chilling sight. Bored snipers lingering for hours in their dens would eventually crawl out and scrawl something on the wall, mementos that remain writ large in fragmented graffiti diaries under aliases such as "Begin" or "Katol."

After the Civil War ended in 1990, Ḥallāk, as a young architect, came across the edifice again: a commanding structure turned eyesore, its crumbling sandstone walls now riddled with bullets. On our tour, Ḥallāk mentioned the pervasive fear that public discussion of the war could rekindle tensions. But with relentless persistence, Ḥallāk rekindled the conversation. For two decades, she headed a campaign to conserve the Barakāts' old house and transform it into a space for personal reckoning. She underscored the kind of museum she had envisioned: a space where one could halt at the ruins and remember, quietly, privately, introspectively, a moment in time during the war. Her and the museum project's innovators' ideal aim was for the ruined house to create a spatial-temporal situation in which the past is not contained by museal design but rather leaks into the present as affective disturbance. For example, one of the planned programs for the memorial was a sound-based performance to activate war memories—through the jingles of radio news flashes that dominated citizens' daily lives during the war. Yet, as Craig Larkin and Ella Parry-Davies note in their article "War Museums in Postwar Lebanon" (2019), Ḥallāk's recourse to prewar narratives of the city also risks reproducing "nostalgic imaginaries of a prewar coexistence" among sects, a notion that Ghādah al-Sammān's novel *Kawābīs Bayrūt* tries to disabuse readers of. The museum in its current guise "risks divorcing the esthetics of the space from the circumstances of its dilapidation, inducting the building into the same economy of nostalgia that underlies much dark tourism in Lebanon."[36]

When I interviewed the museum project's committee members in 2010, before the building became a museum, they had an image of the projected museum as a catalyst for storytelling and collecting—an image very different from what the museum eventually became.[37] They envisioned noninvasive installations that would not alter the structure of the building—for example, through the creation of walkways so that forensic evidence is preserved and not disturbed by visitors. Major aesthetic alterations, however, resulted in the manicuring of bullet holes to make them more pleasing to the gazing eye and in the demolition of a major staircase for a structurally sound one. The municipality even purged some of the ruins of the building, throwing away some of the original art deco tiles, documents, furniture, and sniper barriers. Beit Beirut has officially been open for years now, but visitors only trickle in, and the gate remains bolted for weeks at a time. The municipal authority has yet to appoint a management committee or to recruit staff, and some wings are closed off permanently to visitors. For the project's supporters, the delays reflect the political establishment's unwillingness to interrogate painful memories. The municipality's cultural office says the building is in a "transitional period" while officials establish a legal framework for its operations. The Beirut municipality gradually allocated $19.8 million to renovate the building, preserving some of the old features and traces of the fighting.[38] But the final authorization paperwork needed to open it permanently has not materialized, and Ḥallāk thinks the delay stems from the fear of touching on sensitive issues. Some people of the war generation are apprehensive of the potential effects of this form of museum creation. Their fear is that the space may be turned into a major tourist attraction in which the ghosts of the building would not so much be allowed to speak but rather be silenced by the voices of curators and artists. They are concerned, in other words, that this museum of memory may foster fossilized forgetting rather than lived remembering and in gaining aesthetic potency will suggest a form of closure. These critics see any kind of material intervention or remodeling of the space as disrespectful to the victims of war and the traumatic reality they experienced as well as interference in the building's testimonial function.

Conclusion

One cannot help but wonder whether the plurality of war memories can ever be housed within the walls of a single museum or if in creating such a museum we inevitably delegate our own memory burden to the archivist. Beit Beirut brings this issue into starkest relief in its attempt to engage Lebanon's "postmemory"[39] generation, whose access to and engagement with the Civil War will largely be dependent on such memory forums. The building is indeed haunted, but not everyone—including, surprisingly, the postmemory generation—wants to disturb the ghosts out of their quiet repose. The students who accompanied me on my tour with Ḥallāk have no memory of the Civil War, only inherited stories. After the tour, one of them, whose relative was interned in Khiam, told me she felt uncomfortable in the museum because it walled off experiences unassociated with Beirut.

Lebanon's civil society is clearly haunted by remains of war, past and present, real or imagined, but it is also experiencing a watershed moment in which the political regimes that kindled and retained war in its various guises are finally being confronted in a truly collective counterpublic fashion. The insufferable levels of inequality, environmental abuse, and political disenfranchisement stand to be renegotiated through a collective engagement with the inequities of the present. The next chapter accounts for such counterpublic encounters.

6

Revolutionary Ruins

In the contemplation of current events in the Middle East and beyond, the sense of the growing piles of wreckage is palpable. Perpetual images of Gaza in ruins resonate with other images of destruction; the ruins of Palmyra that once moved philosophers to imagine new ways of organizing society have become Palmyra in ruins.[1] In Palestine, the occupation of the West Bank has grown only more ruinous since the Oslo Accords of 1994 as Gaza remains under a state of siege. The ongoing Civil War in Syria has turned the country into fields of rubble, ruined an entire generation, and generated a ballooning refugee crisis.[2] While we might think of Palestine and Syria as the exceptions, in fact neoliberalism and its ruinous effects the world over have pushed people to the brink of what the anthropologist Ghassan Hage calls "the borderline between the bearable and the unbearable life."[3] So what can an attunement to ruins teach us about global struggles for justice, when "wreckage upon wreckage"[4] is piling up before us today? Circling back to "A Possible Poem on Dahiya," we get an impending sense of ruination through Bayḍūn's proleptic ruins: "We are surprised when we see this heaped rubble, and when we don't see it again. We are surprised at the immense horror, but we don't weep. The tear of remorse, if it exists, is bigger than a rock and it will crush us. . . . The heaps and the rubble fall in our memories too and in our inner selves."[5]

Unlike for the woebegone ancient poet who entreats his fellow travelers to weep with him (*Qifā nabkī*) as he stands before the ruins (*al-wuqūf 'alā al-aṭlāl*) of lost time, in Bayḍūn's contemporary poem there is a refusal to weep because "the tear of remorse, if it exists, is bigger than a rock and it will crush us." Instead, the contemporary poet's declaration "we will not weep" underscores, in the collective, resistance to obsoletion and oblivion,

23. A ray of hope shines through a crack in the Teatro al-Kabīr (Grand Theatre) in central Beirut, December 18, 2019. Photograph by Rola Khayyat.

a sentiment shared by protesting crowds in Lebanon in 2019 as they defiantly pushed back against precarious life conditions inflicted by decades of corruption and authoritarianism. Protesters were clear: they did not want reforms; they wanted an affective revolution that would upend desiccated structures of feelings and the corrupt leaders who perpetuate them.

Toward a Global Southern Counterpublics

Hope began to crackle, if fleetingly, through the global debris as a tidal wave of uprisings began sweeping the globe in 2019. Forming a human chain from South America to East Asia to northern Europe to the Middle East, protesters around the world united over a common grievance: a demand for a dignified life. Largely leaderless and populated by the young, the tide of uprisings against the ruination created by neoliberalism, austerity measures, ecological disaster, economic inequality, inept governance, rampant corruption, and sectarianism over the previous decades was guided by a collective rally for change that used rubble as its medium. In Latin America, Chile's riots followed mass protests in Ecuador, Argentina, and Honduras. The Middle East and North Africa witnessed demonstrations in Algeria, Sudan, Egypt, Iraq, and Lebanon. In eastern Europe—Romania, Slovakia, the Czech Republic, Serbia, and Georgia—governing foundations were rocked by uprisings. In Chile, commuters jumped subway turnstiles in protest of a fare hike, and the protests went viral, sending the country into turmoil. Similarly, Lebanon was set ablaze on October 15, 2019, by the government's indifference to massive wildfires that ravaged more than three thousand acres of trees south of Beirut shortly before it proposed a tax hike for calls made via the internet, one of the many proposed austerity measures meant to offset Lebanon's staggering $86 billion debt. This proposal ignited a nationwide protest, with students, once again, at the helm. The simultaneity of these uprisings throughout the world entangles some of the ruins explored in this book with global constellations of ruins in what I call "global southern counterpublics." The sense of effervescing elation among the protesters during the early days of the uprisings in Lebanon cannot, however, be reduced to a narrative that concentrates only on the struggle against the ruination of inept governance but ignores its affective dimension. As the anthropologist Ghassan Hage explains, "The Lebanese struggle shares its preoccupation with questions such as 'life' and 'dignity' with many other global struggles against neoliberalism, from the Spanish Indignados to the [French] Gilets Jaunes [Yellow Vests]. This is so precisely because neoliberalism is always experienced not just as a subjection to poverty but also as a crushing of the totality of one's economic and symbolic worth."[6]

The early days of the uprisings in Lebanon were characterized by a strong proletarian and nonsectarian component unprecedented in previous popular uprisings: a grassroots spontaneous movement that did not refract itself through a sectarian prism and that attempted to free itself from the shackles of dominant forms of affiliations. Protesters were no longer satisfied by cosmetic change but demanded an overhaul of the senses. Among the many memorable protest posters I encountered was a banner that read RESPECT EXISTENCE OR EXPECT RESISTANCE, a mantra resonating with the rising tide of anger against ungrievable modes of governance. The global uprisings in 2019 reveal the entanglement of local contexts in Lebanon with regional and global power structures, resistances, and repressive apparatuses.

A Counterpublic Pacific Resistance

'Abbās Bayḍūn recently published the article "Īdīyūlūjīyā al-ḥirāk" (Ideology of the Movement, 2020), in which he defines the contours of a new revolutionary ethos emerging from the Lebanese uprisings, or *al-ḥirāk* (the movement), as they are locally known:

> لقد تخلّق وسط المجتمع قطاع سلمي لا يؤسس على العنف المسلح ولا يعود إليه ولا ينصبه مثالاً، رغم أن أجزاء كثيرة من الحراك لا تزال تحل "المقاومة" في قلب إيديولوجيتا، إلا أن سلميتها المعلنة ومثالها السلمي ليسا بدون موقف، بل إن هذه السلمية في مجتمع "مقاوم" تبدو خروجاً وتبدو موقفاً مضاداً وتبدو مهما فهمنا منها اعتراضاً من بعيد أو قريب على السلاح وعلى العنف المسلح لقد حدث ولو بدرجة ضئيلة انقلاب على المجتمع وداخل المجتمع حدث تعدية للمجتمع وبناء على نقده، هل نحلم بلبنان آخر؟![7]

> Peacefulness, insisting on it and adhering to it, is a counterposition. . . . A peaceful sector has been created among society that is not based on

> armed violence and does not return to it or set it up as an example. Rather, this pacifism in a "resistance" society appears to be a departure and appears to be a counterstance, and it appears, however important we understand it to be, from a distant or near objection to arms and armed violence. . . . A small coup against society and within society has occurred, even to a small degree, a transgression of society, and based on its criticism do we dream of another Lebanon?![8]

To Bayḍūn, the pacific nature of the uprisings gave birth to a truly counterpublic position on resistance unprecedented in Lebanon, one devoid of armed struggle and in fact publicly disavowing violence as a means of resistance. Armed with courage and obstinacy instead, the people began redefining the contours of a new ethos of resistance before it all came to an explosive halt.

Resistant Rubble

Many of the protests were well underway as I wrote this chapter, including Lebanon's and Iraq's twin October Revolutions (Thawrat Tishreen). Although some of the global insurrections of 2019 were repressed, all sought in their idiosyncratic goals, as Gordillo puts it, "to interrupt the ongoing ruination unleashed on the planet."[9] The uprisings can be revisited through the lens of the reoccupied ruin: as the ultimate unsilencing of a people buried far too long beneath the hegemonic rubble of empty promises. The people's occupation of derelict and obsolete buildings in the uprisings of Lebanon and Iraq, for example, helped foster a new sense of community that transcended sectarian divide-and-conquer governance. Under the new political structure advocated by the Iraqi October Revolution, the informal confessional system of Iraq, like Lebanon's, would be eliminated. This demand was underscored by a common Lebanese chant during the uprisings: "Killon ya'anī killon!," or "All of them means all of them!"[10] The people's drive to reclaim and repurpose the symbolic ruins of inept governance in Lebanon and Iraq highlights not only their reclamation of public space but also their advocation of feminist, antipatriarchal, and antihomophobic modalities of being and belonging, a rallying call that galvanized and enabled, to borrow Léopold Lambert's words, their "right to the ruin." To Lambert, "the ruin implies a tragic situation, but the negation of the right to the ruin goes even further: it is an absolute re-writing of history as it attempts to erase a part of history."[11] Similarly, the people's sense of empowerment during the uprisings in Lebanon in 2019 resulted in their appropriation—and brief revival—of iconic yet abandoned Civil War ruins, those unintended rem(a)inders of war with genealogies similar to those of the memory sites I explored in the previous chapter. The productive powers of ruins are especially poignant in moments of upheaval. For the common people who occupied the derelict spaces of warfare past, the ruins embodied the end of oppressive modalities of governance and the opening of new horizons of being and belonging.

I was a visiting professor in the Department of English at the American University of Beirut when on October 17, 2019, the country hurtled headlong into a cycle of uprisings. On the seventh day of protests, days before a nationwide mass closure of universities and schools sent the country into lockdown, I received an impassioned collective email from my undergraduate students with the subject line "Patriotic Duties." The email underscored my students' role in "thwarting the country from ruin" and thereby exonerating themselves from attendance in the traditional classroom. Instead, we met for a public teach-in in the belly of an abandoned war relic that had stood silent yet resistant for more than two decades in the heart of downtown Beirut. "The Egg" (al-Bayda), as the defunct cinema was colloquially known, morphed overnight from an eyesore to an incubator of revolutionary fervor, awash with public conferences, rallies, and even raves. Ordinary citizens translated their self-claimed "right to the ruin" by occupying the abandoned structure and converting it into an open space of debate and pedagogy, later titled "the Eggupation" (an English-only play on words). According to anthropologist Nikolas Kosmatopoulos, who launched one of the first teach-ins at the Egg, "One person half-jokingly suggested to call it Eggupation, which we all found provocative and creative. The Egg was hatched." Other abandoned buildings were also reaccessed in downtown Beirut, such as the Grand theatre des milles et une nuits, or the Teatro al-Kabīr, as it is known in Arabic, built in the 1930s by the famous architect Youssef Aftimos, who also conceived the

Barakāt Building (Beit Beirut), the subject of the previous chapter. This iconic landmark, the Teatro al-Kabīr, was abandoned after the Civil War, and Solidère closed it to the public. Since 1990, its future has continued to be debated. It was slated to become yet another boutique hotel, inaccessible to the public. Meanwhile, it has held numerous meetings and sit-ins and welcomed opera singer Michel Roger, whose music reanimated the old ruinous structure and restored the building's former glory for a moment before it was reclosed for safety purposes.

At the Egg, the activities ranged from discussions about "capitalism in crisis"[12] to poetry recitals. Fittingly, my Arabic translation studies class had been reading 'Abbās Bayḍūn's poem "Ḥujūrāt" (Rooms, 1986) on the day we met in the Egg. The opening stanza of "Ḥujūrāt" sets the tone for the pruning work to come in negotiating the terms and limits of living with dignity. In his poem, Bayḍūn evokes the *aṭlāl* of pre-Islamic times, the stones that conjured up melancholic trips down memory lane, precisely to bid them farewell.

> And I bid farewell to these stones that have begun to babble and have
>   blackened all at
> once.
> Those stones we skipped over as we ran.
> I leave it now, where only a door remains to me
> Since that night I stopped being the gardener of my life.
> A wicked vine grew among the grasses, and no one weeded out the
>   follies whose roots
> have hardened.
> I am no longer the gardener of my life.
> I leave it for new tenants and friends who earned it with their betrayals.[13]

In the spirit of Bayḍūn's poem of reckoning, the grassroots movements in Lebanon began the work of reclaiming the people's agency and restoring their role as "gardeners" of their own lives. In other words, they began the long process of bidding adieu to the *zu'amā'* (leaders) of yore, those akin to the "wicked vine . . . among the grasses . . . whose roots / have hardened," in order to make "room" for the verdant growth of a new future forged out of repurposed remains.

Derelict Ruins of Rebellion: The People's Eggupation

Abandoned and obsolete landmarks shaped the ruinous topography of the uprisings from Lebanon to Iraq because derelict and dilapidated places were where the most poignant reappropriation of public space occurred. In Lebanon, such reappropriation took place in the iconic Egg, remembered mostly as an old cinema by locals who watched their first movie in its shell before it fell into eventual ruin. As in its neighbor, Beit Beirut, snipers nested in the Egg while targeting the Armenian church across the street, and like its other neighbor, the Murr Tower, the Egg faced arrested development after the Civil War when the joint-stock company Solidère took Beirut Central District hostage as part of its redevelopment project. Solidère spared the Egg demolition because of its unique structure but

24. A public teach-in at the Egg in the early days of the October Revolution, October 23, 2019. Photograph by the author.

continued to vault its doors against the public. Rabīʿ Jābir's novel *Berytus, une ville sous terre* (Berytus, Underground City, 2006),[14] seems prophetic in its counterpublic vision of the Egg's potential to resist capitalist ruination.

Becoming "al-Balad"

Small groups of people could be seen clambering up a precarious ladder to hoist flags from the Egg's roof while graffiti on the walls called for a revolutionary change to women's and gay rights. Daily, the Egg's walls resounded with the din of students, professors, artists, and curious onlookers, while nightly music transformed a once defunct space into a (questionably safe) rave hall. If we agree with Gordillo that "rubble is potentially disruptive of existing places and relations because it often turns what used to be private or state property into a de facto part of the commons" and that "rubble is matter that belongs to no one and to everyone and that radiates around it a collective spatiality,"[15] then the voids of the Central District became spaces of commerce for street vendors, impromptu public

25. A man walks past graffiti in Arabic: "Its name is al-Balad (the Town) not Solidère," December 28, 2019. Photograph by Rola Khayyat.

forums for political debate, spaces of music and festivities, logistics and amenities, gatherings, leisure, rest, effervescence, and defiance.

Tim Edensor notes that "abandoned ruins, being in unpoliced places, attract practices often frowned on elsewhere"; therefore, "ruins are often characterized by affective collective endeavors that tend towards the carnivalesque."[16] The Egg is significant in that it was abandoned for years until it was revivified into a carnivalesque space of sociality, collectivity, reckoning, and pedagogy in 2019. The fact that a similar occupation would have been immediately repressed by police if it occurred anywhere else speaks volumes of the people's experimentation with their "right to the ruin." The move to occupy the Egg was guided by an effort to turn this node of rubble into an existential marker of defiance. In an area that caters exclusively to the political and financial elite by fencing off the vast majority of the Lebanese people, the Eggupation signaled the people's takeover of the city center by hatching a new urban plan graphically brought to life through the Lebanese architect Antoine Atallah's map. Atallah's remapping of Beirut transforms the Central District back to its former incarnation as "al-Balad" (the Town) by being occupied, appropriated, and reorganized by protesters and the general public. It captures the hitherto unprecedented appropriation of public ruins since Solidère defaced the Central District in the postwar years. As Atallah maintains, during the uprising "the Central District became again a place built by the people, for the people."[17]

Candles in Marty's Square in Beirut spelled GAZA RESISTS, while the songs of the Lebanese singer and songwriter Ahmed Qaabur, known for rendering Palestinian protest poetry into song, threaded Beirut, Damascus, and Baghdad into "one collective cry." Unlike the Lebanese singer Fayrūz's nostalgic songs that glorified a folkloric Lebanon centered on Mount Lebanon, the current street chants and songs addressed a transnational geography that exceeded the boundaries of Lebanon. Songwriters adapted "Bella ciao," the anthem of the Italian antifascist resistance in the 1940s, as the rallying song of the October Revolution. The lyrics "Oh, my people rise, this is our cause, burn the idols of politics that you created. Don't lose your country and raise the flag of Lebanon" formed the song's new opening lines. Such songs do not yearn for a fictional Golden Age but agitate for an intersectional, antisectarian identity as well as gender and environmental rights and express unrelenting hostility toward neoliberal capitalism. This new modality of resistance forged out of years of rampant ruination seeks a civic model of governance. Civil resistance to a corrupt and now practically defunct sectarian system has become as urgent as national liberation from occupation. In Beirut's Riad al-Solh Square, a group of protesters gathered around a beating drum and chanted, "From Iraq to Beirut, one revolution, and it won't die," while graffiti on the surrounding walls read, "Gaza on the mind, Iran on the mind, Baghdad on the mind, we all rise up." Meanwhile, in Baghdad protesters held a banner stating, "From Baghdad to Beirut, we shall continue." Protesters did not just want reforms; they wanted an affective revolution that would unseat desiccated structures of feeling and the corrupt leaders who perpetuate them.

A new mode of resistance emerged from the uprisings in Lebanon, one that addressed the hostage crisis of the Lebanese system itself, which heavily discriminates against women on the basis of nationality, gender, and confessional delineation. Despite cosmetic reforms, the country's legal system is rife with laws that discriminate against women; for instance, Lebanese mothers (including me) cannot pass their citizenship on to their children, while divorce, property rights, and child custody are decreed by religious law, which is heavily unfair toward women. Protesters defined women's demands as people's basic rights to a viable life, given that women are the most vulnerable category of citizen. A woman named Malak Alawye is credited with literally and metaphorically kicking off the fear barrier by physically resisting a minister's armed bodyguard and inspiring women to take to the streets to demand their basic legal rights. Turning what were formerly publicly ungrievable issues into highly public grievable ones, one of the more powerful rallying calls, "Al-thawra unthā" (The revolution is female), placed women on the front burner of social justice. As many street chants reminded us, *thawra* in Arabic is, after all, a feminine word.

Counterpublic News

From the beginning of the uprisings, a fresh crop of news sources sprang up from the verdant efforts of grassroots initiatives. This specific category of outlet was particularly important in that it countered the mainstream media's approach in covering the mobilizations. Most Lebanese television channels avoid broadcasting state violence and, in some cases, even manipulate facts on the ground, which has led to the urgency for alternative sources of information that more accurately reflect the voices normally quelled by political diatribe and censorship. Daleel Thawra (Directory of a Revolution) went live on Instagram on October 24, 2019, attracting more than twenty-three thousand followers. The page inventoried the Lebanese uprisings based on five distinct categories: (1) "Events," such as organized protests, public talks, and group mobilizations; (2) "Resources" for protesters, such as safety tips and access to specific services; (3) "Inspiration," or videos showing notable moments from the mobilization (e.g., the women's march and the human-chain event); (4) "Urgent Needs" on the ground, such as requests for supplies or even blood donations; and (5) "Directory," an extensive list of local organizations and key contacts.[18] The platform crowdsourced all its information, and citizens were interpolated into the process of production by submitting edits, requests, and additional information. Diasporic members managed content remotely in English and Arabic. The decentralized nature of the editorial team, with its orientation toward collective action, evoked Tarek El-Ariss's conception of cyberspace as an alternative counterpublic sphere. El-Ariss defines the contours of "Arab cyberspace" as a space where "the marginal and the mainstream constantly intersect, decentralizing power as one coherent regime of oppression and the activist as its site of resistance,"[19] a definition that resonates with the polyphonic nature of the alternative news platforms that emerged from Lebanon's protesting crowds. El-Ariss's pulse on the emancipatory potential of Arab cybersphere finds its apotheosis in a recently launched Beirut-based independent media organization aptly named the Public Source. The Public Source is dedicated to crowdsourcing political commentary on the October Revolution from local eyewitness perspectives—whereby writers are encouraged to grapple with still smoldering ruins, "both in the moment and after the dust has settled—in the service of public interest."[20] According to its own pitch, the Public Source is "loyal only to its editorial independence" as it "exists on the margins of the Lebanese mediascape dominated by the political agendas of ruling parties through relations of patronage."[21] In the political commentary section titled "Dispatches from the October Revolution" on the Public Source's website, the independent scholar and political scientist Julia Choucair parses the term *oligarchy* in the context of Lebanon's ruling class, begging the all too important question of what comes next: "What is more idealistic? To believe we will be the first to disperse wealth through procedural democracy[?] Or to recognize that we may be standing in a long line of revolutionary moments that did achieve greater equality?"[22] Choucair's questions confront the daunting void of what comes next as the people publicly debate forms of governance most conducive to delivering a bearable life.

Solidarity events in Lebanon transcended borders through another decentralized platform, Meghterbin Mejtemiin (United Diaspora), covering events over five continents and more than fifty cities and extending the cartography of the movement both literally and metaphorically. Through grassroots virtual organizing, Meghterbin Mejtemiin connected solidarity events across the globe with local needs arising at any given moment. Perhaps the most notable output of the Lebanese uprising was its own newspaper, *17 Teshreen* (17 October),[23] which saw three thousand copies of its first edition grabbed up within minutes of hitting the streets. The Lebanese uprisings were not restricted to the urban center—cities such as Tripoli, Saida, and Nabatieh witnessed even more consistent mobilizations than the capital, Beirut—but they remained underrepresented in mainstream media coverage. As a result, groups such as Saida Tantafed,[24] Save the Bisri Valley,[25] Tripoli Revolution 2019,[26] and Tyre Revolution[27] emerged to address the importance of non-Beiruti decentralized mobilizations.

Artistic Refus(e)al

Not only news outlets but also a spate of recyclable artwork[28] culled from the rubble of protestor activity began proliferating after the October uprisings. One such mural shows the bare-handed prying open of the cement blockades that cordoned off protesters from entering the contentious parliamentary square in downtown Beirut (see fig. 26). The streets of

26. The artist Roula Abdo pries open the blockades with a mural in front of Parliamentary Square in Beirut's downtown, February 1, 2020. Photograph by Rola Khayyat, printed with permission from Roula Abdo and Art of Change.

Lebanon from Beirut to Tripoli were literally lined with traces of violence against protesters. In response, artists repurposed into countermonumental design the rubble of excessive state violence and the antiprotest remains of that violence, such as spent tear gas canisters, tattered remains of gas masks, shards of glass, discarded soda cans and bottle caps. By recycling the refuse of violence into artistic production, the artists began crafting their own countermemories from the many deposits of protesters' experiences, ironically using waste to rescue collective efforts of resistance from the dustbin of history. Their art upends our notions of memory, of waste, and of recycling by forcing us to rethink the processes of valuation and devaluation that cast objects as discardable rubble. Rising from the remains of recyclable waste picked up from protest squares in Tripoli,

Al-Thawra unthā (The Revolution Is a Woman) (see fig. 27) comes to life in a mosaic structure of a woman defiantly wielding a Lebanese flag over Beirut's Martyr's Square. This grand female structure crafted out of protestors' waste and the state's antiprotest waste rubs shoulders with another iconic sculpture, a collaborative effort between the Lebanese artist Hayat Nazer and hundreds of protesters, to create a phoenix-shaped sculpture out of the tattered ends of protesters' tents, destroyed by government supporters (see fig. 28).

By rendering waste visible and valuable, this recent spate of artistic detritus compels the viewer to look beyond the discarded rubble's materiality and instead at the throbbing affects, narratives, histories, stories, and losses embodied therein. In the introduction to their collected volume *Waste-Site Stories: The Recycling of Memory* (2002), Brian Neville and Johanne Villeneuve underscore how the reemergence of waste into our world as art "renders visible the potential inversion of value and nonvalue, memory and its involution: oblivion," such that "things that have fallen by the wayside, acquire an unforeseen value precisely because they are resistant to oblivion, because they are at once ephemeral and fixed."[29] By the same token, through monumentalizing tensions between government violence and the protesters' resistance, recycled-materials artwork uses the remains of violence to galvanize nonviolent forms of collective consciousness into counternarratives of resistance. If, as Judith Butler argues, "rage can be crafted—it's sort of an art form of politics"[30]—then, as resistance emblems, the artwork cobbled together from protestor and state law enforcement rubble underscores that remembrance through rubbish is an emblem of a subversive nature that cannot be dictated or controlled by the institutions of political power. By making artistic use of both military and nonmilitary refuse, the recycled-materials artwork on display subverts dominant categories and formulations of beauty to help make us sensitive to what it is to live while caught up in the vortex of violence. Waste, as Walter Moser posits, is "fundamentally volatile; it is at once permanent and unstable."[31] Crafted out of discarded rubble, this cultural-artistic work points to the paradoxical act of remembering what is otherwise deemed forgettable. The displayed artworks operate as performances of recycling memory by taking over public space and performing the artistic refus(e)al

27. *Al-Thawra unthā* (The Revolution Is a Woman), sculpted by the Lebanese architect Pierre Abboud out of discarded materials and both military and protestor waste picked up from protesters' camps in Beirut and Tripoli, January 25, 2020. Photograph by Rola Khayyat, printed by permission of Pierre Abboud.

28. Protesters decked in Christmas attire and a vendor of Lebanese flags in front of *The Phoenix* by Hayat Nazer, December 25, 2019. Photograph by Rola Khayyat, printed with permission from Hayat Nazer.

to forget those who have resisted being silenced; they make their resistance a tangible tactile presence, enjoining the viewer to halt before them, however ephemeral they may be, and to remember a critical moment in time. This spate of recycled-materials artworks reminds us that rubble can be transformed into a powerful tool of resistance against the forces of oblivion once memory begins to wane. Ultimately, the experience of resistance can be powerfully articulated from its remains, its narratives sifted from among recycled matter and memory, as in the experience of South Lebanon's most famous leftist former detainee, Suha Bshāra, whom we encountered in chapter 3, when she and her fellow prisoners made rosary beads from olive pits, parchment from toilet paper, and sweaters from the tattered remains of clothing.

October Revolutions: From Lebanon to Iraq

Cross-regional aspects of the Lebanese uprisings resonated with aspects of the uprisings of other countries across the Global South. Protest scenes from Lebanon and Iraq bore uncanny resemblances to each other—for instance, in the reclamation of previously deserted concrete buildings by demonstrators calling out for the downfall of a regime. Thousands of Iraqi antigovernment protesters occupied an abandoned high-rise building in the center of Baghdad, locally known as the "Turkish Restaurant" (so named because of the restaurant that occupied its top floor in the 1980s), turning it into a bustling protest center replete with makeshift electricity and elevators. The mass squat started after a second wave of mass demonstrations against Prime Minister Adel Abdul Mahdi's government began on the night of October 24, 2019. The demonstrators wanted to end the post-2003 political order, which they saw as endemically corrupt and which had failed to deliver a livable life. Abdul Mahdi had promised reforms and a broad cabinet reshuffle but never followed through. Once a commercial center, this six-story building fell into disarray when it was bombed twice during the US-led invasion of Iraq in 2003 and was subsequently abandoned, a hollowed-out shell. The protesters claimed it was previously a snipers' nest, and its present occupation by the people was driven in part by an attempt to thwart a repeat of a similar fate. Protesters occupied all eighteen floors of the building. Inside, they danced, smoked *shisha*, played backgammon, and chanted for the downfall of the ruling elites. Like downtown Beirut's Burj al-Murr, the Turkish Restaurant's towering height provided an umpire's view of strategic quarters, such as Baghdad's Tahrīr (Liberation) Square, making it possible to record potential police repression. Some protesters even redubbed the landmark "Mount Uhud" in reference to a mountain in Medina where early Muslims battled those who sought to destroy the nascent religion in 625 CE.[32] The Muslims lost this battle because instead of holding their base on Mount Uhud, they disobeyed orders and went to loot the battlefield. The religious-mythic lesson from this story for the Turkish Restaurant squat was the imperative to hold on to the ruin or fall into ruin.

In 2019, it seemed as though a new chapter had opened up for Lebanon and the Global South as the people continued to rise up against rampant neoliberal ruination—a critical mass with women at its forefront, occupying ruins in defiance of precarious life. From Algeria to Sudan, from Iraq to Lebanon, people rallied, demanding an end to corruption and authoritarianism, demanding a revolution of all the sensoria. Ruins in the hands of the crowds were not about what had been lost but about what remained, about hope amid the wreckage of war. By opening up the constellations of ruins in Lebanon's uprisings to insurrections around the globe, I hope to show here how the emergence of a global southern counterpublic could slowly but surely transform wreckage into ruins of resistance. But this historical moment of collective sociality and communitarian building was violently undone in Lebanon on August 4, 2020, when ruination once again engulfed the country, following on the heels of a global pandemic.

Conclusion

Return to Ruin—on Planetary Pandemics and Explosions

A novel virus known as COVID-19 is coursing through the planet, corralling people in their homes, severing economic sinews, exposing the most vulnerable, and challenging existences the world over. Into the maelstrom of Lebanon's uprisings and economic meltdown in 2019 came COVID-19, a curse "worse than war."[1] War remains the preferred metaphor for the pandemic from the Global North to the Global South, but discrepancies abound. The coronavirus flattens difference with regard to whom it attacks, but it exacerbates privilege in terms of who has access to care, exposing the precarity of the Global North's supposedly stable social and political networks.[2] The impact of the virus in the United States, the United Kingdom, and other powerful and rich countries of the Global North blurs the boundaries between metaphor and reality, as Ilyās Khūrī aptly states in his essay "Saramāģū: Al-Wabā' wa al-'ama al-abyad" (Saramago: Epidemic and White Blindness, 2020):

> لكن المسافة بين الحاضر والكناية تبدو سريعة التلاشي. فالكورونا تتحول اليوم ، إلى ما يشبه الكناية، معها نكتشف الوحشية التي تقتل مسنّي أوروبا بلا رحمة، وجشع الرأسمالية التي تضحّي بحيوات البشر على مذبح إله السوق، وجنون العظمة الذي يقود أمريكا إلى الكارثة.
>
> كورونا صارت آلة يتكنّى بها الاستبداد، كي يواصل حربه على الفقراء، وهذا ما نشهده في لبنان، حيث تتصرف الأوليغارشية ومافيا الفاسدين وكأن كورونا قدمت لهما رأس الانتفاضة.
>
> هل ستنتصر المافيا على الانتفاضة، أم أن البركان الذي يستعد للانفجار سوف يحرق الوباءين معاً: كورونا والنظام؟[3]

> Today's epidemic is real and not metaphorical, but the distance between present and metaphor seems to fade. Today, corona is becoming a metaphor for the brutality that ruthlessly kills the elderly in Europe, the greed of capitalism that sacrifices human lives at the altar of the market god, and the paranoia that drives America to disaster.
>
> Corona has become a mechanism for tyranny to continue to wage its war on the poor, which is what we are witnessing in Lebanon via the oligarchy and the corrupt mafia, as if corona offered them the severed head of the uprising. Will the mafia prevail over the uprising, or will the volcano that is preparing to explode burn the two epidemics together: corona and the system?

Wars remain within the horizon of expectation for the inhabitants of Lebanon. In 2020, the country pedaled back to the Lebanese Civil War years, when lockdowns were the norm as people "sheltered in place" for what seemed like frozen time. Shortages of fuel, water, power, and food staples were omnipresent. Yet despite and amid war and its remains, life persisted. In time, people eked out modalities for survival and living with war. But the virus has discombobulated even the most war seasoned of nations. In September 2019, about one-third of the Lebanese population lived below the poverty line. In 2020, when the pandemic struck, that segment was closer to half the population.[4] That year, Lebanon's banks vaporized depositors' money and in one fell swoop froze dollar withdrawals, inaugurating austerity.[5] The Lebanese lira, which had long been exchanged at roughly 1,500 liras to one US dollar through a so-called feat of "financial engineering"[6] by Riad Salameh, the longtime governor of the Lebanese Central Bank, started losing its value at an alarmingly fast rate. The Central Bank's series of dizzying circulars, each decreeing contradictory exchange rates, exacerbated the instability of the lira and provoked a frenzied run on the banks. In other words, COVID-19 "arrived" in Lebanon on the heels of economic catastrophe and social upheaval.[7] I use the term *arrived* to allude to 'Abbās Bayḍūn's article "Sīyāsāt kūrūnā" (Corona Policies, 2020), in which he riffs on sectarianism by asking, "On which flight did the virus 'arrive' in Lebanon?" Finger-pointing at an incoming priest from Italy or at an incoming flight from Iran (implicating

Hizbullah) only underscores the omnipresence of demagoguery in Lebanon, laments Bayḍūn.[8]

Two months into the lockdown, from my balcony overlooking the Mediterranean Sea in the heart of Beirut I could hear sirens calling the occasional defiant walker (and now swimmer) off the formerly bustling corniche promenade. But when night fell, an unusual silence reigned over Rās Beirut (Central Beirut). I could even hear the lapping of waves on the beach, a sound normally muffled by car horns, the cacophony of schoolchildren, and the rumble of diesel-belching generators. The American University of Beirut campus declared an early shutdown and pivoted to remote teaching weeks before the virus arrived in the United States. I did not bid my students farewell at the time of our seemingly early closure because the early shutdown seemed out of sync with the rest of the world. During lockdown, the campus was slowly taken over by cats, the eager children of quarantined professors (my twin toddlers included), and a skeleton administration. We were the lucky ones with free reign of one of the only green spaces in Beirut as the virus brought laxity to the stringent university rules about keeping children (and cats) off its neatly manicured lawns. As my twin daughters giggled and ran amok hither and thither, the majority of Beirutis remained quarantined in their apartment blocks.

Outside the campus, virus reminders abounded, but so did signs of economic disaster. A visit to our local supermarket entailed full personal-protection gear, quick temperature checks at the entrance, and a body-sanitizing spritz. Masked and gloved, we contemplated with disbelief the inflated prices slapped onto imported goods. Each week the prices of imports inflated until they eventually became unaffordable or were discontinued. Diapers, a weekly staple for any parent of toddlers, was one of the fast-vanishing imports. Lebanon manufactures few of its own products, so local replacements were not always an option.

After the lockdown, the Lebanese lira went into free fall, and prices increased almost by the day. The government promised aid to needy families, but it squabbled about distributing the aid for so long that by the time an agreement was reached, the sum per person had been devalued to less than US$100. On April 25, 2020, the lira hit an all-time low: about 4,000–4,200 liras to one US dollar, a devaluation of more than 60 percent.

Salaries at the American University of Beirut also took a hit, devaluing by nearly 70 percent. After the usual infighting, the government announced its economic "rescue plan,"[9] which consisted of appealing to the International Monetary Fund (IMF) for a loan. Should the IMF eventually approve the request, Lebanon will have to contend with austerity measures that will only increase poverty. But even that will happen only if the notoriously corrupt Lebanese state can even meet the minimum reforms that the IMF requires.[10]

After the lockdown, protesters, now masked, were back on the streets of Tripoli,[11] Beirut, Sidon, and Tyre, hurling Molotov cocktails at banks for allowing big depositors to smuggle billions out of the country,[12] while the poorest could no longer afford basic food staples.[13] The army responded with extreme violence, using tear gas and both rubber and live bullets to crush the protesters. On the night of April 27, 2020, the army shot and killed twenty-six-year-old Fawaz al-Samman and wounded dozens of others during protests in Tripoli, Lebanon's poorest coastal city. The victim, a motorbike mechanic, had been struggling to eke out support for his wife and infant daughter after his income nosedived from the crisis. The killing refanned the flames of uncontainable outrage with an unprecedented edge of desperation. The threat of the virus was slowly starting to fade, but only to be replaced by the everyday despair of no longer being able to afford the necessities.

Whither Arabic Pandemic Literature?

History is littered with disease and quarantines. How have these moments been anticipated, suffered, and remembered in literary history? When thinking about literary responses to pandemics, many are quick to cite *La peste* (*The Plague*), published by the French Algerian writer Albert Camus in 1947, which recounts the cholera epidemic that engulfed the Algerian city of Oran in 1849, and *Ensaio sobre a cegueira* (*Blindness*, 1995) by the Nobel Prize winner José Saramago.[14] But what insights does Arabic literature have to offer? The same year Camus published *The Plague*, the Iraqi poetess Nazek al-Malaika (1923–2007) published her groundbreaking free-verse poem "Al-Kolera" (Cholera), which depicts the cholera epidemic that ravaged Egypt in the closing months of 1947.[15] Ancient epidemic-related literature from the Middle East and North Africa also includes hygiene guidance, travel books, and *ḥadīth*s (sayings, actions, or silent approval attributed to the Prophet Muhammad and used as guidance for everyday life). Works by the ninth-century Iraqi writer Ibn Abi al-Dunya (823–94 CE), for example, issued guidance on how to combat disease. In *Kitāb al-awba'ī* (The Book of Pestilences), he included a *ḥadīth* that describes fever as an expiation of sin:

عَنْ جَابِرٍ أَنَّ رَسُولَ اللَّهِ صَلَّى اللَّهُ عَلَيْهِ وَسَلَّمَ دَخَلَ عَلَى أُمِّ السَّائِبِ أَوْ أُمِّ الْمُسَيَّبِ
فَقَالَ مَا لَكِ يَا أُمَّ السَّائِبِ أَوْ يَا أُمَّ الْمُسَيَّبِ تُزَفْزِفِينَ قَالَتْ الْحُمَّى لَا بَارَكَ اللَّهُ فِيهَا
فَقَالَ لَا تَسُبِّي الْحُمَّى فَإِنَّهَا تُذْهِبُ خَطَايَا بَنِي آدَمَ كَمَا يُذْهِبُ الْكِيرُ خَبَثَ الْحَدِيدِ

> The Messenger of Allah, peace and blessings be upon him, entered the home of Umm Sa'ib and he said, "What ails you, O Umm Sa'ib? You are shivering."
>
> She said: "It is a fever. Allah has not blessed it."
>
> The Prophet said: "Do not curse fever. Verily, it removes the sins of the children of Adam, just as a furnace removes dirt from iron."[16]

In "Al-Wabā' wa al-adab al-'arabī al-ḥadīth" (The Epidemic and Modern Arab Literature), published on April 6, 2020, Ilyās Khūrī notes a surprising lack of plague-related literature in modern Arabic literary history, an absence that is especially surprising with respect to the cholera and Ebola epidemics of the 1920s.[17] Among the few modern Arab pandemic novels Khūrī cites is *Ebola 76*, published by the Sudanese writer Amir Taj al-Sir's in 2012, which describes the Ebola epidemic that hit the Congo and extended to Anzara, southern Sudan, in 1976; Andrée Chedid's *Le sixième jour* (The Sixth Day, 1962) (it is said the cholera victim dies on the sixth day), which recounts a Cairene grandmother's attempts to protect her son from the ravages of cholera in Egypt; and Rabī' Jābir's *Amīrkā: Riwāyah* (*Amerika*: *A Novel*, 2009), which dedicates a chapter to a Syrian Lebanese émigré's memories of the "Spanish" flu epidemic in America that reaped fifty million souls worldwide, more victims than the First World War.[18]

Why, muses Khūrī, is there a dearth of contemporary Arabic pandemic literature? Why did the Arabic novel not pay attention to the epidemics, locusts, and famine of the First World War? (He does cite one exception: the novel *Al Raghīf* [The Loaf, 1939] by Tawfīq Yūsuf 'Awwād [b. 1911].) Has the Nahda[19] (Awakening) and modernity, Khūrī wonders aloud, "washed away our memories of tragedies, or is Arab culture still searching for a lost relationship to a forgotten past and a present afflicted by the semiblindness that struck the protagonists of Saramago's novel *Blindness*?"[20] Khūrī turns a critical lens on contemporary Arabic poetry as well, citing only a handful of pandemic poems, such as Aḥmad Shawqī's "Qānūn al-ghāba" (Law of the Jungle), which introduces children to the "cursed disease" resulting from "sin that angered God," and Ali Al-Jarem's "Al-Wabā'" (The Epidemic), a poem, he says, that "lacks human experience."[21] Among the pandemic poems Khūrī critiques is al-Malaika's "Cholera," which, he argues, details the victims' suffering while "the poet keeps a safe distance from the plague."[22] Pandemic literature, decrees Khūrī, cannot be a mirror of human experience if it is not borne of the moment. The belatedness of the pandemic literature he cites compromises its capacity to bear witness to the plagues under scrutiny, for the poet keeps "reinterpreting and incorporating the past in a new context."[23]

If we are to follow Khūrī's dictum that pandemic literature cannot be a mirror of reality unless born of it, then contemporary poets, especially the war-seasoned ones such as 'Abbās Bayḍūn, are critically poised to describe the everyday lived reality of today's novel and deadly virus. Bayḍūn, as per his wont, does carefully render life lived in our new viral reality. He writes of quarantine on April 11, 2020, in a poem titled "Umthūlat al-'adad" (Number Example), "Isolation, where days collapse upon each other . . . I wash my hands to the count of thirty . . . and I brush my hair twenty times, I am safe in my bathroom, kitchen, and balcony. . . . My assertions and expectations are assured if I counted correctly."[24] Bayḍūn shifts our focus from a countdown for a more just life that exceeds the epidemiological virus toward a deadlier one: the complete disregard for life's worth by the political elite. On the heels of what appears to be a northern counterpublic uprising in the United States after the death of George Floyd at the hands of a Minnesota police officer, on his Facebook page Bayḍūn brings the question back to Lebanese politics: "We object to racism in America," he quips, "but we don't care that in Lebanon it is the basis of politics." "Corona policies in Lebanon," he continues, are inseparable from Lebanese politics but rather build on it and provoke it. "The choice between domestic quarantine and hunger is ambiguous, but the matter becomes more ambiguous when it comes to violating the embargo in the Palestinian camp in Sabra. What alternative exists for those living in squalor?"[25] As if in answer to his own question, Bayḍūn penned a poem on April 17, 2020, eerily titled "Daqīqa nawawīyya" (A Nuclear Minute), in which he anticipates the ruination that awaited Lebanon yet again on August 4, 2020:

دقيقة نوويّة
. . .
هذه بالتأكيد دقيقة نووية
كأن يبدأ العالم منها
كأن يصبح الجميع تحت الأمر
. . .
لقد أخرجوا شاعراً من المصح
وسلموه أن يبتكر
فيروس الجنون
أن يقلب بلداناً على بلدان
وأن يوزع الحياة في أنابيب[26]

. . .
This is definitely a nuclear minute,
from which the world begins,
as if everyone is under its command,
And in complete obedience,
. . .
They took a poet out of the sanatorium
And let him innovate
The virus of insanity,
To turn countries against countries
And to distribute life in tubes

Bayḍūn's poetic attunement to the explosive potentiality of the ruin takes us full circle to the type of sensibilities toward ruins that I have

29. Mushroom clouds of ammonium nitrate fill the sky above the American University of Beirut campus, August 4, 2020. Photograph by Rola Khayyat.

explored in this book. Yet to write about ruins in real time in Lebanon is itself a precarious act of interpretation, one that resists closure. Lebanon's current situation is one of crisis, one of ruination, one that threatens to continually erupt. On August 4, 2020, I was putting finishing touches on my book manuscript when a mere four kilometers away from my blinking cursor one of the largest nonnuclear anthropogenic explosions in global history tore through Beirut's port, sheathing the city in what Bayḍūn once described in relation to Ḍāḥiya as "an odyssey of rubble."[27] Shortly after 6:00 p.m. on that day, Lebanon returned to ruin once again.[28] Later I would discover that the initial explosion registered seismic waves equivalent to a 3.3-magnitude earthquake. As the entire house shook, my window screens, false ceilings, and door hinges blew out. War is the subject of my academic practice, but never before had I lived through anything like this. The slow-motion-like sensorial nature of the deafening dual blasts made the experience unlike the "usual" bombings I experienced in my childhood. My knee-jerk reaction was to think that the blast was an Israeli rocket launched on the heels of border skirmishes a week earlier, a conjecture corroborated in the moment by friends calling in to report low-flying jets. To be attuned to the seasonality of war in this country means to know that the end of summer is often the "preferred" time for elective bombings. At that deafening moment when the second blast went off, my thoughts raced to my loved ones, those who had lived through wars and those who were experiencing for the first time a calamity of this magnitude. Cycles of violence in Lebanon thread generations into one continuous chain of life. My mother is no stranger to war, having raised five children in wartime Lebanon. Today, her memoir, *Brownies and Kalashnikovs: A Saudi Woman's Memoir of American Arabia and Wartime Beirut* (2009), which recounts her survival of an explosion a stone's throw from where I was seated at the time of the port blast, resounds loudly. She writes of the opening chapter of the Lebanese Civil War on September 17, 1975:

> I lay in my bed and stared silently out of the window, a square of pitch-black night, as I listened to the insanity of people killing and people dying. It did not feel real. There was nothing to distract me from the ugliness surrounding me. Where was my mother and why was I alone without her? I lay on my hospital bed in darkened solitude while butchery and screaming violence continued outside my window. I was jolted from my fitful sleep the following morning in sheer panic by a thundering explosion that came from the direction of the sea, a five-minute walk from the hospital. I did not expect to survive, thinking that the hospital had been the target of the explosion.[29]

Shortly after the second port blast went off in August 2020, pink plumes of toxic gas blanketed the skies, tainting the airways of humans and nonhumans in as yet unfathomable ways. For decades, Lebanon has been mired in what the anthropologist Ghassan Hage describes as "the ungovernability of waste" in the form of toxic gases and chemicals in the water, soil, and atmosphere.[30] The Beirut port blast is but another instance of environmental violence caused by the rendition of otherwise innocuous materials (fertilizer in this case) into a deadly fireworks display. As the geographer Mazen Labban explains, Beirut was "accidentally" enrolled in the routes of extractive capital when 2,750 tons of ammonium nitrate were carelessly transferred to a dockside warehouse in 2014 from a cargo ship sailing from the Black Sea to the port of Mozambique and left there to fester for six years until they exploded.[31] Although unintentional, the blast that killed more than 150, injured more than 5,000, displaced up to 300,000, and caused an estimated $2 billion or more in damage to the city was a crisis caused by political and environmental negligence.[32] An "accidental" spark caused by fireworks ignited the ammonium nitrate dumped and stored for years in the port, creating an indescribable fireworks display, which, as Theodor Adorno aptly writes, "are apparitions par excellence."[33] The humanitarian crime of neglecting 2,750 tons of explosive materials for six years in the heart of Beirut criminalizes the ineptitude of the Lebanese government, past and present, which has made people's lives and livelihoods go up in apparitional smoke.

The day after the blast was a different kind of brutal. As the initial shockwaves subsided, the rage returned. Hospitals already heaving with COVID-19 cases were now overwhelmed by the swelling number of dead and wounded. Cascading reports told of people still buried beneath the rubble and friends hospitalized. The port blasts were the kiss of death in an already implosive situation. On the heels of economic collapse, a viral surge, and imminent lockdown, the single-day vaporization of the only lifeline for severely dwindling imports seemed indeed like a curse worse than war. The blast destroyed the main grain-storage silos and stocks of medical equipment, thus initiating a new round of deprivation, hyperinflation, and calamity. As Heiko Wimmen of the International Crisis Group wrote at the time, "The blast will accelerate the Lebanese economy's tailspin, immiserating a larger and larger part of the 6.8 million-strong population."[34] On August 6, 2020, the Lebanese Central Bank issued hollow promises to businesses and individuals seeking to repair the devastating damage.[35] The liquidity crisis meant that access to state-provided electricity tapered off to just a few hours per day as fuel became a scarcity. As usual, Lebanese politicians responded to the country's political-economic crisis with characteristic dispassion, bickering among themselves over the scale of losses and who should take the blame. Negotiations with the IMF over an economic-rescue package reached a stalemate in this instance, too. A state of emergency was declared in the aftermath of the explosion, but it was mostly civilian volunteers from all over the country who worked to clear away the metaphorical and physical rubble. This latest preventable explosion of world-historical size and destructive power, second in magnitude only to a nuclear explosion, unleashed a new wave of popular fury. Political elites began facing, once again, the wrath of the country's citizens, as they did in October 2019, when hundreds of thousands rallied against the politicians in charge. Activist groups that played a prominent role in the October Revolution started mobilizing again, reviving their popular slogan that demanded the removal of the country's entrenched elites: "Killon yaʿanī killon" (All of them means all of them). A major protest on August

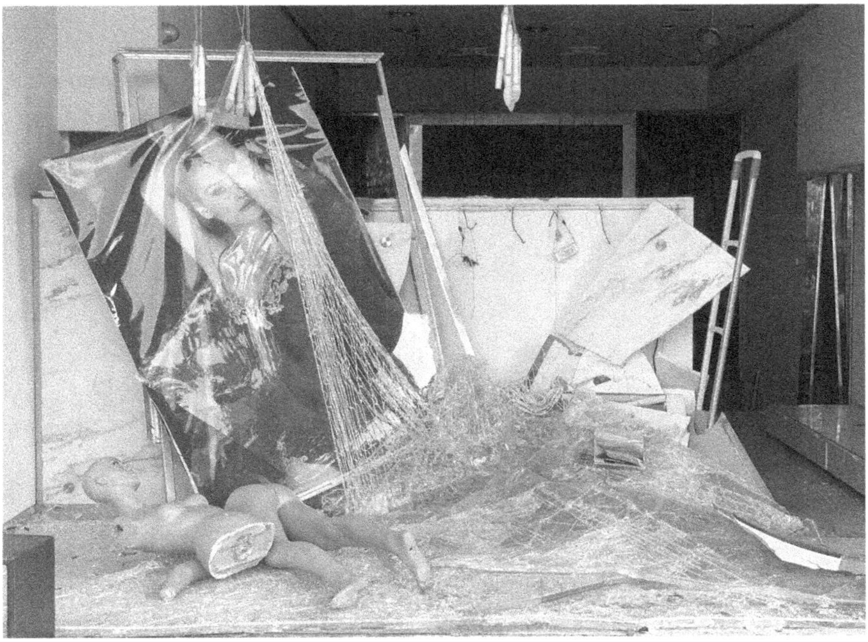

30. A storefront in central Beirut reduced to broken glass and a dead manikin as a result of the twin port blasts on August 4, 2020. Photograph by the author, August 5, 2020.

8, 2020, aptly depicted a row of nooses dangling a short distance from the blast site, awaiting justice to be served.

Two days before the one-year anniversary of the blast, on August 2, 2021, some of the cleared debris, such as scrap metal from the destroyed hangars, made its way into a gargantuan sculpture dubbed *The Gesture* (see fig. 31) by the Lebanese architect and installation artist Nadim Karam. Culled from the remains of this massive moment of human atrocity, *The Gesture*, weighing in at thirty-five tons, towers over ground zero at eighty-two feet tall. Offsetting the structure's imposing presence is a delicate dove in the sculpture's hand, which according to Karam, is a gesture "of solidarity and hope to the city by asserting the power of creativity over violence."[36] By monumentalizing raw ruins that continue to pulsate in the lives of the blast survivors, *The Gesture*'s artistic intervention as an "act of memory" becomes at once a glaring gesture toward the absence of governmental support for the blast survivors.[37] In an interview, Nadim Karam told me that the jagged and corrugated slabs of steel that comprise the towering figure of *The Gesture* were kept intact to reflect the unfinished narrative of the blast's survivors, the shards of pain and memory that lodge themselves deep in the viscera of our very being as we dwell in a place of seemingly perpetual war such as Beirut. As an "act of memory," the debris-based sculpture viscerally captures the rawness of the port blast for the survivors who still carry their memories like a wound in perpetuity. Karam's ruin structure's temporary status as an installation is also a fleeting gesture toward the precarity of fixing memory in a city like Beirut, which he grimly states, "I have the impression that I died here more than one time." But Karam's gesture still gestures toward hope, despite its heavy subject matter, for in Karam's words *The Gesture* embodies "*alam*" (pain), "but it also embodies *amal* (hope) because it is still standing tall."[38]

Yet the Beirut port has not always been just a transactional place of trade and commerce as well as an incubator of pain. Ghādah al-Sammān insists it was once a "literary port," where she met one of the most influential twentieth-century Egyptian writers and intellectuals, Taha Hussein (1889–1973), for the first and last time, after an appointment set up by the Lebanese novelist, short-story writer, journalist, and translator Suhail Idris (d. 2008). At the time, al-Sammān writes, Lebanon was "the Arab capital

31. *The Gesture* by the Lebanese architect Nadim Karam towers over the port of Beirut in commemoration of the one-year anniversary of the twin port blasts, August 7, 2021. Photograph courtesy of Nadim Karam.

of writers, publishing, joy and development," a country that transacted in ideas, narratives, stories, and faith. Al-Sammān refutes static commemorative categories such as "memorial day" in relation to August 4, 2020, because "every day we live in Lebanon is like that, and every day has its victims in a certain sense." She goes even further to argue that "there is a so-called 'International Refugee Day,' but most of those who remained in Lebanon are, in essence, refugees, because the homeland is no longer a homeland but has become alienation, and the harshest types of alienation are those that a person experiences in his homeland."[39]

Hope, Remains

In this book, ruins have signaled the start of a collective regeneration that points not toward the nostalgic past but toward an alternative future forged from resistant ruins, as I have hoped to signal through the work of southern counterpublics. Ruins in the hands of southern counterpublics evoke the past not as a refuge, as in the pre-Islamic poetic tradition, or as a foreign country but as a heterotopic sphere that inspires diverse future imaginaries. By venturing south, literally and metaphorically, I was able to apprehend the assemblage of ruins described in this book, which have long remained invisible to too many eyes. There, I examined ruins in the context of two war museums curated to evoke a homogenizing narrative that co-opted variable forms of resistance under one morally political banner. I analyzed the ruins of a destroyed fort turned prison-museum with a haunting afterlife and fields of rubble that awakened muted memories. By sifting through the ruins of Khiam and Mleeta, I was able to excavate narratives that emerged from the voids, beneath which such stories repose. I turned to the October 2019 Lebanese uprisings, or *ḥirāk* (the movement), a revolutionary democratic Lebanese response to Lebanon's economic crisis, in order to reflect on popular attempts to repurpose rubble into generative markers of antigovernmental defiance in what Léopold Lambert calls the people's "right to the ruin."[40] I examined counterartistic design cobbled together from the military's and protesters' waste (used tear gas canisters, spent bullets, tattered clothing) during the uprisings and countercarceral artwork eked out of prison detritus, as described in the memoirs of South Lebanon's famous female former detainee, Suha Bshāra, about her grueling ten-year (1988–98) internment in the infamous Khiam Detention Center. It is my hope that the heterogeneity of memorial practices explored in this book recovers the value of individual witness, uncommemorated sites, memorial objects, and oral and textual narratives, which, relegated to the margins of memory, otherwise seem destined for oblivion.

The chapters in this book have amassed like ruins, incorporating palimpsestic layering and contact with different media and genres. I have sought to show the multiple meanings of ruins in both their literary and material senses and how these meanings connect and collide. In chapter 6, I redirected our gaze to the ruination at the core of the nation and how this ruination led to a general strike that rippled throughout the Global South and beyond. By analyzing a constellation of both metaphorical and material nodes of rubble, I have hoped to show how neglected wreckage transforms, if fleetingly, into a productive trope for resistant thought and action. The narratives and ethnographic journeys in this book, then, are not just about material matter but also about the potentiality of the ruin defined by disturbances and, more importantly, rebellion. I have argued that common to all the works under study is the repurposing of ruins into valuable markers of resistance against precarious life conditions.

Before I end my venture south, I would like to return to ʿAbbās Bayḍūn's poetic gaze at the rubble, a gaze that "looks for a blade of grass in the cracks, for a handkerchief, a tasseled carpet, a rosary, a broken walking stick" to guide us out of this global ruinous morass because "there are no suitable words to calculate the immensity of earthquakes, planetary explosions, and outbursts of nature."[41] Perhaps the unique admixture of ruins and hope that this book has set out to capture is best encapsulated in Huda Barakāt's recent reflection, "Sawt sārikh fīl bariyya" (A Voice Crying in the Wilderness), in which she beholds the environmental devastation caused by the Beirut port blasts: "The land is a wasteland and a wilderness. It is that which ends at the verge of the water and summons the sea with all its might. Like the sea of Beirut that exploded and became a desert. A deserted sea," reflects Barakāt. "Yet it is not allowed to die, in spite of the bodies that have accumulated in its depths. Hope remains because we will it to. Look at the greenness of the wheat sprouting from the bags of nitrate."[42] By "greening"[43] over the bags of nitrate, Barakāt superimposes hope on the unbearable levels of ruination Lebanon perpetually faces. In the same spirit, this book has strived to show how ruins are not only about what has been lost but also about what remains, about hope amid the ruination. For in the end there is something that cannot be ruined: the collective will to a dignified life.

Notes

Bibliography

Index

Notes

Introduction

1. In 2006, over the course of thirty-three days, an Israeli air and land assault on Lebanon killed more than a thousand civilians, left scores of southern villages completely flattened, displaced hundreds of thousands from their homes, and left huge swathes of agricultural land peppered with cluster bombs. This war effectively turned Lebanon, especially the South, once again into an extended ruin, with al-Ḍāḥiya at its "urban" reach. Israel's indiscriminate bombing of South Lebanon, as the geographer Derek Gregory maintains, rendered it a zone of indistinction that lethally blurred civilians and combatants ("'In Another Time Zone, the Bombs Fall Unsafely . . . ': Targets, Civilians and Late Modern War," *Arab World Geographer* 9, no. 2 [2006]: 88–111). It was Israel's mistaken assumption that Hizbullah (Party of God), a Shīʿite militant grassroots organization and Lebanese political party, could be eliminated by force. See also Gilbert Achcar and Michel Warschawski, *The 33-Day War: Israel's War on Hezbollah in Lebanon and Its Consequences* (Boulder, CO: Paradigm, 2007). In "Weak Seed and Poisoned Land: Slow Violence and the Toxic Infrastructures of War in South Lebanon," *Environmental Humanities* 10, no. 1 (2018): 86–106, Vasiliki Touhoulioti offers a trenchant account of the continued violence of undetonated bombs supplied by the United States that Israel blanketed southern Lebanon with in the July War of 2006, disabling a civilian population with shrapnel and cancers that do not go away. See also Syrine Hout, "Recounting Memories of Resistance in 33 Days," *Arab Studies Quarterly* 38, no. 2 (2016): 481–99.

2. ʿAbbās Bayḍūn, "A Possible Poem on Dahiya," trans. Issa J. Boullata, in *Lebanon, Lebanon*, ed. Anna Wilson (London: Saqi, 2006), 19, emphasis added.

3. According to Mona Harb, "al-Dahiya is an eponym for the southern suburb of Beirut, which remained unnamed until, by dint of habit, its proper name came to be al-Dahiya al-Janubiya (southern suburb)" ("Story of a Name," in *Beyroutes*, supplement of Beiroutes: A Guide to Beirut 22 [2010]: 71). It delineates a specific geographic territory that extends south of the capital city over an area equal to that of municipal Beirut, housing half a million residents. The name "al-Ḍāḥiya" also "homogenizes" and "stigmatizes" diverse neighborhoods as monolithic and as a distinct other. For a genealogical history of

Ḍāḥiya, see Harb, "Story of a Name"; and Lara Deeb and Mona Harb, *Leisurely Islam: Negotiating Geography and Morality in Shi'ite South Beirut* (Princeton, NJ: Princeton Univ. Press, 2013).

4. It is worth quoting the following lines from *Leisurely Islam*: "'Beirut is ours,' 'Beirut is a red line,' proclaimed the former prime minister Hariri's advocates. Hizbullah labeled Dahiya 'the rebel that never dies' and the 'territory of the proud and the glorious.' The March 8 sit-in in downtown Beirut was described by Beirutis as 'Dahiya-fication' and an 'invasion of our city,' ignoring the multisectarian makeup of the protesters. Opinion pieces in newspapers rejected the migrants that were 'ruralizing' Beirut and were desolate over the transformation of its neat streets into picnic areas where people danced dabkeh, smoked argileh, and ate kaak and corn on the cob sold by vendors" (Deeb and Harb, *Leisurely Islam*, Kindle ed., loc. 49).

5. Bayḍūn, "A Possible Poem on Dahiya," 17–21, last ellipses in the original.

6. Bayḍūn, "A Possible Poem on Dahiya," 18.

7. The watchdog group New Weapons Committee indicted Israel for using experimental weapons, including DIME (dense inert metal explosive) bombs, in Lebanon in 2006. A type of nonconventional "low collateral damage" weapon, DIME bombs are filled with microparticles of highly toxic metals (see Defense Update, "Dense Inert Metal Explosive (DIME)," n.d., at defense-update.com/products/d/dime.htm, accessed Jan. 7, 2018). According to Touhouliotis, "The debate around uranium weapons continued in 2008, when a Lebanese newspaper published results from urine analyses conducted on a group of patients from the heavily bombed southern suburbs of Beirut who had symptoms of dizziness, nausea, and fatigue. Lebanese physicist Mohammed Ali Kobeissi found industrial and enriched uranium in their urine fourteen months after the war, leading him to conclude that Israel had used weapons with a particularly insolvent type of uranium" ("Weak Seed and Poisoned Land," 91).

8. Bayḍūn, "A Possible Poem on Dahiya," 19.

9. For example, a Human Rights Watch report issued in 2007 stopped tallying civilian deaths from the war at the cease-fire declaration, despite the massive amounts of unexploded remnants of war; see Human Rights Watch, *Why They Died: Civilian Casualties in Lebanon during the 2006 War* (New York: Human Rights Watch, Sept. 2007), at https://www.hrw.org/sites/default/files/reports/lebanon0907.pdf. For an extensive report on cluster bombs and the damage they caused, see Human Rights Watch, *Flooding South Lebanon: Israel's Use of Cluster Munitions in Lebanon in July and August 2006* (New York: Human Rights Watch, Feb. 2008), at https://www.hrw.org/report/2008/02/16/flooding-south-lebanon/israels-use-cluster-munitions-lebanon-july-and-august-2006. Those who died after the cease-fire not only were *not* casualties, the investigation suggested, but also remained causally separate from war. As Touhouliotis remarks in her investigation of the belated effects of war on South Lebanon residents: "It is striking that there were not more voices in Lebanon like Green Line clamoring for more certainty on the toxic effects of Israel's

weapons and intent on broadening the categories of casualty and causality. Interviews with important figures in South Lebanon who bore responsibility for the war wounded, either as their political representatives or as their caregivers, revealed that they were similarly invested in uncertainty about toxic contamination, a temporally restricted understanding of war, and a limited conception of war injury" ("Weak Seed and Poisoned Land," 93).

10. The name "South Lebanon" (Janūb Lubnān) refers to the province of South Lebanon, which stretches south of the Awālī River; is bounded on the west by the Mediterranean coast; encompasses the ancient port cities of Sidon (Ṣaydā) and Tyre (Ṣūr); goes all the way to Ra's al-Nāqūrah on the Israeli border and then inland from the Mediterranean Sea along the Lebanese–Israeli border through the Western Beka' to Mount Hermon (Jabal al-Shaykh) on the Lebanese–Syrian border; and encompasses Jabal 'Amel, the historical heartland of Lebanese Shī'ism.

11. See Harb, "Story of a Name."

12. Bayḍūn, "A Possible Poem on Dahiya," 21.

13. Bayḍūn, "A Possible Poem on Dahiya," 19.

14. See Carole Dagher, *Bring Down the Walls: Lebanon's Post-war Challenge* (New York: St. Martin's Press, 2000), 43. Dagher uses the Arabic word *al-atrāf* (sidelines or extremities) in her discussion of the marginality of South Lebanon and its Shī'ite communities.

15. Judith Butler, *Frames of War: When Is Life Grievable?* (London: Verso, 2009).

16. Lucia Volk, *Memorials and Martyrs in Modern Lebanon* (Bloomington: Indiana Univ. Press, 2010).

17. Munira Khayyat, *A Landscape of War: Ecologies of Resistance and Survival in South Lebanon* (Berkeley: Univ. of California Press, 2022).

18. See Hans Gebhardt, Dorothee Sack, Ralph Bodenstein, Andreas Fritz, and Jens Hanssen, *History, Space and Social Conflict in Beirut: The Quarter of Zokak El-Blat* (Beirut: Orient-Institut; Würzburg, Germany: Ergon Verlag in Kommission, 2005); and Samir Khalaf, *Civil and Uncivil Violence in Lebanon: A History of the Internationalization of Communal Contact* (New York: Columbia Univ. Press, 2002).

19. See, for example, Saree Makdisi, "Laying Claim to Beirut: Urban Narrative and Spatial Identity in the Age of Solidère," *Critical Inquiry* 23, no. 3 (Spring 1997): 661–705. For a discussion of the broader implications of postwar memory, see Sune Haugbølle, *War and Memory in Lebanon* (New York: Cambridge Univ. Press, 2010); Craig Larkin, *Memory and Conflict in Lebanon: Remembering and Forgetting the Past* (Abingdon, UK: Routledge, 2012); Felix Lang, *The Lebanese Post–Civil War Novel: Memory, Trauma, and Capital* (New York: Palgrave Macmillan, 2016); Claire Launchbury, Nayla Tamraz, Roger Celestin, and Eliane Dalmolin, "War, Memory, Amnesia: Postwar Lebanon," *Contemporary French and Francophone Studies* 18, no. 5 (2014): 457–61; and John Nagle, "Ghosts, Memory, and the Right to the Divided City: Resisting Amnesia in Beirut City Centre," *Antipode* 49, no. 1 (2017): 149–68.

20. See, for example, miriam cooke, *War's Other Voices: Women Writers on the Lebanese Civil War* (Cambridge: Cambridge Univ. Press, 1987); Ghenwa Hayek, *Beirut, Imagining the City: Space and Place in Lebanese Literature* (London: I. B. Tauris, 2014); Hanna Kifah, *Feminism and Avant-Garde Aesthetics in the Levantine Novel: Feminism, Nationalism, and the Arabic Novel* (New York: Palgrave Macmillan, 2016); and Robyn Creswell, *City of Beginnings: Poetic Modernism in Beirut* (Princeton, NJ: Princeton Univ. Press, 2019).

21. Films on the Civil War have been censored since the 1990s on the grounds that conflict-related discussions and images threaten civil peace. Examples of censored films include Randa Chahal Sabag's *Civilisées* [A Civilized People] (Canal Plus, 1999). Simon El Habre was forced to excise six minutes of his documentary *The One-Man Village* (Mec film, 2009). See Lina Khatib, "Lebanese Cinema and the Representation of War," in *Film in the Middle East and North Africa: Creative Dissidence*, ed. Josef Gugler (Austin: Univ. of Texas Press, 2011), 134–46.

22. See Kaelen Wilson-Goldie, "Contemporary Art Practices in Post-war Lebanon: An Introduction," in *Out of Beirut*, ed. Suzanne Cotter (Oxford: Modern Art Oxford, 2006), 82–83; Chad Elias, *Posthumous Images: Contemporary Art and Memory Politics in Post–Civil War Lebanon* (Durham, NC: Duke Univ. Press, 2018).

23. Joanne Randa Nucho, *Everyday Sectarianism in Urban Lebanon: Infrastructures, Public Services, and Power* (Princeton, NJ: Princeton Univ. Press, 2016); Aseel Sawalha, *Reconstructing Beirut: Memory and Space in a Postwar Arab City* (Austin: Univ. of Texas Press, 2010).

24. Sune Haugbølle coined this term in *War and Memory in Lebanon*.

25. Michael Warner, *Publics and Counterpublics* (New York: Zone Books; Cambridge: MIT Press, 2002), 119.

26. Warner, *Publics and Counterpublics*, 56.

27. Warner, *Publics and Counterpublics*, 36.

28. Warner, *Publics and Counterpublics*, 36.

29. See David Zeitlyn, "Anthropology in and of the Archives: Possible Futures and Contingent Pasts; Archives as Anthropological Surrogates," *Annual Review of Anthropology* 41 (2012): 461–80; Michel-Rolph Trouillot, *Silencing the Past: Power and the Production of History* (Boston: Beacon, 2001). For feminist and familial perspectives on the archive as alternative to imperial productions, see Munira Khayyat, Yasmine Khayyat, and Rola Khayyat, "Pieces of Us: The Intimate as Imperial Archive," *Journal of Middle East Women's Studies* 14, no. 3 (2018): 268–91; and Ayşe Gül Altınay, María José Contreras, Marianne Hirsch, Jean Howard, Banu Karaca, and Alisa Solomon, eds., *Women Mobilizing Memory* (New York: Columbia Univ. Press, 2019).

30. Laleh Khalili, *Heroes and Martyrs of Palestine: The Politics of National Commemoration* (Cambridge: Cambridge Univ. Press, 2007).

31. Volk, *Memorials and Martyrs in Modern Lebanon*, 20.

32. Ken Seigneurie, *Standing by the Ruins: Elegiac Humanism in Wartime and Postwar Lebanon* (New York: Fordham Univ. Press, 2011).

33. Avery Gordon, *Ghostly Matters: Haunting and the Sociological Imagination* (Minneapolis: Univ. of Minnesota Press, 2008), 22.

34. Jabal 'Āmil (جبل عامل) is a mountainous region of South Lebanon named after the Saleh Al Amel, a Christian Yemenite tribe who settled in Syria, Palestine, parts of Jordan, and South Lebanon. The area was known in ancient times as Jabal 'Amilah and later as Jabal 'Amil (Jabal Amel) or Belad Bechara.

35. It must be added here that the South is not the only marginalized region in Lebanon, although it is the place that I take up in this book because of its position at the forefront of war. The North, the Beka', and other regions are at times equally absent in national politics and Lebanese studies and are consigned not only to the physical and social margins but also to literatures on the margins or "borderlands."

36. Hasan Sharif, "South Lebanon: Its History and Geopolitics in South Lebanon," in *South Lebanon*, Special Report no. 2, ed Elaine Hagopian and Samih Farsoun (Detroit: Arab American Univ. Graduates, 1978), 10–11.

37. The Palestinian exodus of 1948, also known as the Nakba (النكبة), literally "Disaster," "Catastrophe," or "Cataclysm."

38. The Cairo Agreement of 1969, which gave the Palestinian militants use of the South Lebanon borderland as a base for military missions against Israel, consecrated the borderland as battlefield.

39. Indeed, there is always already a sense that war might return to Lebanon at any given moment. On the subject of the immanence of war in Lebanon, see Sami Samir Hermez, *War Is Coming: Between Past and Future Violence in Lebanon* (Philadelphia: Univ. of Pennsylvania Press, 2017), which addresses the temporality, memory, and futurity of war in the life-worlds of young urban elites and former fighters, and Hiba Bou Akar, *For the War Yet to Come: Planning Beirut's Frontiers* (Stanford, CA: Stanford Univ. Press, 2018), which explores the materiality of war in relation to urban planners.

40. Ḥasan Dāwūd, "They Destroy and We Build," trans. Boullata, in *Lebanon, Lebanon*, ed. Wilson, 24–25.

41. For a lengthier discussion of the genesis of Hizbullah, see Augustus Richard Norton, *Hezbollah: A Short History* (Princeton, NJ: Princeton Univ. Press, 2007). See also Augustus Richard Norton, *Amal and the Shi'a: Struggle for the Soul of Lebanon* (Austin: Univ. of Texas Press, 1987); Lara Deeb, *An Enchanted Modern: Gender and Public Piety in Shi'i Lebanon* (Princeton, NJ: Princeton Univ. Press, 2006); Amal Saad-Ghorayeb, *Hizbu'llah: Politics and Religion* (London: Pluto Press, 2002); and Na'īm Qāsim, *Hizbullah: The Story from Within*, trans. Dalia Khalil (London: Saqi, 2005). Other work on Hizbullah includes Joseph Alagha, *The Shifts in Hizbullah's Ideology: Religious Ideology, Political Ideology,*

and Political Program (Amsterdam: Amsterdam Univ. Press, 2006); Abdallah Balqaziz, *Ḥizbullah min al-taḥrīr ila al-rad: 1982–2006* [Hizbullah from Liberation to Deterrence: 1982–2006] (Beirut: Markaz Dirāsāt al-Waḥdah al-ʻArabīyah, 2006); Houchang Chehabi, *Distant Relations: Iran and Lebanon in the Last 500 Years* (London: Center for Lebanese Studies and Tauris, 2006); Emile El-Hokayem, "Hizbullah and Syria: Outgrowing the Proxy Relationship," *Washington Quarterly* 30, no. 2 (Spring 2007): 35–52; Sabrina Mervin, ed., *Les mondes chiites et l'Iran* (Paris: Karthala, 2007); Waddah Sharara, *Dawlat Ḥizbullah: Lubnan mujtamaan Islamiyah* [The Hizbullah State: Lebanon as an Islamic Society] (Beirut: Dār al-Nahar, 2006). See also Deeb and Harb, *Leisurely Islam*; Bashir Saade, *Hizbullah and the Politics of Remembrance: Writing the Lebanese Nation* (Cambridge: Cambridge Univ. Press, 2016); Ahmad Nizar Hamzeh, *In the Path of Hizbullah* (Syracuse, NY: Syracuse Univ. Press, 2004); Joseph Daher, *Hezbollah: The Political Economy of Lebanon's Party of God* (Florence, Italy: European Univ. Institute, 2019).

42. Lara Deeb, "Exhibiting the 'Just Lived Past': Hizbullah's Nationalist Narratives in a Transnational Political Context," *Comparative Studies in Society and History* 50, no. 2 (2008): 374.

43. Augustus Richard Norton, "Hizballah and the Israeli Withdrawal from Southern Lebanon," *Journal of Palestine Studies* 30, no. 1 (2000): 22–35.

44. Hatim El-Hibri, *Visions of Beirut: The Urban Life of Media Infrastructure* (Durham, NC: Duke Univ. Press, 2021); Tarek El-Ariss, *Trials of Arab Modernity: Literary Affects and the New Political* (New York: Fordham Univ. Press, 2013); Zeina Halabi, ed., *Unmaking of the Arab Intellectual: Prophecy, Exile, and the Nation* (Edinburgh: Edinburgh Univ. Press, 2017).

45. Gastón R. Gordillo, *Rubble: The Afterlife of Destruction* (Durham, NC: Duke Univ. Press, 2014), 5.

46. Bhakti Shringarpure, *Cold War Assemblages: Decolonization to Digital New York* (Milton Park, UK: Routledge, Taylor & Francis Group, 2020), 9.

47. Shringarpure, *Cold War Assemblages*, 8.

48. See Tim Edensor, "The Ghosts of Industrial Ruins: Ordering and Disordering Memory in Excessive Space," *Environment and Planning D: Society and Space* 23 (2005): 829–49; Tim Edensor, *Industrial Ruins: Space, Aesthetics, and Materiality* (Oxford: Berg, 2005); Dylan Trigg, *The Memory of Place: A Phenomenology of the Uncanny* (Athens: Ohio Univ. Press, 2012); Yael Navaro-Yashin, "Affective Spaces, Melancholic Objects: Ruination and the Production of Anthropological Knowledge," *Journal of the Royal Anthropological Institute* 15 (2009): 1–18; and Yael Navaro-Yashin, *The Make-Believe Space: Affective Geography in a Postwar Polity* (Durham, NC: Duke Univ. Press, 2012).

49. Ann Laura Stoler, "Imperial Debris: Reflections on Ruins and Ruination," *Cultural Anthropology* 23, no. 2 (2008): 191–219; see also Ann Laura Stoler, "Introduction: 'The Rot Remains': From Ruins to Ruination," in *Imperial Debris: On Ruins and*

Ruination, ed. Ann Laura Stoler (Durham, NC: Duke Univ. Press, 2013), 1–36; and Ann Laura Stoler, *Duress: Imperial Durabilities in Our Times* (Durham, NC: Duke Univ. Press, 2016).

50. Stoler, "Introduction," 9.

51. The village of Arnūn is on the edge of the zone occupied by Israel. In February 1999, after being "annexed" by Israel and the South Lebanon Army (discussed in more detail in chapter 3), the village was liberated by a mass demonstration of Lebanese students. In April, it was reoccupied by Israel. In May and June, the South Lebanon Army withdrew from the Jezzine salient.

52. The term *ṣāmidūn* is a play on the word *ṣumūd*, which means "steadfast" but also colloquially refers to the act of sitting down.

53. A Crusader-era fortress that the Israelis used during their occupation of South Lebanon.

54. The word *khiam* literally means "encampment."

55. For "the shadows," see Laleh Khalili, *Time in the Shadows: Confinement in Counterinsurgencies* (Stanford, CA: Stanford Univ. Press, 2012).

56. Anna Lowenhaupt Tsing, *The Mushroom at the End of the World: On the Possibility of Life in Capitalist Ruins* (Princeton, NJ: Princeton Univ. Press, 2015), 23.

57. Ilyās Khūrī, *Zamān al-iḥtilāl* [The Age of Occupation] (Beirut: Mu'assasat al-Abḥāth al-'Arabiyyah, 1985), 219. For a genealogy of the military borderland, see Mundhir Maḥmūd Jābir, *Sharīṭ al-Lubnānī al-muḥtal: Masālik al-iḥtilāl, masārāt al-muwājahah, maṣā'ir al-ahālī* [The Occupied Lebanese Border Strip: Occupation Routes, Paths of Confrontation, the Fate of Its Occupants] (Beirut: Mu'assasat al-Dirāsāt al-Filasṭīnīyah, 1999).

58. Yael Navaro-Yashin, "Diversifying Affect," *Cultural Anthropology* 33, no. 2 (2017): 211.

59. See, for example, Caitlin DeSilvey, *Curated Decay: Heritage beyond Saving* (Minneapolis: Univ. of Minnesota Press, 2017).

60. Quoted in Gordillo, *Rubble*, 32.

61. See, for example, Susan Stewart, *The Ruins Lesson: Meaning and Material in Western Culture* (Chicago: Univ. of Chicago Press, 2020), in which the poet-critic explores the West's fascination with ruins in literature, visual art, and architecture, covering a vast chronological and geographical range from the ancient Egyptians to T. S. Eliot.

In the introduction to *Ruins of Modernity* (Durham, NC: Duke Univ. Press, 2010), the editors, Julia Hell and Andreas Schönle, go through a list of art and writing about ruins and observe: "This story of imperial legacies, (colonial) empires, and their ruins is familiar, and it seemed to be a story of European ruins" (3). They mention Friedrich Ratzel's *Die Erde und das Leben* (1902), W. B. Sebald's *Rings of Saturn* (1998), Christopher Woodward's *In Ruins: A Journey through History, Art and Literature* (2001), Denis Diderot's *Salon of 1767* (1767), and Walter Benjamin's *The Arcades Project* (1989).

62. Suzanne Pinckney Stetkevych, *The Mute Immortals Speak: Pre-Islamic Poetry and the Poetics of Ritual* (Ithaca, NY: Cornell Univ. Press, 1993), 10–11.

63. Nathalie Khankan, "Re-perceiving the Pre-Islamic Nasīb," *Journal of Arabic Literature* 33, no. 1 (2002): 1–23.

64. The *qaṣīdah* is a metrical and monorhyme Master Arabic poetic structure that dominated Arabic poetry from pre-Islamic times until the first half of the twentieth century.

65. Jaroslav Stetkevych, *The Zephyrs of Najd: The Poetics of Nostalgia in the Classical Arabic Nasīb* (Chicago: Univ. of Chicago Press, 1993), 26–27. In this work, Stetkevych deals with the ways in which the *aṭlāl* and other motifs of the *nasīb* evolved in the later Arabic poetic tradition.

66. See Huda J. Fakhreddine, *Metapoesis in the Arabic Tradition: From Modernists to Muḥdathūn* (Leiden: Brill, 2015); Stetkevych, *The Zephyrs of Najd*; Andras Hamori, *On the Art of Medieval Arabic Literature* (Princeton, NJ: Princeton Univ. Press, 1974); Stefan Sperl, *Mannerism in Arabic Poetry: A Structural Analysis of Selected Texts* (Cambridge: Cambridge Univ. Press, 1989); Seigneurie, *Standing by the Ruins*; Hilary Kilpatrick, "Literary Creativity and the Cultural Heritage: The Aṭlāl in Modern Arabic Fiction," in *Tradition, Modernity, and Postmodernity in Arabic Literature: Essays in Honor of Professor Issa F. Boullatta*, ed. Kamal Abdel-Malek and Wael Hallaq (Leiden: Brill, 2000), 42; Tarek El-Ariss, "Return of the Beast: From Pre-Islamic Ode to the Contemporary Novel," *Journal of Arabic Literature* 47, nos. 1–2 (2016): 62–90; Elliott Colla, *Conflicted Antiquities: Egyptology, Egyptomania, Egyptian Modernity* (Durham, NC: Duke Univ. Press, 2007); Elizabeth M. Holt, *Fictitious Capital: Silk, Cotton, and the Rise of the Arabic Novel* (New York: Fordham Univ. Press, 2017); Birget Embaló, "The City, Mythical Images and Their Deconstruction: The Image of Beirut in Contemporary Works of Arabic Literature," in *Myths, Historical Archetypes and Symbolic Figures in Arabic Literature: Towards a New Hermeneutic Approach*, ed. Angelika Neuwirth, Birgit Embaló, Sebastian Günther, and Maher Jarrar (Stuttgart, Germany: Steiner, 1999), 583–603.

67. The amorous prelude of the pre-Islamic ode encapsulates the ruins motif known as the *aṭlāl*. See Stetkevych, *The Zephyrs of Najd*, and Hussein 'Aṭwān, *Muqaddimāt al-qaṣīdah al-'Arabīyya* [Introduction to the Arabic Ode], 3 vols. (Cairo: Dār al- Ma'rifa bi-Misr, 1970).

68. Marc Augé, *Oblivion* (Minneapolis: Univ. of Minnesota Press, 2004).

69. Convinced of his genius, al-Mutanabbī (d. 356 CE) in his youth felt impelled to compose verses in emulation of the Qur'ān, which earned him the sobriquet "the would-be prophet."

70. Ann Laura Stoler, *Along the Archival Grain: Epistemic Anxieties and Colonial Common Sense* (Princeton, NJ: Princeton Univ. Press, 2009), 255.

71. Adrian Forty, introduction to *The Art of Forgetting*, ed. Adrian Forty and Susanne Kuchler (Oxford: Berg, 1999), 1–18.

1. Shu'arā' al-Janūb

1. Khūrī, *Zamān al-iḥtilāl*, 219. *Zamān al-iḥtilāl* is a collection of vehement editorials that Khūrī wrote for the leftist Beiruti newspaper *Al-Safīr* during the Israeli invasion of Lebanon in 1982.

2. Khūrī, *Zamān al-iḥtilāl*, 220.

3. Warner, *Publics and Counterpublics*, 119.

4. Warner, *Publics and Counterpublics*, 136.

5. See, for example, miriam cooke, *Women Write War: The Centring of the Beirut Decentrists* (Oxfordshire, UK: Centre for Lebanese Studies, 1987).

6. See Sune Haugbølle, "Counterpublics of Memory: Memoirs and Public Testimonies of the Lebanese Civil War," in *Publics, Politics, and Participation: Locating the Public Sphere in the Middle East and North Africa*, ed. Seteney Shami (New York: Columbia Univ. Press, 2010), 124.

7. The two Arabic terms—*mashhad*, that which is grasped with the eye, and *arḍ*, that which is underfoot, land—evoke an inchoative process: a way of being, of dwelling, all directed through the poet's lingering gaze.

8. Born Ali Ahmad Said Esber.

9. Elise Salem Manganaro, *Constructing Lebanon: A Century of Literary Narratives* (Gainesville: Univ. Press of Florida, 2003), 137.

10. Nizār Qabbānī, *Ilā Bayrūt al-unthā . . . ma' ḥubbī: Muqaddimah wa 5 qaṣā'id* [To Beirut, the Woman . . . With My Love: Introduction and 5 Poems] (Beirut: Manshurāt Nizār Qabbānī, 1981).

11. Adūnīs, "The Desert: Diary of Beirut under Siege, 1982," trans. in Salem Manganaro, *Constructing Lebanon*, 138.

12. Tawfīq Yūsuf 'Awwād, *Ṭawāḥin Bayrūt* [Death in Beirut] (Beirut: Dār al-Ādāb, 1972), 2.

13. Gilles Deleuze and Félix Guattari, *Kafka: Toward a Minor Literature*, trans. Dana Polan (Minneapolis: Univ. of Minnesota Press, 1986), 16–17.

14. Raymond Williams, *Marxism and Literature* (Oxford: Oxford Univ. Press, 1977), 132–34.

15. It must be added here that the South is by no means populated only by Shī'ites, although I have taken up their poetic thread here. The borderland is also home to Druze, Christian (Maronite and Greek Catholic), and Sunni communities. These communities have been just as profoundly affected by the history being recounted here but in different ways because of the role of institutions such as the church, geographical locations, social positions, political alliances, and many other factors that are beyond the scope of this chapter.

16. Jacques Derrida, *Acts of Literature*, ed. Derek Attridge (New York: Routledge, 1992).

17. See Fadi A. Bardawil, *Revolution and Disenchantment: Arab Marxism and the Binds of Emancipation* (Durham, NC: Duke Univ. Press, 2020).

18. Translated and quoted in Yvonne Albers, "Turning the Page: Reading 1979 in and through the Cultural Journal *Mawaqif*," *TRAFO—Blog for Transregional Research*, 2018, at https://trafo.hypotheses.org/9858.

19. Albers, "Turning the Page."

20. 'Abbās Bayḍūn,"Al-Ḥadātha al-ān: Bahth fi-lḥarakāt al-shu'arā'al-shabbān al-lubnāniyīn" [Modernity Now: Research on the Movement of Young Lebanese Poets], *Mawāqif* 34 (1979): 5, 3.

21. Bayḍūn, "Al-Ḥadātha, al-ān," 3.

22. Fawwaz Traboulsi, *A History of Modern Lebanon* (London: Pluto Press, 2007), 165, quoted in Bardawil, *Revolution and Disenchantment*, Kindle ed., loc. 5676.

23. Bayḍūn, "Al-Ḥadātha, al-ān," 5.

24. See Christopher Stone, "Ziyad Rahbani's 'Novelization' of Lebanese Musical Theater or the Paradox of Parody," *Middle Eastern Literatures* 8, no. 2 (July 2005): 151–70.

25. Ziyād Raḥbānī, *Shī fāshil* [A Failure] (Beirut: Mukhtārāt, 1994), 150, ellipses in the original.

26. Al-Majlis al-Thaqāfī li-Lubnān al-Janūbī [Cultural Council of South Lebanon], *Al-Muqāwamah fī al-ta'bīr al-adabī* [Resistance in Literary Expression] (Beirut: Dār al-Farabi, 1985).

27. The Cultural Council of South Lebanon (al-Majlis al-Thaqāfī li-Lubnān al-Janūbī) was a nongovernmental cultural institution dedicated to the "plight of the South" and founded in 1964.

28. The Jabhat al-Muqāwamah al-Waṭanīyyah al-Lubnāniyyah (Front national de la résistance libanaise), known as Jammoul based on its Arabic acronym, was catalyzed on the heels of the Israeli invasion of Beirut in September 1982. The Front comprised an amalgam of leftist political parties, including the Lebanese Communist Party, the Organization of Communist Action–Lebanon, the Arab Socialist Action Party–Lebanon, the Arab Democratic Party, the Lebanese Armed Revolutionary Faction, the Popular Front for the Liberation of Palestine, and the Democratic Front for the Liberation of Palestine.

29. Quoted in Salem Manganaro, *Constructing Lebanon,* 148.

30. Ḥabīb Ṣādiq, introductory statement in al-Majlis al-Thaqāfī li-Lubnān al-Janūbī, *Al-Muqāwamah,* 16.

31. Perhaps the most profound act of literature came from the poet Khalīl Ḥāwī, whose suicide on the day of the Israeli invasion testified to the im/possibility of bearing witness.

32. The Lebanese scholar Suhayl Idrīs (1925–2008) founded one of the most prominent literary journals, *Al-Ādāb*, in 1953 in Beirut.

33. For a discussion of Majallat *al-Ādāb*'s engagement with the politics of literature, see Muhsin al-Musawi, *The Postcolonial Arabic Novel: Debating Ambivalence* (Leiden:

Brill, 2003), 184–85; Yoav Di-Capua, "Arab Existentialism: An Invisible Chapter in the Intellectual History of Decolonization," *American Historical Review* 117, no. 4 (2012): 1061–91; Seigneurie, *Standing by the Ruins*, 5–8.

34. Quoted and translated in M. M. Badawi, "Commitment in Contemporary Arabic Literature," *Cahiers d'histoire mondiale* 14, no. 4 (1972): 868.

35. Idrīs's journal, *Al-Ādāb*, became the mouthpiece for progressive writers and advocates of *iltizām* in the 1950s and 1960s as well as a battleground for the two competing trends. In his editorial note to the first volume of January 1953, Idrīs announced that "the policy of the periodical was to publish and promote the cause of Adab Multazim" (quoted in Badawi, "Commitment in Contemporary Arabic Literature," 867).

36. Translated and quoted in Salem Manganaro, *Constructing Lebanon*, 148.

37. In fact, the poet and journalist 'Abbās Bayḍūn (one of the Poets of the South) was responsible for the cultural pages in the pan-Arab daily *As-Safīr* between 1967 and 1997.

38. Ḥasan 'Abdallāh, "Al-Tasalul ilal-waṭan al-asīr" [Infiltration into the Captive Homeland], *Al-Safīr* 3, no. 121 (June 12, 1993): 14.

39. 'Abdallāh, "Al-Tasalul ilal-waṭan al-asīr," 14.

40. 'Abdallāh, "Al-Tasalul ilal-waṭan al-asīr," 14.

41. Ralph Waldo Emerson, quoted in W. J. T. Mitchell, *Picture Theory: Essays on Verbal and Visual Representation* (Chicago: Univ. of Chicago Press, 1994), 29.

42. The *mu'allaqāt* are the most famous—and among the earliest—examples of the *qaṣīdah* (commonly translated as "ode"), a form that frequently runs to some 120 lines. The term *qaṣīdah* may derive from the root *qaṣada*, "to aim" or "to go forward," or from *qasar*, "to break," in reference to the mandatory division of the line into two rhythmically equal parts. For the work of some prominent critics who have examined Imru' al-Qays's life and poetry, see Aḥmad Makkī al-Ṭāhir, *Imru' al-Qays: Amīr shu'arā' al-jāhiliyyah* [Imru' al-Qays: Prince of Pre-Islamic Poets] (Cairo: Dār al- Ma'ārif, 1968); Ahmad Makki al-Tahir, "Imru' al-Qays," in *Dictionary of Literary Biography*, vol. 311: *Arabic Literary Culture: 500–925*, ed. Michael Cooperson and Shawkat M. Toorawa (Detroit: Thomson Gale, 2005), 212–24; Shawqī Ḍayf, *Tārīkh al-adab al-'Arabī 1: Al-'Aṣr al-jāhilī* [History of Arabic Literature: The Pre-Islamic Age] (Cairo: Dār al-Ma'ārif, 1960); Īliyyā Ḥāwī, *Imru' al-Qays: Shā'ir al-mar'a wa-l-ṭabī'a* [Imru' al-Qays: Poet of Women and Nature] (Beirut: Dār al-Thaqāfa, 1970); Muḥammad Ṣāliḥ Samak, *Amīr alshi'r fī l-'aṣr al-qadīm Imru' al-Qays* [Prince of Poetry in the Ancient Era: Imru' al-Qays] (Cairo: Dār Nahḍat Miṣr, 1974).

43. Mitch Rose and John Wylie, "Animating Landscape," *Environment and Planning D: Society and Space* 24 (2006): 475.

44. It is worth noting that 'Abbās Bayḍūn won the Sheikh Zayed Award in 2017 for his book *Kharīf al barā'a* (The Autumn of Innocence).

45. 'Abbās Bayḍūn, "Al-Shi'ir lam yabda'" [The Poem Has Not Started Yet], *As-Safīr*, Apr. 30, 2013.

46. Yumnā al-ʻĪd, *Al-Kitābah taḥawwul fī al-taḥawwul: Muqārabah li-l-kitābah al-adabīyah fī zaman al-ḥarb al-Lubnāniyyah* [Writing Shifts in Transition: An Approach to Literary Writing at the Time of the Lebanese War] (Beirut: Dār al-Ādāb, 1993), 134.

47. Bayḍūn, "Al-Shiʻir lam yabda'."

48. ʻAbbās Bayḍūn, "Ṣūr" [Tyre], in *Al-Aʻmāl al-shiʻrīyah* [The Complete Works of Poetry] (Beirut: Al-Mu'assasah al-ʻArabīyyah li-l-Dirāsāt wa-l-Nashr, 2007), 33–46.

49. Adūnīs, *Kalām al-bidāyāt* [Word Beginnings] (Beirut: Dār al-Ādāb, 1989), 76.

50. Bayḍūn, "Ṣūr," in *Al-Aʻmāl al-shiʻrīyah*, 33.

51. Bayḍūn, "Ṣūr," in *Al-Aʻmāl al-shiʻrīyah*, 33.

52. Bayḍūn, "Ṣūr," in *Al-Aʻmāl al-shiʻrīyah*, 55.

53. Bayḍūn, "Ṣūr," in *Al-Aʻmāl al-shiʻrīyah*, 55.

54. Bayḍūn, "Ṣūr," in *Al-Aʻmāl al-shiʻrīyah*, 55.

55. Bayḍūn, "Ṣūr," in *Al-Aʻmāl al-shiʻrīyah*, 57.

56. Bayḍūn, "Ṣūr," in *Al-Aʻmāl al-shiʻrīyah*, 57.

57. Bayḍūn, "Ṣūr," in *Al-Aʻmāl al-shiʻrīyah*, 61.

58. Hannah Arendt, *The Origins of Totalitarianism* (New York: Harcourt, Brace & World, 1966), 293.

59. Bayḍūn, "Ṣūr," in *Al-Aʻmāl al-shiʻrīyah*, 44.

60. "Wave" is my rendering of the movement of meters because the word for a meter in Arabic poetry, *baḥr*, literally means "sea."

61. Bayḍūn, "Ṣūr," in *Al-Aʻmāl al-shiʻrīyah*, 51.

62. Stetkevych, *The Mute Immortals Speak*, 18.

63. The original Arabic is given in Labīd ibn Rabīʻa, "The Muʻallaqah of Labīd ibn Rabīʻah," in *The Muʻallaqat for Millennials: Pre-Islamic Arabic Golden Odes*, trans. and ed. Suzanne Pinckney Stetkevych and Khalid Stetkevych (Olaya, Saudi Arabia: King Abdullazizz Center For World Culture [Ithra], King Fahad National Library, 2020), 221.

64. The translation is given in Labīd ibn Rabīʻah, "Muʻallaqah of Labīd ibn Rabīʻah," in *The Muʻallaqat for Millennials*, trans. and ed. Stetkevych and Stetkevych, 221.

65. Bayḍūn, "Ṣūr," in *Al-Aʻmāl al-shiʻrīyah*, 56.

66. Translated from the Arabic by Sharif S. Elmusa in Elise Salem Manganaro, "Bearing Witness: Recent Literature from Lebanon," *Literary Review* 37, no. 3 (Spring 1994): 382.

67. Bayḍūn, "Ṣūr," in *Al-Aʻmāl al-shiʻrīyah*, 54.

68. Bayḍūn, "Ṣūr," in *Al-Aʻmāl al-shiʻrīyah*, 48.

69. Bayḍūn, "Ṣūr," in *Al-Aʻmāl al-shiʻrīyah*, 52.

70. Bayḍūn, "Ṣūr," in *Al-Aʻmāl al-shiʻrīyah*, 63.

71. Bayḍūn, "Ṣūr," in *Al-Aʻmāl al-shiʻrīyah*, 64.

72. Adūnīs, *Kalām al-bidāyāt*, 78.

73. Bayḍūn, "Ṣūr," in *Al-Aʻmāl al-shiʻrīyah*, 64.

74. Bayḍūn, "Ṣūr," in *Al-Aʻmāl al-shiʻrīyah*, 66.

75. Bayḍūn, "Ṣūr," in *Al-Aʻmāl al-shiʻrīyah*, 66.

76. Bayḍūn, "Ṣūr," in *Al-A'māl al-shi'rīyah*, 60.

77. Quoted in Heonik Kwon, *Ghosts of War in Vietnam: Studies in the Social and Cultural History of Modern Warfare* (Cambridge: Cambridge Univ. Press, 2008), 38.

78. Quoted in translation in Richard Serrano, *Neither a Borrower, nor a Lender: Forging Traditions in French, Chinese and Arabic Poetry* (Oxford: Legenda, 2002), 29.

79. Stetkevych, *The Mute Immortals Speak*, 20.

80. Bayḍūn, "Ṣūr," in *Al-A'māl al-shi'riyah*, 74.

81. On the topic of committed literature, see Ken Seigneurie, "Introduction: A Survival Aesthetic for Ongoing War," in *Crisis and Memory: The Representation of Space in Modern Levantine Narrative*, ed. Ken Seigneurie (Wiesbaden, Germany: Reichert, 2004), 11–32; al-Musawi, *The Postcolonial Arabic Novel*, 184–85, 190–91; Di-Capua, "Arab Existentialism"; Verena Klemm, "Different Notions of Commitment (*Iltizam*) and Committed Literature (*al-Adab al-Multazim*) in the Literary Circles of the Mashriq," *Arabic & Middle Eastern Literature* 3, no. 1 (2000): 51–62.

82. Fakhr al-Dīn's collection of children's poems *Thalāthūn qaṣīdah lil atfāl* (Thirty Poems for Children, 2013) won the Sheikh Zayed Book Award in 2014.

83. Jawdat Fakhr al-Dīn, "Ayyām fī qaryatī-al-mahjūrah" [Days in My Deserted Village], in *Al-A'māl al-shi'riyyah* [The Complete Works of Poetry] (Beirut: Al-Mu'assasah al-'Arabīyah li-l-Dirāsāt wa-l-Nashr, 2006), 147.

84. Fakhr al-Dīn, "Ayyām fī qaryatī-al-mahjūrah," in *Al-A'māl al-shi'riyyah*, 148.

85. Fakhr al-Dīn, "Ayyām fī qaryatī-al-mahjūrah," in *Al-A'māl al-shi'riyyah*, 149.

86. From Sūrat al-Naml; see Muhsin Jasim al-Musawi, *Arabic Poetry: Trajectories of Modernity and Tradition* (London: Routledge, 2006), 76.

87. Fakhr al-Dīn, "Ayyām fī qaryatī-al-mahjūrah," in *Al-A'māl al-shi'riyyah*, 149.

88. Navaro-Yashin, "Affective Spaces, Melancholic Objects," 5.

89. Fakhr al-Dīn, "Ayyām fī qaryatī-al-mahjūrah," in *Al-A'māl al-shi'riyyah*, 147.

90. Fakhr al-Dīn, "Ayyām fī qaryatī-al-mahjūrah," in *Al-A'māl al-shi'riyyah*, 148.

91. Fakhr al-Dīn, "Ayyām fī qaryatī-al-mahjūrah," in *Al-A'māl al-shi'riyyah*, 148.

92. Jawdat Fakhr al-Dīn, "Al-Qaṣīdah nafusaha" [The Qaṣīdah Itself], in *Al-A'māl al-shi'riyyah*, 96.

93. Fakhr al-Dīn, "Al-Qaṣīdah nafusaha," in *Al-A'māl al-shi'riyyah*, 96.

94. Jawdat Fakhr al-Dīn, "Iḥḏarū mawtanā fī al-janūb" [Beware of Our Death in the South], in *Al-A'māl al-shi'riyyah*, 25.

95. Fakhr al-Dīn, "Iḥḏarū mawtanā fī al-janūb," in *Al-A'māl al-shi'riyyah*, 25.

96. Maurice Blanchot, *The Space of Literature* (Lincoln: Univ. of Nebraska Press, 1983), 22.

97. Shawqī Bizī', "Al-Shā'ir" [The Poet], in *Ka'annī gharībuka bayna al-nisā'* (As Though I Am Your Stranger among Women) (Beirut: Dār al-Ādāb, 1994), 5.

98. Shawqī Bizī', "Al-'Ā'id" (He who returns), in *'Anāwīn sarī'ah li-waṭan maqtūl: Shi'r* [Quick Headlines for a Murdered Nation: Poetry] (Beirut: Dār al-Ādāb, 1982), 58.

99. Bizī', "Al-'Ā'id," in *'Anāwīn sarī'ah li-waṭan maqtūl*, 58.

100. Ḥasan 'Abdallāh, "Min ayna adkhulu al-watan?" [Where Do I Enter the Homeland?], in *Adhkuru annanī aḥbabtu* [I Remember That I Loved] (Beirut: Dār al-'Awdah, 1972), 86.

101. 'Abdallāh, "Min ayna adkhulu al-watan," in *Adhkuru annanī aḥbabtu*, 86.

102. Ḥasan 'Abdallāh, "Adhkuru annanī aḥbabtu" [I Remember That I Loved], in *Adhkuru annanī aḥbabtu*, 47.

103. 'Abdallāh, "Adhkuru annanī aḥbabtu," in *Adhkuru annanī aḥbabtu*, 47.

104. Maurice Blanchot, *The Writing of the Disaster*, trans. Anne Smock (Lincoln: Univ. of Nebraska Press, 1995), 11.

105. 'Abdallāh, "Adhkuru annanī aḥbabtu," in *Adhkuru annanī aḥbabtu*, 48–49.

106. 'Abdallāh, "Adhkuru annanī aḥbabtu," in *Adhkuru annanī aḥbabtu*, 51–56.

107. Stetkevych, *The Mute Immortals Speak*, 248, 249.

108. Muḥammad 'Alī Shams al-Dīn, "Fatiha lil-nār fī kharā'ib al-jasad" [Open Fire in the Ruins of the Body], in *Al-A'māl al-shi'riyyah* [The Complete Works of Poetry] (Beirut: Al-Mu'assasah al-'Arabiyyah li-l-Dirāsāt wa-l-Nashr, 2009), 24.

109. Mūsā al-Ṣadr to Ḥusayn Ḥusaynī, July 14, 1975, quoted in Fouad Ajami, *The Vanished Imam: Musa al Sadr and the Shia of Lebanon* (Ithaca, NY: Cornell Univ. Press, 1986), 136.

110. Shams al-Dīn, "Fatiha lil-nār fī kharā'ib al-jasad," in *Al-A'māl al-shi'riyyah*, 25.

111. Shams al-Dīn, "Fatiha lil-nār fī kharā'ib al-jasad," in *Al-A'māl al-shi'riyyah*, 24.

112. Shams al-Dīn, "Fatiha lil-nār fī kharā'ib al-jasad," in *Al-A'māl al-shi'riyyah*, 25.

113. Muḥammad 'Alī Shams al-Dīn, "Mūshaḥ ila a'midat al-rīḥ al-janūbīya" [Ode to the Pillars of the Southern Wind], in *Al-A'māl al-shi'riyyah*, 25.

114. Al-Musawi, *Arabic Poetry*, 25.

115. Shams al-Dīn, "Mūshaḥ ila a'midat al-rīḥ al-janūbīya," in *Al-A'māl al-shi'riyyah*, 27.

116. Shams al-Dīn, "Mūshaḥ ila a'midat al-rīḥ al-janūbīya," in *Al-A'māl al-shi'riyyah*, 27.

117. Shams al-Dīn, "Mūshaḥ ila a'midat al-rīḥ al-janūbīya," in *Al-A'māl al-shi'riyyah*, 27.

118. Shams al-Dīn, "Mūshaḥ ila a'midat al-rīḥ al-janūbīya," in *Al-A'māl al-shi'riyyah*, 27, 28.

119. Shams al-Dīn, "Mūshaḥ ila a'midat al-rīḥ al-janūbīya," in *Al-A'māl al-shi'riyyah*, 29, 30.

2. Haunted by Home in Wartime and Postwar Lebanese Fiction

1. Jorge Luis Borges, "Funes, His Memory," in *Collected Fictions*, trans. Andrew Hurley (New York: Viking Penguin, 1998), 135.

2. Augé, *Oblivion*.

3. Augé, *Oblivion*, ix.

4. Augé, *Oblivion*, 20.

5. Lang, *The Lebanese Post–Civil War Novel*, 120.

6. Ilyās Khūrī, "Al-Riwāya wa-al-riwā'ī wa-al-ḥarb" [The Novel, the Novelist, and the War], *Al-Mulḥaq al-thaqāfī li-al-nahār*, Jan. 22, 2006, 14.

7. Many members of the generation of "Civil War novelists" are unaccounted for in this chapter, including Ḥanān al-Shaykh (b. 1945), Amīn Ma'lūf (b. 1949), Rashīd al-Ḍa'īf (b. 1945), and Hudā Barakāt (b. 1952), to name a few.

8. Kifah, *Feminism and Avant-Garde Aesthetic in the Levantine Novel*, 4.

9. Ghada Samman, *Beirut '75*, trans. Nancy N. Roberts (Fayetteville: Univ. of Arkansas Press, 1995).

10. The publication date mentioned here is the date of the first edition of the Arabic novel (1976). Transliterations of characters' names are mine.

11. Dedication in Ghādah al-Sammān, *Kawābīs Bayrūt* (Beirut: Manshurāt Dār al-Ādāb, 1976), translated by Nancy N. Roberts as Ghada Samman, *Beirut Nightmares* (London: Quartet Books, 1997).

12. The Lebanese Phalange, also known as the Kataeb Party, was founded in 1936 by Pierre Gemayel and named after the nationalist right-wing Phalange movement in Spain. The Lebanese Phalange began as a small but potent party that espoused a form of nationalism in direct opposition to Arabism, a driving force behind the Arab nationalist movement that emerged in the early twentieth century and played a major role in the struggle for independence in many Arab countries. In agitating for sovereignty from the yoke of French Mandatory rule over Lebanon, the Lebanese Phalange were also agitating for their own ascendancy within a newly established Lebanese state and central government. During the Lebanese Civil War, the Lebanese Phalange maintained close ties to Israel and were involved in the 1982 Sabra and Shatila massacre, in which Phalange militiamen killed hundreds of Palestinian refugees. Today, the Lebanese Phalange is one of the largest political parties in Lebanon and is part of the March 14 Alliance, which is a coalition of parties that oppose Syrian interference in Lebanese affairs.

13. Haugbølle, *War and Memory in Lebanon*, 9.

14. Haugbølle, *War and Memory in Lebanon*, 39.

15. Stoler, "*Imperial Debris*," 196.

16. Samman, *Beirut Nightmares*, 325, 137. The original Arabic version:

17. Samman, *Beirut Nightmares*, 97.

18. Samman, *Beirut Nightmares*, 6.

19. In Arabic, *bayt* means "house" but also refers to a line of poetry.

20. Al-Mutanabbī, "Lakī yā manāzil fi al-qulūb manāzil" [O Dwellings, in Our Hearts You Dwell], in *Sharḥ dīwān al-Mutanabī* [Explanation of al-Mutanabī], 4 vols., ed. 'Abd al-Raḥmān al-Barqūqī (Beirut: Dār al-Kitāb al-'Arabī, 1986), 3:366.

21. Samman, *Beirut Nightmares*, 47.

22. Samman, *Beirut Nightmares*, 75, 356.

23. Huda Fakhreddine, "Defining Metapoesis in the 'Abbāsid Age," *Journal of Arabic Literature* 42 (2011): 209.

24. Al-Sammān, *Kawābīs Bayrūt*, 186, my translation.

25. Stoler, "Imperial Debris," 207.

26. Marianne Hirsch and Nancy K. Miller, *Rites of Return: Diaspora Poetics and the Politics of Memory* (New York: Columbia Univ. Press, 2011), 17.

27. Samman, *Beirut Nightmares*, 213, 214.

28. Al-Sammān, *Kawābīs Bayrūt*, 152–53.

29. Samman, *Beirut Nightmares*, 167.

30. Samman, *Beirut Nightmares*, 139.

31. Samman, *Beirut Nightmares*, 311.

32. Ghassan Kanafani, *Fi al-adab al-Sahyuni* [On Zionist Literature] (1967; reprint, Nicosia, Cyprus: Rimal, 2015), 11.

33. See Elizabeth M. Holt, "Resistance Literature and Occupied Palestine in Cold War Beirut," *Journal of Palestine Studies* 50, no. 1 (2021): 3–18.

34. Ghādah al-Sammān, *Rasā'il Ghassān Kanafānī ila Ghāda al-Sammān* [Ghassān Kanafānī's Love Letters to Ghāda al-Sammān] (1992; reprint, Beirut: Dar al-Taliya, 1993), 13.

35. Samman, *Beirut Nightmares*, 322, 323.

36. Samman, *Beirut Nightmares*, 286, 143.

37. Samman, *Beirut Nightmares*, 136, 51.

38. For the English translation, see Mahmud Darwish, *Memory for Forgetfulness: August, Beirut, 1982*, trans. Ibrahim Muhawi (Berkeley: Univ. of California Press, 1995).

39. Maḥmūd Darwīsh, *Dhākirah lil-nisyān: Al-zamān, Bayrūt: Al-makān, yawm min Āb 1982* [*Memory for Forgetfulness: The Time, Beirut: The Place, a Day in August 1982*] (Cairo: Dār al-Thaqāfah al-Jadīdah, 1989), 157.

40. Darwīsh, *Dhākirah lil-nisyān*, 157.

41. Samman, *Beirut Nightmares*, 185.

42. Jacques Derrida, *Specters of Marx: The State of the Debt, the Work of Mourning, and the New International*, trans. Peggy Kamuf (New York: Routledge, 1994), 168.

43. Derrida, *Specters of Marx*, 168.

44. Samman, *Beirut Nightmares*, 30.

45. Tim Edensor, "Waste Matter: The Debris of Industrial Ruins and the Disordering of the Material World," *Journal of Material Culture* 10, no. 3 (2005): 326.

46. Svetlana Boym, "Ruinophilia: Appreciation of Ruins," in *Atlas of Transformation*, ed. Zbynek Baladrán and Vik Havránek (Zurich: JRP Ringier, 2008), at http://monumenttotransformation.org/atlas-of-transformation/html/r/ruinophilia/ruinophilia-appreciation-of-ruins-svetlana-boym.html.

47. Darwīsh, *Dhākirah lil-nisyān*, 207.

48. Darwish, *Memory for Forgetfulness*, 162.

49. Samman, *Beirut Nightmares*, 375.

50. Samman, *Beirut Nightmares*, 376.

51. Samman, *Beirut Nightmares*, 375.

52. Augé, *Oblivion*, 87–89.

53. Augé, *Oblivion*, 17.

54. Samman, *Beirut Nightmares*, 376.

55. Ḥasan Dāwūd, *Bināyat Mātīld* (Beirut: Dār al-Tanwīr, 1983), translated by Peter Theroux as Hasan Daoud, *The House of Mathilde* (London: Granta, 1999), 5. In Arabic: "لم تعد البناية صالحةً للسكن" (Dāwūd, *Bināyat Mātīld*, 9).

56. Sawalha, *Reconstructing Beirut*, 109.

57. Daoud, *The House of Mathilde*, 4.

58. Daoud, *The House of Mathilde*, 5.

59. Daoud, *The House of Mathilde*, 126, 58, 148.

60. Petra Rau, quoted in Emma Zimmerman, "A 'Tottering Lace-like Architecture of Ruins': The Wartime Home in Elizabeth Bowen's *The Heat of the Day*," *Literary Geographies* 1, no. 1 (2015): 43.

61. Daoud, *The House of Mathilde*, 31.

62. Daoud, *The House of Mathilde*, 33.

63. Daoud, *The House of Mathilde*, 149.

64. Gaston Bachelard, *The Poetics of Space* (Boston: Beacon Press, 1969), 224.

65. Bachelard, *The Poetics of Space*, 224.

66. Daoud, *The House of Mathilde*, 129, 149.

67. Daoud, *The House of Mathilde*, 179.

68. Dāwūd, *Bināyat Mātīld*, 7.

69. Daoud, *The House of Mathilde*, 3.

70. Marianne Hirsch and Leo Spitzer, *Ghosts of Home: The Afterlife of Czernowitz in Jewish Memory* (Berkeley: Univ. of California Press, 2010), 81.

71. Abū Tammām, "Lā anta anta wa-lā al- diyāru diyāru" [You Are Not You and the Abodes Are Not Abodes], in *Dīwān Abī Tammām* [Collected Works of Abū Tammām], 2 vols., ed. Muḥyī al-Dīn Ṣubhī (Beirut: Dār Sādir, 1997), 1:321. Translated by Suzanne Stetkevych in *Abu Tammam and the Poetics of the Abbasid Age* (Leiden: Brill), 81. See also Ḥusayn b. Aḥmad al-Zawzanī, *Sharḥ al-mu'allaqāt al-sab'* [Explanation of the Seven *Mu'allaqāt*] (Beirut: Dār al-Jīl, n.d.), 7–10, and Miguel Ángel Vázquez and Robert G. Havard, "Poetic Pilgrimages: From Baghdad to Andalucía, Abū Tammām's *Lā anta anta wa-lā al-diyāru diyāru*," in "The Arabic Literature of al-Andalus," special issue of *Journal of Arabic Literature* 34, nos. 1–2 (2003): 122–37.

72. Abū Tammām, "Lā anta anta wa-lā al- diyāru diyāru," trans. Suzanne Pinckney Stetkevych, in Suzanne Pinckney Stetkevych, *Abu Tammam and the Poetics of the Abbasid Age* (Leiden: Brill, 1991), 81.

73. Bachelard, *Poetics of Space*, 27.

74. Daoud, *House of Mathilde*, 8.

75. Daoud, *House of Mathilde,* 149.

76. Daoud, *House of Mathilde,* 129.

77. According to Craig Larkin, "The Ṭā'if Accord of 1990, which ended Lebanon's prolonged civil war, essentially reconfigured the National Pact but also held an elusive promise of the abolition of confessionalism and the implementation of full democracy. Its key reforms, incorporated within thirty-one constitutional amendments, included Christian–Muslim parity in Parliament; a political troika made up of a weakened Maronite president, a Sunni prime minister, and a strengthened Shī'ite Speaker; electoral reform and boundary extensions; an independent judiciary; administrative decentralization; and the creation of the Constitutional Council, the Socio-economic Council, and a National Committee to study and propose means to ensure the abolition of confessionalism" (*Memory and Conflict in Lebanon,* 53).

78. See Nizar Saghieh, "Dhākirat al-ḥarb fil-nizām al-qānūnī al-lubnānī" [Memory of the War in the Lebanese Legal System], in *Memoire pour l'avenir,* ed. Amal Makarem (Beirut: Éditions Dar an-Nahar, 2002), 255.

79. Elias Khoury, "The Novel, the Novelist, and the Lebanese Civil War," Fourth Farhat J. Ziadeh Distinguished Lecture in Arab and Islamic Studies, Department of Near Eastern Languages and Civilization, Univ. of Washington, Seattle, 2006, at http://depts.washington.edu/nelc/pdf/event_files/ziadeh_series/2006lebanon-eliaskhoury.pdf.

80. Makdisi, "Laying Claim to Beirut," 662.

81. Lebanon remains a country "without an official history," especially a country without a history of its long civil war. To date, school curricula do not include Lebanon's recent history, even though the Ṭā'if Accord stipulated it should be. Although historians composed curriculum that would be binding on all schools, every school still decides for itself which history book to use (or exclude). See Saree Makdisi, "Beirut, a City without History?," in *Memory and Violence in the Middle East and North Africa,* ed. Ussama Samir Makdisi and Paul A. Silverstein (Bloomington: Indiana Univ. Press, 2006), 201–14.

82. Lang, *The Lebanese Post–Civil War Novel,* 65.

83. Ilyās Khūrī, *Yālū: Riwāyah* (Beirut: Dār al-Ādāb), translated as Elias Khoury, *Yalo,* by Peter Theroux (New York: Archipelago, 2008), 55, 56, 128.

84. Khoury, *Yalo,* 127.

85. Khoury, *Yalo,* 181.

86. El-Ariss, "Return of the Beast," 67.

87. Brad Evans and Bracha Ettinger, "Art in a Time of Atrocity," *New York Times,* Dec. 16, 2016.

88. The village of Yālū is located thirteen kilometers southeast of Ramallah and is identified by Edward Robinson as the ancient Canaanite city of Aijalon. After the Arab–Israeli War of 1948, it was formally annexed by Jordan. During the Six-Day War of 1967, the Israel Defense Forces expelled all of Yālū's inhabitants, destroyed the village, and occupied the village of "Yālū." A recreational space named Canada Park was built atop

the ruins of the village. For further information, see "Palestinian Emigration and Israeli Land Expropriation in the Occupied Territories," *Journal of Palestine Studies* 3, no. 1 (1973): 106–18, and Meron Benvenisti, *Sacred Landscape: The Buried History of the Holy Land since 1948* (Berkeley: Univ. of California Press, 2000).

89. Khoury, *Yalo*, 159, 108.

90. Khoury, *Yalo*, 117, 84, 197.

91. Tūr 'Abidīn (Syriac for "Mountain of the Servants of God") is a hilly region of southeastern Turkey on the border with Syria.

92. Khoury, *Yalo*, 295, 155.

93. Michel Foucault, "On the Archaeology of the Sciences: Response to the Epistemology Circle," in *The Essential Works of Foucault, 1954–1984*, vol. 1, trans. Robert Hurley, ed. Paul Rabinow and Nikolas Rose (New York: New Press, 2003), 392.

94. Khūrī, *Yālū*, 317.

95. Khoury, *Yalo*, 176.

96. The philosopher and sociologist Maurice Halbwachs first coined the term *collective memory*.

97. James Edward Young, *At Memory's Edge: After-Images of the Holocaust in Contemporary Art and Architecture* (New Haven, CT: Yale Univ. Press, 2000), xi.

98. Michel de Certeau, *The Practice of Everyday Life*, trans. Timothy J. Tomasik (Minneapolis: Univ. of Minnesota Press, 1998), xi. De Certeau defines *bricolage* as "artisan-like inventiveness" (*The Practice of Everyday Life*, xviii).

99. Marianne Hirsch, "The Generation of Postmemory," *Poetics Today* 29, no. 1 (2008): 103.

100. Khoury, *Yalo*, 204.

101. Khoury, *Yalo*, 204.

102. Augé, *Oblivion*, 20.

103. Blanchot, *The Writing of the Disaster*, 11.

104. Andreas Huyssen, *Present Pasts: Urban Palimpsests and the Politics of Memory* (Stanford, CA: Stanford Univ. Press, 2003), 7.

105. Khoury, *Yalo*, 205.

106. Khoury, *Yalo*, 84. Arabic original: "لكن الحرب علمت يالو أن يصدق عينيه لا عيون الكلمات" (Khūrī, *Yālū*, 93).

107. Khūrī, *Yālū*, 112.

108. Khoury, *Yalo*, 100.

109. Khoury, *Yalo*, 307.

110. Khoury, *Yalo*, 220.

111. Khoury, *Yalo*, 314.

112. Khoury, *Yalo*, 317.

113. Fabio Caiani, "'My Name Is Yalu': The Development of Metafiction in Ilyas Khuri's Work," *Middle Eastern Literatures* 10, no. 2 (2008): 148.

114. Khoury, *Yalo*, 222.

115. Derek Walcott, "Ruins of a Great House," in *Collected Poems 1948–1984* (New York: Farrar, Straus and Giroux, 1987), 20.

3. Khirbet Khiam

1. I capitalize "Resistance" in contexts where it refers specifically to Hizbullah's Islamic Resistance or to the Hizbullah notion of "Resistance memory" or "Resistance museum." I use the lowercase term *resistance* when I refer to Lebanese resistance to occupation in general or to resistance as a concept.

2. Stewart, *The Ruins Lesson*, 261.

3. Mona Harb and Lara Deeb, "Culture as History and Landscape: Hizbullah's Efforts to Shape an Islamic Milieu in Lebanon," *Arab Studies Journal* 19, no. 1 (2011): 13.

4. Lara Deeb, "Exhibiting the 'Just Lived Past': Hizbullah's Nationalist Narratives in a Transnational Political Context," *Comparative Studies in Society and History* 50, no. 2 (2008): 377.

5. See Deeb, "Exhibiting the 'Just Lived Past,'" 377.

6. Harb and Deeb, "Culture as History and Landscape," 27.

7. Marianne Hirsch, "Introduction: Practicing Feminism, Practicing Memory," in *Women Mobilizing Memory*, ed. Altınay et al., 20.

8. On the "security zone," see Hussein A. Amery, "The Litani River of Lebanon," *Geographical Review* 83, no. 3 (July 1993): 233.

9. On Khiam, see Neve Gordon, "Outsourcing Violations: The Israeli Case," *Journal of Human Rights* 1, no. 3 (2002): 321–37; Human Rights Watch, "Torture in Khiam Prison: Responsibility and Accountability," Oct. 27, 1999, at https://www.hrw.org/en/news/1999/10/27/torture-Khiam-prison-responsibility-and-accountability?print; Amnesty International, "Israel/South Lebanon: The Khiam Detainees: Torture and Ill Treatment," May 6, 1992, at https://www.amnesty.org/en/documents/mde15/008/1992/en/; Robert Fisk, "Relatives Let into Israelis' Jail of Death," *Independent* (United Kingdom), Feb. 2, 1995, at http://www.independent.co.uk/news/world/relatives-let-into-israelis-jail-of-death-1571094.html; Khalili, *Time in the Shadows*, 101–38; David Hirst, "South Lebanon: The War That Never Ends?," *Journal of Palestine Studies* 28, no. 3 (1999): 5–18; Claire Launchbury, "Staging Khiam: Documentary, Theater, and Archive in Postwar Lebanon," *Contemporary French and Francophone Studies* 18, no. 5 (2014): 514–22.

10. Jim Quilty, "Prison. Museum. Ruin," *Daily Star* (United Kingdom), Aug. 24, 2006, at http://mobile.dailystar.com.lb/News/Lebanon-News/2006/Aug-24/43009-prison-museum-ruin.ashx.

11. Hans Wehr and J. Milton Cowan, *A Dictionary of Modern Written Arabic: (Arabic–English)* (Wiesbaden, Germany: Harrassowitz, 1979), s.v. *laḥd*, 859.

12. Named after the South Lebanese river. See Amery, "The Litani River of Lebanon," 233.

13. The full text of Resolution 425 and related Resolutions 426 and 427 can be found at the United Nations website at www.un.org/documents.

14. Traboulsi, *A History of Modern Lebanon*, 221–22.

15. Michael Taussig, *Shamanism, Colonialism, and the Wild Man: A Study in Terror and Healing* (Chicago: Univ. of Chicago Press, 1987), 51–73, 128.

16. Soha Bechara, *Resistance: My Life for Lebanon* (Brooklyn, NY: Soft Skull Press, 2003), 80. In 2000, Suha Bshāra, with Gilles Paris, published the French-language memoir *Résistance*, with translations into Arabic (2000) and English (2003). Three film biographies about Bshāra's life also appeared in 2000. For the French-language memoir, see Souha Béchara, with Gilles Paris, *Résistante* (n.p.: J. C. Latts, 2000); for the Arabic version, see Souha Bechara, *Muqawama* (Beirut: Dar al-Saqi, 2002); and for the English version, see Bechara, *Resistance*. For her name, I use the transliteration "Suha Bshāra."

17. Roberta Arnold, "Command Responsibility: A Case Study of Alleged Violations of the Laws of War at Khiam Detention Center," *Journal of Conflict and Security Law* 7, no. 2 (2002): 191–231.

18. James E. Young, *The Texture of Memory: Holocaust Memorials and Meaning* (New Haven, CT: Yale Univ. Press, 1993), 123.

19. See Julie Flint, "Town Tells of Day of Torture," *Guardian*, Feb. 24, 1986.

20. Arnold, "Command Responsibility," 193.

21. Arnold, "Command Responsibility," 193.

22. Arnold, "Command Responsibility," 193.

23. Bechara, *Resistance*, 54.

24. Jim Holstun, "Antigone Becomes Jocasta: Soha Bechara, Résistante, and Incendies," *Mediations: Journal of the Marxist Literary Group* 29, no. 1 (Fall 2015): 9.

25. Bilal Khrais, "Lebanon's Women Warriors," *Al Jazeera*, Apr. 24, 2010, at https://www.aljazeera.com/videos/2010/4/24/lebanons-women-warriors.

26. Quoted in Olivia Snaije, "Seeing Yourself Re-made as Fiction," *Daily Star* (United Kingdom), Feb. 2, 2011, http://www.dailystar.com.lb/Culture/Film/Feb/02/Seeing-yourself-re-made-asfiction.ashx#axzz1PJ051RPc.

27. Quoted in Holstun, "Antigone Becomes Jocasta," 9.

28. Diana Taylor, *Disappearing Acts: Spectacles of Gender and Nationalism in Argentina's "Dirty War"* (Durham, NC: Duke Univ. Press, 1997), 144.

29. Jayce Salloum, dir., *Untitled Part I: Everything and Nothing* (France/Canada, 2001).

30. For further reading on this subject, see Barbara Harlow, "Prison Memoirs of Political Detainees," in *Resistance Literature* (New York: Methuen, 1987), 117–54.

31. Bechara, *Resistance*, 126.

32. In Salloum, *Untitled Part I*; ellipses indicate pauses in speech.

33. Butler, *Frames of War*, 142.

34. Bechara, *Resistance*, 65–66.

35. Marc Abizeid, "Ex-resistance Fighter Pays Tribute to Secular 'Martyrs,'" *Daily Star* (United Kingdom), Apr. 10, 2009, at http://www.dailystar.com.lb/News/Politics/Apr/10/Ex-resistance-fighter-pays-tribute-to-secularmartyrs.ashx#axzz2POIUbypv.

36. Bechara, *Resistance*, 141.

37. Bechara, *Resistance*, 104, 105.

38. Bechara, *Resistance*, 109.

39. Souha Bechara and Cosette Ibrahim, *Ahlumu bi-zinzānah min karaz* [I Dream of a Prison Cell (Made) of Cherries] (Beirut: Dār al-Saqi, 2011), Kindle ed., loc. 70.

40. Jim Holstun, "Antigone Becomes Jocasta: Soha Bechara, *Résistante*, and *Incendies*," *Mediations: Journal of the Marxist Literary Group* 29, no. 1 (Fall 2015): 4.

41. Bechara and Ibrahim, *Ahlumu bi-zinzānah min karaz*, Kindle ed., loc. 480; quotations are my translations in all instances.

42. Bechara and Ibrahim, *Ahlumu bi-zinzānah min karaz*, Kindle ed., loc. 480.

43. See Bechara, *Resistance*, 97–102.

44. Bechara and Ibrahim, Ahlumu bi-zinzānah min karaz, Kindle ed., loc. 783.

45. Nawal Qasim Baidoun, *Memoirs of a Militant: My Years in the Khiam Women's Prison*, trans. Michelle Hartman and Caline Nasrallah, ed. Malek Abisaab (Northampton, MA: Olive Branch Press, 2022), 158.

46. Baidoun, *Memoirs of a Militant*, 14.

47. Baidoun, *Memoirs of a Militant*, 20.

48. Michelle Hartman and Malek Abisaab, introduction to Baidoun, *Memoirs of a Militant*, 11.

49. Lila Abu-Lughod, "The Romance of Resistance: Tracing Transformations of Power through Bedouin Women," *American Ethnologist* 17 no. 1 (1990): 41.

50. Sophia Stamatopoulou-Robbins, *Waste Siege: The Life of Infrastructure in Palestine* (Stanford, CA: Stanford Univ. Press, 2020).

51. Judith Butler, Zeynep Gambetti, and Leticia Sabsay, introduction to *Vulnerability in Resistance*, ed. Judith Butler, Zeynep Gambetti, and Leticia Sabsay (Durham, NC: Duke Univ. Press, 2016), 6.

52. Sune Haugbølle, "The (Little) Militia Man: Memory and Militarized Masculinity in Lebanon," *Journal of Middle East Women's Studies* 8, no. 1 (2012): 115–39.

53. Khalili, *Time in the Shadows*, 170.

54. Khayyat, *A Landscape of War*, Kindle ed., loc. 30–31.

55. Abu-Lughod, "The Romance of Resistance," 41.

56. In Salloum, *Untitled Part I*.

57. Gordon, *Ghostly Matters*, 8.

58. Caitlin DeSilvey, "Palliative Curation: Art and Entropy on Orford Ness," in *Ruin Memories: Materiality, Aesthetics and the Archaeology of the Recent Past*, ed. Bjørnar Olsen and Þóra Pétursdóttir (London: Routledge, 2014), 87. See also DeSilvey, *Curated*

Decay, and Caitlin DeSilvey, "Observed Decay: Telling Stories with Mutable Things," *Journal of Material Culture* 11, no. 3 (2006): 318–38.

59. Quoted in Amnesty International, "Lebanon: Where Is the Door? Letter from an Amnesty International Delegation Visiting Khiam Prison in South Lebanon," May 29, 2000, at https://www.amnesty.org/en/documents/mde18/008/2000/en/.

60. Diana Taylor, quoted in Hirsch and Miller, *Rites of Return*, 13.

61. Young, *Texture of Memory*, xii.

62. Harb and Deeb, "Culture as History and Landscape," 19.

63. *Sajīn al-Janūb* [Prisoner of the South], documentary film (Munīr Bū Samrā, 2000).

64. Susan Sontag, *Regarding the Pain of Others* (New York: Farrar, Straus and Giroux, 2003).

65. Taylor, *Disappearing Acts*, 141.

66. Mahmud Darwish, *A River Dies of Thirst: Journals*, trans. Catherine Cobham (Brooklyn, NY: Archipelago, 2009), 12.

67. Bayḍūn, "A Possible Poem on Dahiya," trans. Boullata, in *Lebanon, Lebanon*, ed. Wilson.

68. Ali, interviewed by the author, Khiam memorial, July 20, 2010.

69. Irene Kacandes, *Talk Fiction: Literature and the Talk Explosion* (Lincoln: Univ. of Nebraska Press, 2001).

70. Harb and Deeb, "Culture as History and Landscape," 40.

71. DeSilvey, "Palliative Curation," 87.

72. Gordillo, *Rubble*, 225.

73. Robert Bevan, *The Destruction of Memory* (London: Reaktion, 2006), 8. Among this literature, see Nadia Abu El-Haj, *Facts on the Ground: Archaeological Practice and Territorial Self-Fashioning in Israeli Society* (Chicago: Univ. of Chicago Press, 2001); Gordillo, *Rubble*; Andrew Herscher, *Violence Taking Place: The Architecture of the Kosovo Conflict* (Stanford, CA: Stanford Univ. Press, 2010); Eyal Weizman, *Hollow Land: Israel's Architecture of Occupation* (London: Verso, 2012); Eyal Weizman, *The Least of All Possible Evils: Humanitarian Violence from Arendt to Gaza* (London: Verso, 2012); Andreas Huyssen, *Twilight Memories: Marking Time in a Culture of Amnesia* (New York: Routledge, 1995); and, in museum and heritage studies, Tony Bennett, Fiona Cameron, Nélia Dias, Ben Dibley, Rodney Harrison, Ira Jacknis, and Conal McCarthy, *Collecting, Ordering, Governing: Anthropology, Museums, and Liberal Government* (Durham, NC: Duke Univ. Press, 2017); Léopold Lambert, *Weaponized Architecture: The Impossibility of Innocence* (Barcelona: dpr-Barcelona, 2012). For a transdisciplinary approach, see Lucia Alias, *Designs of Destruction: The Making of Monuments in the Twentieth Century* (Chicago: Univ. of Chicago Press, 2018), which provides an important study of the homology between the reification of monumental forms and ideology.

74. Pierre Nora, "Between Memory and History: Les lieux de mémoire," *Representations* 26 (1989): 13.

75. Laurie Beth Clark, "Ruined Landscapes and Residual Architecture," *Performance Research* 20, no. 3 (2015): 84.

76. Tony Bennett, *The Birth of the Museum* (London: Routledge, 1995), 24, 186.

77. Paul Connerton, *How Societies Remember* (Cambridge: Cambridge Univ. Press, 1989), 22.

78. Quoted in Olivia Snaije, "Seeing Yourself Re-made as Fiction," *Daily Star* (United Kingdom), Feb. 2, 2011, http://www.dailystar.com.lb/Culture/Film/Feb/02/Seeing-yourself-re-made-asfiction.ashx#axzz1PJ051RPc.

79. Edensor, *Industrial Ruins*, 115.

80. De Certeau, *The Practice of Everyday Life*, 160.

81. Robert Ginsberg, *The Aesthetics of Ruins* (Amsterdam: Rodopi, 2004), 322.

4. Curating Resistance

1. See the Mleeta website at www.mleeta.com, accessed Aug. 1, 2010.

2. See Jad Naṣrallah, "Bayt al-'Aynkabūt' yunsaj fī al-Ḍāḥiya wa-l-iftītāḥ al-rasmi masā'an" [The Spider's Web Has Been Woven in Ḍāḥiya and Its Official Opening Is This Evening], *Al-Akhbār* (Lebanon), July 25, 2007.

3. For a nuanced reading of the politics of concealment in Mleeta, see Hatim El-Hibri, *Visions of Beirut: The Urban Life of Urban Infrastructure* (Durham, NC: Duke Univ. Press, 2021).

4. Toufoul Abou Hodeib, "Sanctity across the Border: Pilgrimage Routes and State Control in Mandate Lebanon and Palestine," in *The Routledge Handbook of the History of the Middle East Mandates*, ed. Cyrus Schayegh and Andrew Arsan (London: Routledge, 2015), 387–88.

5. Harb and Deeb, "Culture as History and Landscape," 20.

6. Jacques Rancière, *The Future of the Image*, trans. Gregory Elliot (2007; reprint, London: Verso, 2009), 15.

7. Henri Lefebvre, *The Production of Space*, trans. Donald Nicholson-Smith (Oxford: Blackwell, 1992), 38–39.

8. Jacques Rancière, *The Politics of Literature*, trans. Julie Rose (Cambridge: Polity, 2011), 12.

9. Or, as the inscription on the placard indicates, "The Merkava 4 symbolizes the neutralization of the Israeli sophisticated military machine in the fight against the will and steady faith of the Resistance fighters."

10. The Israeli military historian Martin van Creveld has called the Israeli invasion of Lebanon in 1982 Israel's "greatest folly" (quoted in David Hirst, *Beware of Small States: Lebanon, Battleground of the Middle East* [New York: Nation Books, 2010], 135). In entering the "quagmire" of Lebanon, Israel, through unspeakable acts of violence and destruction, tarnished the military reputation it had forged in the

numerous Arab–Israeli wars and, most crucially, created its most formidable foe to date. It had entered Lebanon to fight one foe, but upon defeating that foe, it rode a wave of hubris and created another much more dangerous and effective one: the Party of God.

11. Marianne Hirsch and Leo Spitzer, "What's Wrong with This Picture? Holocaust Photographs in Contemporary Narratives," *Journal of Modern Jewish Studies* 5, no. 2 (2006): 237.

12. Hirsch and Spitzer, "What's Wrong with This Picture?"

13. Part of a network of bunkers and tunnels dug out by guerrilla fighters over a span of three years.

14. El-Hibri, *Visions of Beirut*, 144.

15. Harb and Deeb, "Culture as History and Landscape," 26.

16. Mleeta's head architect, interviewed by the author, July 21, 2011; all quotations from the architect come from this interview.

17. Tim Ingold, "The Temporality of the Landscape," *World Archaeology* 25, no. 2 (1993): 152–53.

18. Quoted in Ingold, "Temporality of the Landscape," 171.

19. The eagle sparrow on Mleeta's logo was chosen to represent the fighters, reflecting their "strength, agility and refusal to suffer defeat," per the museum's website (www.mleeta.com).

20. Nora, "Between Memory and History," 7.

21. From the Mleeta website at www.mleeta.com, my emphasis.

5. Toward an Archive of Unintended Detritus

1. Forty, introduction to *The Art of Forgetting*, ed. Forty and Kuchler.

2. Forty, introduction to *The Art of Forgetting*, ed. Forty and Kuchler.

3. Jeanette Bicknell, "Architectural Ghosts," *Journal of Aesthetics and Art Criticism* 72, no. 4 (2014): 436.

4. Stoler, *Along the Archival Grain*, 255.

5. Gastón R. Gordillo, *Rubble: The Afterlife of Destruction* (Durham, NC: Duke Univ. Press, 2014), 164.

6. Forty, introduction to *The Art of Forgetting*, ed. Forty and Kuchler.

7. Sara Fregonese, *War and the City: Urban Geopolitics in Lebanon* (London: I. B. Tauris, 2019), 118.

8. Sawalha, *Reconstructing Beirut*, 271.

9. Elias, *Posthumous Images*, Kindle ed., loc. 671.

10. Gordillo, *Rubble*, 41.

11. Umam Documentation & Research, "The Collection," n.d., at http://www.Umam-dr.org/en/home/categories/13/our-collection, accessed Oct. 20, 2020.

12. See Umam Documentation & Research, *The "War" through Its Memorials: Photo Exhibition in Progress*, Haret Hreik, Lebanon, June 12–29, 2009, at https://www.Umam-dr.org//eventdetail/77/77/.

13. See Umam Documentation & Research, "About Us: Mission Statement," n.d., at https://www.Umam-dr.org/en/home/about-Umam/1/advance-contents/3/mission-statement, accessed Oct. 23, 2020.

14. Umam Documentation & Research, Memory at Work: A Guide for Lebanese on Peace and War, database, n.d., at http://www.memoryatwork.org/, accessed Oct. 19, 2020. The digital archive was funded after the 2006 war as part of the restoration of the Hangar and digitization program by the Dutch Ministry of Foreign Affairs through the Prince Claus Fund for Culture and Development.

15. Rema Hammami, "Palestinian NGOs since Oslo: From NGO Politics to Social Movements?," *Middle East Report* 214 (2000): 19.

16. Hammami, "Palestinian NGOs since Oslo," 19.

17. On the subject of the wartime missing, see Lamia Joreige's documentary *Huna wa rubbamā hunāk* [Here and Perhaps Elsewhere] (03 productions, 2003), which is also concerned with the problem of giving form to the traces of the missing in the physically and socially fractured urban landscape of post–Civil War Beirut. Whereas Umam's *The "War" through Its Memorials* exhibition focused on portrait snapshots of the disappeared, Joreige draws on photographs of former checkpoints along the Green Line, where some of these individuals and many thousands of others were abducted. See also Fushat Amal (Space for Hope), an online memorial project featuring an interactive memory map that attempts to reclaim the identities of the disappeared through oral memory, at https://www.actforthedisappeared.com, and the Lebanese photographer Dalia Khamissy's work on the missing at https://www.mnemoscape.org/dalia-khamissy—the-missing-of-lebanon. Khamissy's work examines how personal items such as school bags, clothing, and cigarette packets trigger narrative responses from the families of the disappeared. Lebanese visual artist and photographer Rola Khayyat's work poignantly engages the conundrum of Lebanese civil war memory: https://rolakhayyat.com/past-projects/.

18. Quoted in Jim Quilty, "Putting Flesh and Bones on the Specter of Dahiyeh," *Daily Star* (United Kingdom), June 8, 2007.

19. Craig Larkin and Ella Perry Davies, "War Museums in Postwar Lebanon: Memory, Violence, and Performance," *Nationalism and Ethnic Politics* 25, no. 1 (2019): 78–96, reprinted in *Power-Sharing after Civil War: Thirty Years since Lebanon's Taif Agreement*, ed. John Nagle and Mary-Alice Clancy (New York: Routledge, 2022), 96.

20. Lokman Slīm, interviewed by the author, Dec. 14, 2012.

21. Edensor, "Ghosts of Industrial Ruins."

22. Trevor L. Hoag, "Ghosts of Memory: Mournful Performance and the Rhetorical Event of Haunting (Or: Specters of Occupy)," *Liminalities: A Journal of Performance Studies* 10, nos. 3–4 (2014): 2.

23. Sāliḥ Barakāt, gallery owner and curator, interviewed by the author, Feb. 12, 2012.

24. Kaelen Wilson-Goldie, "Walid Raad and the Atlas Group," Bidoun, n.d., at https://www.bidoun.org/articles/walid-raad-and-the-atlas-group, accessed June 9, 2012.

25. According to Chad Elias, the Western hostage crisis refers to the systematic kidnapping in Lebanon of ninety-six foreign nationals—mostly American and Western European—between 1982 and 1992. The hostages were held by a group calling itself Islamic Jihad. The kidnapping of the Westerners was part of an effort to obtain the release of four Lebanese members of the Iraqi-based and Shiite-aligned al-Da'wa al-Islamiyya Party imprisoned in Kuwait for orchestrating a series of attacks on key foreign and Kuwaiti installations" (*Posthumous Images*, Kindle ed., loc. 3833). For a discussion of the politics of the Western hostage crisis, see Hala Jaber, *Hezbollah: Born with a Vengeance* (New York: Columbia Univ. Press, 1997).

26. Walīd Ra'ad, Atlas Group Archive (1989–2004), online, mixed media, n.d., at www.theatlasgroup.org/, accessed May 29, 2018.

27. Ra'ad, Atlas Group Archive.

28. Quoted in Edward Said, *Beginnings: Intention and Method* (New York: Basic Books, 1975), 292.

29. For an in-depth exploration of the concept of martyrdom in relation to experimental documentaries, see Elias, *Posthumous Images*.

30. See Yo-Yo Ma, "Bach Project," n.d., at https://bach.yo-yoma.com, accessed Sept. 11, 2018.

31. Betty Gilbert-Sleiman, "The Reform of History School Textbooks in Lebanon: Collecting Conflict Memories in a Peace-Building Process (1996–2001)," in *Archives, Museums and Collecting Practices in the Modern Arab World*, ed. Sonja Mejcher-Atassi and John Pedro Schwartz (London: Routledge, 2016), 134. See also the website Beit Beirut, at www.beitbeirut.org, first accessed June 1, 2011.

32. Quoted in Gilbert-Sleiman, "Reform of History School Textbooks in Lebanon," 134.

33. Quoted in *Naharnet*, "Beit al-Madina to Recall Horrors of Civil War," Oct. 17, 2008, at www.middle-east-online/com/english/i?d=28346.

34. Quoted in Gilbert-Sleiman, "Reform of History School Textbooks in Lebanon," 136.

35. On September 9, 2017, the students and I toured Beit Beirut with Mona Ḥallāk as guide and interlocutor.

36. Larkin and Parry-Davies, "War Museums in Postwar Lebanon," 84.

37. The project's committee members were anthropologists and historians specializing either in Beirut's urban and social fabric or in heritage-restoration problems.

38. Gilbert-Sleiman, "Reform of History School Textbooks in Lebanon," 136.

39. Hirsch, "Generation of Postmemory."

6. Revolutionary Ruins

1. In 1782, Constantin-François de Chassebœuf, the Comte de Volney, journeyed to Syria and Egypt to learn Arabic and study "Oriental" cultures. Seven years later he published *Les ruines, ou, Méditation sur les révolutions des empires*, in which he looks to the rise and fall of Babylon, Ethiopia, and Palmyra to comprehend "what concerns the happiness of mankind in a state of society." Volney introduces his subject as he meditates on the desert ruins of Palmyra: "Here, said I to myself, an opulent city once flourished. This was the seat of powerful empire. . . . [T]hese ruinous galleries present the outlines of public places." He continues: "Who knows but that hereafter some traveller like myself will sit down upon the banks of the Seine, the Thames, or the Zuyder sea, where now, in the tumult of enjoyment, the heart and the eyes are too slow to take in the multitude of sensations; who knows but he will sit down on solitary amid silent ruins, and weep a people inurned, and their greatness changed into an empty name?" (Comte de Volney [Constantin-François de Chassebœuf], *The Ruins; or, A Survey of the Revolutions of Empires*, trans. James Marshall, with an introduction by Jonathan Wordsworth [West Yorkshire, UK: Orley, 2000], 9–10).

2. Gordillo, *Rubble*, 301.

3. From an intriguing public talk by Ghassan Hage titled "Academia in the Revolution" in Jibrān Park, downtown Beirut. In this impromptu lecture, which I attended on October 27, 2019, Hage troubled the role of the academic in revolutionary discourse, questioning intellectual labor with respect to envisioning the nonconfessionalism emerging from the cracks of the old order. Hage underscored a new way of looking at Lebanon's "monoreality" as now "multiple" and questioned the ways in which such realities can move from being minor realities to major realities.

4. Walter Benjamin, *Illuminations*, trans. Harry Zohn, ed. Hannah Arendt (New York: Schocken, 1969), 257–58.

5. Bayḍūn, "A Possible Poem on Dahiya," trans. Boullata, in *Lebanon, Lebanon*, ed. Wilson, 19.

6. Hage, "Academia in Revolution."

7. ʿAbbās Bayḍūn, "Īdīyūlūjīyā al-ḥirāk" [Ideology of the Movement], *:24*, n.d., at https://24.ae/article/544295/أيديولوجيا-الحراك, accessed Apr. 6, 2020.

8. Ellipses in my English translation indicate omission of text given in the Arabic version.

9. Gordillo, *Rubble*, 267.

10. On the subject of the Lebanese Uprisings, see Jillian Schwedler, "Thinking Critically about Regional Uprisings," *Middle East Report* 292, no. 3 (Fall–Winter 2019), at https://merip.org/2019/12/thinking-critically-about-regional-uprisings/.

11. Léopold Lambert, "#PALESTINE /// The Right to the Ruin: Civilizational Absence in the Post-Nakba Landscapes," *Funambulist* 14, no. 6 (2013): 41. See also Lambert, *Weaponized Architecture*, 159.

12. See Nikolas Kosmatopoulos, "Unhatching the Egg in Lebanon's 2019 Protests: Activism, Purity and the Real-Estatization of Civil Society," *South Atlantic Quarterly* 120, no. 2 (Fall 2021): 446–55.

13. ʻAbbās Bayḍūn, "Ḥujūrāt" [Rooms], in *Al-Aʻmāl al-shiʻrīyah*, 61.

14. Rabee Jaber, *Berytus, une ville sous terre*, trans. Charlotte Woillez and Simon Corthay (Paris: Gallimard, 2006).

15. Gordillo, *Rubble*, 265.

16. Edensor, *Industrial Ruins*, 30.

17. Antoine Atallah, "Al Balad," *Beirut Bright Side* (blog), Nov. 14, 2019, at http://www.beirutsbrightside.com/al-balad/.

18. See the Daleel Thawra website at www.daleelthawra.com, accessed Oct. 29, 2019.

19. Tarek El-Ariss, *Leaks, Hacks, and Scandals* (Princeton, NJ: Princeton Univ. Press, 2019), 362.

20. See the Public Source website at https://thepublicsource.org, accessed Feb. 1, 2020.

21. Public Source website. Describing how it came to be, the Public Source states at its website: "With the spark of revolution, we precipitated our publishing date and launched the platform with Dispatches from the October Revolution to convey the spirit of the day and offer insider observations into the multi-front struggle against the governing political-economic order. This section is open to all workers, organizers, activists, and agitators, students and intellectuals, theorists, and academics, artists, and researchers to share ideas, collective experiences, and analyses at this critical historical moment" (see Public Source, "About," n.d., at https://thepublicsource.org/about, accessed Feb. 1, 2020).

22. Julia Choucair, "What Is Oligarchy?," Public Source, Feb. 18, 2020, at https://thepublicsource.org/what-is-oligarchy.

23. See the Meghterbin Mejtemiin website at https://17teshreen.com, accessed Dec. 20, 2020.

24. The Saida Tantafed website also follows other everyday mobilizations by activists and the people of Saida. The group reports on an otherwise undocumented aspect of the Lebanese struggle from the South as the people fight for their rights, such as access to public spaces. One noteworthy post showed masked men dressed in red overalls (in reference to the Netflix program *La casa de papel*), cutting the chains around the gates of the public Kenayat Park (منتزه الكينايات), thereby reclaiming their right to access a public garden normally cordoned off for private usage.

25. Active since 2015, the Save the Bisri Valley group intensified its organizing in early November 2019 to halt the planned construction of a dam, funded in large part by the World Bank, in the Bisri Valley between Jezzine and the Chouf Mountains. Through social media platforms, the campaign has been educating people on the devastating ecological and economic consequences of this project while creatively mobilizing people to join the fight. The group's Facebook page includes informative videos with English

subtitles clearly explaining the issue, and it used to have live coverage of the creative "camp as resistance" movement.

26. Tripoli has been dubbed عروس الثورة (*'arūs al-thawra*), "bride of the revolution" or the "crown jewel of the revolution," because of its relentless political activity. Despite its daily mobilizations and events, creative chants, and targeted actions, this northern city has not received enough media attention. The Tripoli Revolution 2019 Facebook page inventories the events happening in this active city in a detailed calendar.

27. In Ṣūr, the mobilizations may be smaller in number, but they are notable in their importance. Under the very strict patronage of leading political factions, the defiance of the people of Ṣūr comes at great personal risk as they protest in front of local banks, gather to hold public debates, and even enjoy their own revolutionary concerts in derelict buildings turned revolutionary dance centers.

28. On February 6, 2020, Beit Beirut hosted a book event for the recent publication of Mariejoe Raidy's compilation of revolution street art by some two hundred artists, *The Silent Leaders: The Lebanese Revolution Art Book*. The event, however, was interrupted by angry protesters, who stormed in, complaining that the book, which sells for a whopping $120 in a country bereft of dollars, is literally capitalizing on the revolution by monetizing its cultural output.

29. Brian Neville and Johanne Villeneuve, "Introduction: In Lieu of Waste," in *Waste-Site Stories: The Recycling of Memory*, ed. Brian Neville and Johanne Villeneuve (Albany: State Univ. of New York Press, 2002), 6.

30. Masha Gessen, "The *New Yorker* Interview: Judith Butler Wants to Reshape Our Rage," *New Yorker*, Feb. 9, 2020, at www.newyorker.com/culture/the-new-yorker-interview/judith-butler-wants-to-reshape-our-rage.

31. Quoted in Neville and Villeneuve, "Introduction," 6.

32. See the Iraqi Civil Society Solidarity Initiative website at https://www.iraqicivilsociety.org/archives/10774, accessed Nov. 1, 2019.

Conclusion

1. Timour Azhari, "'Worse Than the War': Hunger Grows in Lebanon along with Anger," *Al Jazeera Impact*, Apr. 19, 2020, at https://www.aljazeera.com/ajimpact/war-hunger-grows-lebanon-anger-200417222253896.html?fbclid=IwAR2fLTKyzIUGk_vp8_3q3B9MnsRKkUY8Gn2KM5o0wILVRmbyHz4eeAIW_dY.

2. George Packer, "We Are Living in a Failed State," *Atlantic*, June 2020, at https://www.theatlantic.com/magazine/archive/2020/06/underlying-conditions/610261/?fbclid=IwAR2xhGtnq2Czvmll99fir3pZcmzHHJYZMyATYqo4kbxUZCLKa9_ZEXHTnfw.

3. Ilyās Khūrī, "Saramāġū: Al-Wabā' wa al-'ama al-abyad" [Saramago: Epidemic and White Blindness], *Al-Quds al-Arabi*, Apr. 20, 2020, at https://www.alquds.co.uk/-ساراماغو/الوباء-والعمى-الأبيض/. In Arabic, the essay's title is "الوباء والعمى الأبيض."

4. World Bank, "Targeting Poor Households in Lebanon," factsheet, Apr. 21, 2020, at https://www.worldbank.org/en/news/factsheet/2020/04/21/targeting-poor-households-in-lebanon?fbclid=IwAR0jK7XL5VZXd4USaP_AOBve0zo44Y6PpkFH6lVRLkHS9r9AWc6iGTDLP_w; see also Tamara Qiblawi, "75% of Lebanon Needs Aid after Coronavirus, and Hungry Protesters Are Back on the Streets," *CNN World*, Apr. 29, 2020, at https://edition.cnn.com/2020/04/28/middleeast/lebanon-hunger-aid-coronavirus-intl/index.html?fbclid=IwAR18oIvQUWpwG1foDuT9ufZxYqVEr5j5H9DELPFOXxWs3aqp0ixzT7UN1Ww.

5. Timour Azhari, "'Not Legal' but Necessary: Lebanon's Banks Tighten Restrictions," *Al Jazeera Impact*, Feb. 3, 2020, at https://www.aljazeera.com/ajimpact/legal-lebanon-banks-tighten-restrictions-200203163004785.html.

6. *Financial Times*, "Lebanon's Central Bank Governor: 'We're Not a Normal Country,'" Nov. 20, 2017, at https://www.ft.com/content/cf667768-c0bd-11e7-b8a3-38a6e068f464.

7. See, for example, Helen Sullivan, "Dispatch: The Making of Lebanon's October Revolution," *New Yorker*, Oct. 29, 2019, at https://www.newyorker.com/news/dispatch/the-making-of-lebanons-october-revolution; and World Bank, "World Bank: Lebanon Is in the Midst of Economic, Financial and Social Hardship, Situation Could Get Worse," press release, Nov. 6, 2019, at https://www.worldbank.org/en/news/press-release/2019/11/06/world-bank-lebanon-is-in-the-midst-of-economic-financial-and-social-hardship-situation-could-get-worse.

8. ʿAbbās Bayḍūn, "Sīyāsāt kūrūnā" [Corona Policies], *:24*, Apr. 6, 2020, at https://24.ae/article/560736/سياسات%20كورونا?fbclid=IwAR30odTaq08kznMC01W10-8yB1x6kmm0wMsLdeVNnVjXpys9p77O4e7LtxA.

9. *France 24*, "Lebanon Approves Long-Awaited Economic Rescue Plan after Weeks of Unrest," Apr. 30, 2020, at https://www.france24.com/en/20200430-lebanon-approves-long-awaited-economic-rescue-plan-after-weeks-of-unrest.

10. Timour Azhari, "Lebanon to Seek IMF Loan, Says It Needs $10bn in Aid," *Al Jazeera Impact*, Apr. 30, 2020, at https://www.aljazeera.com/ajimpact/lebanon-seek-imf-loan-10bn-aid-200430182046291.html.

11. Martin Chulov, "'You Think We Care about Masks?' Anger and Poverty Grip Lebanese City," *Guardian*, May 1, 2020, at https://www.theguardian.com/world/2020/may/01/care-about-masks-anger-poverty-grip-lebanese-city-tripoli-coronavirus.

12. Youssef Diab, "Scandal of Lebanese Politicians' Transfer of Billions of Dollars Abroad 'Confuses' Banks," *Asharq al-Awsat*, Dec. 29, 2019, at https://english.aawsat.com//home/article/2057301/scandal-lebanese-politicians%e2%80%99-transfer-billions-dollars-abroad-%e2%80%98confuses%e2%80%99-banks.

13. Lina Mounzer, "In Lebanon, a Pandemic of Hunger," *New York Times*, May 6, 2020, at https://www.nytimes.com/2020/05/06/opinion/lebanon-protests-coronavirus.html.

14. A plague is often referred to as *ṭaʿūn* in Arabic; a more general pestilence or epidemic is called *wabāʾ*.

15. See Nazek al-Malaika, “Cholera,” trans. Husain Haddawy, in *The Poetry of Arab Women: A Contemporary Anthology,* edited by Nathalie Handal (New York: Interlink Books, 2001), 176–82. Al-Malaika’s style “was hailed by critics at the time as groundbreaking in its use of free verse rather than the traditional Arabic ode, a form which is now almost 1,500 years old. As such, *Cholera* heralded a new chapter in Arabic poetry and inspired a new wave of Arab poets—called the Pioneer Generation—to experiment with different forms” (Mustafa Abu Sneineh, “Plague and Poetry: How Middle Eastern Authors Have Written about Disease,” *Middle East Eye,* Mar. 27, 2020, at https://www.middleeasteye.net/discover/coronavirus-middle-east-covid-19-writer-plague-poet-book).

16. Quoted and translated in Mira Bajirova, *The Divine Cure of Coronavirus and Widespread Diseases* (Singapore: Partridge, 2020), 241–42.

17. Ilyās Khūrī, “Al-Wabā’ wa al-adab al-‘arabī al-ḥadīth” [The Epidemic and Modern Arab Literature], *:24,* Apr. 6, 2020, https://24.ae/article/560736/%D8%B3%D9%8A%D8%A7%D8%B3%D8%A7%D8%AA%20%D9%83%D9%88%D8%B1%D9%88%D9%86%D8%A7?fbclid=IwAR30odTaq08kznMC01W10-8yB1x6kmm0wMsLdeVNnVjXpys9p77O4e7LtxA.

18. See Amir Tag Elsir, *Ebola 76,* trans. Charis Bredin and Emily Danby (London: Darf, 2015); Andrée Chedid, *The Sixth Day* (1962; reprint, London: Serpent’s Tail, 1987); Rabī‘ Jābir, *Amīrkā: Riwāyah* [America: A Novel] (Casablanca, Morocco: Al-Markaz al-Thaqāfī al-‘Arabī, 2009), translated into French as Rabee Jaber, *Amerika,* trans. Charlotte Woillez and Simon Corthay (Paris: Gallimard, 2013).

19. The Nahda (Arabic: النهضة, *an-nahḍa,* meaning “the Awakening” or “the Renaissance”), also referred to as the Arab Renaissance or Enlightenment, was a cultural movement that flourished in Egypt, Lebanon, and Syria during the second half of the nineteenth century and the early twentieth century.

20. Khūrī, “Al-Wabā’ wa al-adab al-‘arabī al-ḥadīth.”

21. Khūrī, “Al-Wabā’ wa al-adab al-‘arabī al-ḥadīth.”

22. Khūrī, “Al-Wabā’ wa al-adab al-‘arabī al-ḥadīth.”

23. Khūrī, “Al-Wabā’ wa al-adab al-‘arabī al-ḥadīth.”

24. ‘Abbās Bayḍūn, “Umthūlat al-‘adad” [Number Example], *Al-Akhbar,* Apr. 11, 2020, my translation, at https://al-akhbar.com/Literature_Arts/287930?fbclid=IwAR3rcDV4a7Lhk-PPk8moc8xC1WgCYir-NHO_RPWRw-qKS59Rszxd6Qy0Ido.

25. ‘Abbās Bayḍūn, Facebook page, Apr. 6, 2020, at https://www.facebook.com/abbass.beydoun.

26. ‘Abbās Bayḍūn, “Daqīqa nawawīyya” [A Nuclear Minute], Facebook page, posted Apr. 17, 2020, at facebook.com/abbass.beydoun.

27. ‘Abbās Bayḍūn, Facebook page posting, Aug. 4, 2020, at https://www.facebook.com/abbass.beydoun.

28. For a personal reflection on the Beirut port blasts, see Yasmine Khayyat and Rola Khayyat, “Ruminating on Ruins in Beirut,” *Jadaliyya*, Aug. 7, 2020, at https://www.jadaliyya.com/Details/41537.

29. Fadia Basrawi, *Brownies and Kalashnikovs: A Saudi Woman’s Memoir of American Arabia and Wartime Beirut* (Reading, UK: Garnet, 2009), 200.

30. Ghassan Hage, “Introduction: States of Decay,” in *Decay*, ed. Ghassan Hage (Durham, NC: Duke Univ. Press, 2021), 10.

31. See Mazen Labban, “On the #BeirutBlast: Organized Abandonment and the Environmental Violence of Capital,” *Capitalism Nature Socialism* 31, no. 4 (2020): 18.

32. The figures here come from Rami Ruhayem and Paul Adams, “The Inferno and the Mystery Ship,” *BBC News*, Aug. 8, 2020, at https://www.bbc.co.uk/news/extra/x2iutcqf1g/beirut-blast.

33. Theodor W. Adorno, *Aesthetic Theory*, trans. Christian Lenhardt, ed. Gretel Adorno and Rolf Tiedemann (London: Routledge and Kegan Paul, 1984), 120.

34. International Crisis Group, “The Beirut Blast: Accident in Name Only,” Aug. 7, 2020, at https://www.crisisgroup.org/middle-east-north-africa/eastern-mediterranean/lebanon/beirut-blast-accident-name-only?fbclid=IwAR1F_MWKzPJvz9megfW3UbkfwFhISxXnkT8G2LJolCdH4OPIyuEFEsAgXzk.

35. Georgi Azar, “Central Bank to Offer Interest–Free Loans as Damaged Estimated in Billions,” *An–Nahar*, June 6, 2020, at https://en.annahar.com/article/1251194-central-bank-to-offer-interestfree-loans-as-damage-estimated-in-billions.

36. Nadim Karam, interviewed by the author, Dec. 9, 2022.

37. See Karim Merhej, Kareem Chehayeb, and Christina Cavalcanti, “How the Lebanese Government Disabled Hundreds of People—and Then Left Them to Pay for Its Crime,” Public Source, Aug. 5, 2021, https://thepublicsource.org/disability-justice-beirut-blast.

38. Nadim Karam, interview, Dec. 9, 2022.

39. Ghada Samman, “Lebanon? It Left and Never Returned,” *Sawt Beirut International*, Aug. 21, 2021, at https://www.sawtbeirut.com/press/لبنان؟-ذهب-ولم-يعد/.

40. Lambert, *Weaponized Architecture*, 159.

41. Bayḍūn, “A Possible Poem on Dahiya,” trans. Boullata, in *Lebanon, Lebanon*, ed. Wilson, 18.

42. Huda Barakāt, “A Voice Crying in the Wilderness,” *Derivative*, Apr. 9, 2021, at https://thederivative.org/a-voice-crying-in-the-wilderness/.

43. Nadine Sinno coined the term *greening* in “The Greening of Modern Arabic Literature: An Ecological Interpretation of Two Contemporary Arabic Novels,” *Interdisciplinary Studies in Literature and Environment* 20, no. 1 (2013): 118–32.

Bibliography

'Abdallāh, Ḥasan. *Adhkuru annanī aḥbabtu* [I Remember That I Loved]. Beirut: Dār al-'Awdah, 1972.

———. "Al-Tasalul ilal-waṭan al-asīr" [Infiltration into the Captive Homeland]. *Al-Safīr* 3, no. 121 (June 12, 1993): 14.

Abizeid, Marc. "Ex-resistance Fighter Pays Tribute to Secular 'Martyrs.'" *Daily Star* (United Kingdom), Apr. 10, 2009. At http://www.dailystar.com.lb/News/Politics/Apr/10/Ex-resistance-fighter-pays-tribute-to-secularmartyrs.ashx#axzz2POIUbypv.

Abou Hodeib, Toufoul. "Sanctity across the Border: Pilgrimage Routes and State Control in Mandate Lebanon and Palestine." In *The Routledge Handbook of the History of the Middle East Mandates*, edited by Cyrus Schayegh and Andrew Arsan, 383–94. London: Routledge, 2015.

Abu El-Haj, Nadia. *Facts on the Ground: Archaeological Practice and Territorial Self-Fashioning in Israeli Society*. Chicago: Univ. of Chicago Press, 2001.

Abu-Lughod, Lila. "The Romance of Resistance: Tracing Transformations of Power through Bedouin Women." *American Ethnologist* 17, no. 1 (1990): 41–55.

Abu Sneineh, Mustafa Abu. "Plague and Poetry: How Middle Eastern Authors Have Written about Disease." *Middle East Eye*, Mar. 27, 2020. At https://www.middleeasteye.net/discover/coronavirus-middle-east-covid-19-writer-plague-poet-book.

Abū Tammām. *Dīwān Abī Tammām* [Collected Works of Abū Tammām]. 2 vols. Edited by Muḥyī al-Dīn Ṣubhī. Beirut: Dār Sādir, 1997.

Achcar, Gilbert, and Michel Warschawski. *The 33-Day War: Israel's War on Hezbollah in Lebanon and Its Consequences*. Boulder, CO: Paradigm, 2007.

Adorno, Theodor W. *Aesthetic Theory*. Translated by Christian Lenhardt. Edited by Gretel Adorno and Rolf Tiedemann. London: Routledge and Kegan Paul, 1984.

Adūnīs. *Kalām al-bidāyāt* [Word Beginnings]. Beirut: Dār al-Ādāb, 1989.

Aḥmad al-Zawzanī, Ḥusayn b. *Sharḥ al-mu'allaqāt al-sab'* [Explanation of the Seven *Mu'allaqāt*]. Beirut: Dār al-Jīl, n.d.

Ajami, Fouad. *The Vanished Imam: Musa al Sadr and the Shia of Lebanon.* Ithaca, NY: Cornell Univ. Press, 1986.

Alagha, Joseph. *The Shifts in Hizbullah's Ideology: Religious Ideology, Political Ideology, and Political Program.* Amsterdam: Amsterdam Univ. Press, 2006.

Albers, Yvonne. "Turning the Page: Reading 1979 in and through the Cultural Journal *Mawaqif.*" *TRAFO—Blog for Transregional Research,* 2018. At https://trafo.hypotheses.org/9858.

Alias, Lucia. *Designs of Destruction: The Making of Monuments in the Twentieth Century.* Chicago: Univ. of Chicago Press, 2018.

Altınay, Ayşe Gül, María José Contreras, Marianne Hirsch, Jean Howard, Banu Karaca, and Alisa Solomon, eds. *Women Mobilizing Memory.* New York: Columbia Univ. Press, 2019.

Amery, Hussein A. "The Litani River of Lebanon." *Geographical Review* 83, no. 3 (July 1993): 229–37.

Amnesty International. "Israel/South Lebanon. The Khiam Detainees: Torture and Ill Treatment." May 6, 1992. At https://www.amnesty.org/en/documents/mde15/008/1992/en/.

———. "Lebanon: Where Is the Door? Letter from an Amnesty International Delegation Visiting Khiam Prison in South Lebanon." May 29, 2000. At https://www.amnesty.org/en/documents/mde18/008/2000/en/.

Arendt, Hannah. *The Origins of Totalitarianism.* New York: Harcourt, Brace & World, 1966.

El-Ariss, Tarek. *Leaks, Hacks, and Scandals.* Princeton, NJ: Princeton Univ. Press, 2019.

———. "Return of the Beast: From Pre-Islamic Ode to the Contemporary Novel." *Journal of Arabic Literature* 47, nos. 1–2 (2016): 62–90.

———. *Trials of Arab Modernity: Literary Affects and the New Political.* New York: Fordham Univ. Press, 2013.

Arnold, Roberta. "Command Responsibility: A Case Study of Alleged Violations of the Laws of War at Khiam Detention Center." *Journal of Conflict and Security Law* 7, no. 2 (2002): 191–231.

Atallah, Antoine. "Al Balad." *Beirut Bright Side* (blog), Nov. 14, 2019. At http://www.beirutsbrightside.com/al-balad/.

‘Aṭwān, Hussein. *Muqaddimāt al-qasida al-‘Arabiyya* [Introduction to the Arabic Ode]. 3 vols. Cairo: Dār al-Ma‘rifa bi-Misr, 1970.

Augé, Marc. *Oblivion*. Minneapolis: Univ. of Minnesota Press, 2004.

‘Awwād, Tawfīq Yūsuf. *Ṭawāḥin Bayrūt* [Death in Beirut]. Beirut: Dār al-Ādāb, 1972.

Azar, Georgi. “Central Bank to Offer Interest-Free Loans as Damage Estimated in Billions.” *An-Nahar*, June 6, 2020. At https://en.annahar.com/article/1251194-central-bank-to-offer-interestfree-loans-as-damage-estimated-in-billions.

Azhari, Timour. “Lebanon to Seek IMF Loan, Says It Needs $10bn in Aid.” *Al Jazeera Impact*, Apr. 30, 2020. At https://www.aljazeera.com/ajimpact/lebanon-seek-imf-loan-10bn-aid-200430182046291.html.

———. “‘Not Legal’ but Necessary: Lebanon’s Banks Tighten Restrictions.” *Al Jazeera Impact*, Feb. 3, 2020. At https://www.aljazeera.com/ajimpact/legal-lebanon-banks-tighten-restrictions-200203163004785.html.

———. “‘Worse Than the War’: Hunger Grows in Lebanon along with Anger.” *Al Jazeera Impact*, Apr. 19, 2020. At https://www.aljazeera.com/ajimpact/war-hunger-grows-lebanon-anger-200417222253896.html?fbclid=IwAR2fLTKyzIUGk_vp8_3q3B9MnsRKkUY8Gn2KM5o0wILVRmbyHz4eeAIW_dY.

Bachelard, Gaston. *The Poetics of Space*. Boston: Beacon Press, 1969.

Badawi, M. M. “Commitment in Contemporary Arabic Literature.” *Cahiers d’histoire mondiale* 14, no. 4 (1972): 858–79.

Baidoun, Nawal Qasim. *Memoirs of a Militant: My Years in the Khiam Women’s Prison*. Translated by Michelle Hartman and Caline Nasrallah. Edited by Malek Abisaab. Northampton, MA: Olive Branch Press, 2022.

Bajirova, Mira. *The Divine Cure of Coronavirus and Widespread Diseases*. Singapore: Partridge, 2020.

Balqaziz, Abdallah. *Ḥizbullah min al-taḥrīr ila al-rad: 1982–2006* [Hizbullah from Liberation to Deterrence: 1982–2006]. Beirut: Markaz Dirāsāt al-Waḥdah al-‘Arabīyah, 2006.

Barakāt, Huda. “A Voice Crying in the Wilderness—for Tarek El-Ariss.” *Derivative*, Apr. 9, 2021. At https://thederivative.org/a-voice-crying-in-the-wilderness/.

Bardawil, Fadi A. *Revolution and Disenchantment: Arab Marxism and the Binds of Emancipation*. Durham, NC: Duke Univ. Press, 2020.

Basrawi, Fadia. *Brownies and Kalashnikovs: A Saudi Woman’s Memoir of American Arabia and Wartime Beirut*. Reading, UK: Garnet, 2009.

Bayḍūn, ‘Abbās. *Al-A‘māl al-shi‘rīyah* [The Complete Works of Poetry]. Beirut: Al-Mu’assasah al-‘Arabīyah li-l-Dirāsāt wa-l-Nashr, 2007.

———. “Daqīqa nawawiyya” [Nuclear Minute]. Facebook page, posted Apr. 17, 2020. At https://www.facebook.com/abbass.beydoun.

———. “Al-Ḥadātha al-ān: Bahth fi-l ḥarakāt al-shu‘arā’ al-shabbān al-lubnāniyīn” [Modernity Now: Research on the Movement of Young Lebanese Poets]. *Mawāqif* 34 (1979): 3–30.

———. “Īdīyūlūjīyā al-ḥirāk” [Ideology of the Movement]. *:24*, n.d. At https://24.ae/article/544295/أيديولوجيا-الحراك. Accessed Apr. 6, 2020.

———. “A Possible Poem on Dahiya.” Translated by Issa J. Boullata in *Lebanon, Lebanon*, edited by Anna Wilson, 17–21. London: Saqi, 2006.

———. “Al-Shi‘ir lam yabda’” [The Poem Has Not Started Yet]. *Al-Safīr*, Apr. 30, 2013.

———. “Sīyāsāt kūrūnā” [Corona Policies], *:24*, Apr. 6, 2020, at https://24.ae/article/560736/سياسات%20كورونا?fbclid=IwAR30odTaq08kznMC01W10-8yB1x6kmm0wMsLdeVNnVjXpys9p77O4e7LtxA . In Arabic, the title is “سياسات†كورونا.”

———. “Umthūlat al-‘adad” [Number Example]. *Al-Akhbar*, Apr. 11, 2020. At https://al-akhbar.com/Literature_Arts/287930?fbclid=IwAR3rcDV4a7Lhk-PPk8moc8xC1WgCYir-NHO_RPWRw-qKS59Rszxd6Qy0Ido.

Bechara, Soha. *Resistance: My Life for Lebanon*. Brooklyn, NY: Soft Skull Press, 2003.

Bechara, Souha. *Muqawama*. Beirut: Dar al-Saqi, 2002.

Bechara, Souha, and Cosette Ibrahim. *Ahlumu bi-zinzānah min karaz* [I Dream of a Prison (Made) of Cherries]. Beirut: Dār al-Saqi, 2011.

Béchara, Souha, with Gilles Paris. *Résistante*. N.p.: J. C. Latts, 2000.

Benjamin, Walter. *Illuminations*. Translated by Harry Zohn. Edited by Hannah Arendt. New York. Schocken, 1969.

Bennett, Tony. *The Birth of the Museum*. London: Routledge, 1995.

Bennett, Tony, Fiona Cameron, Nélia Dias, Ben Dibley, Rodney Harrison, Ira Jacknis, and Conal McCarthy. *Collecting, Ordering, Governing: Anthropology, Museums, and Liberal Government*. Durham, NC: Duke Univ. Press, 2017.

Benvenisti, Meron. *Sacred Landscape: The Buried History of the Holy Land since 1948*. Berkeley: Univ. of California Press, 2000.

Bevan, Robert. *The Destruction of Memory*. London: Reaktion, 2006.

Bicknell, Jeanette. “Architectural Ghosts.” *Journal of Aesthetics and Art Criticism* 72, no. 4 (2014): 435–41.

Bizī‘, Shawqī. *‘Anāwīn sarī‘ah li-waṭan maqtūl: Shi‘r* [Quick Headlines for a Murdered Nation: Poetry]. Beirut: Dār al-Ādāb, 1978.

———. *Ka'annī gharībuka bayna al-nisā'* [As Though I Am Your Stranger among Women]. Beirut: Dār al-Ādāb, 1994.

Blanchot, Maurice. *The Space of Literature.* Lincoln: Univ. of Nebraska Press, 1983.

———. *The Writing of the Disaster.* Translated by Anne Smock. Lincoln: Univ. of Nebraska Press, 1995.

Borges, Jorge Luis. "Funes, His Memory." In *Collected Fictions,* translated by Andrew Hurley, 131–37. New York: Viking Penguin, 1998.

Bou Akar, Hiba. *For the War Yet to Come: Planning Beirut's Frontiers.* Stanford, CA: Stanford Univ. Press, 2018.

Boym, Svetlana. "Ruinophilia: Appreciation of Ruins." In *Atlas of Transformation,* edited by Zbynek Baladrán and Vik Havránek. Zurich: JRP Ringier, 2008. At http://monumenttotransformation.org/atlas-of-transformation/html/r/ruinophilia/ruinophilia-appreciation-of-ruins-svetlana-boym.html.

Butler, Judith. *Frames of War: When Is Life Grievable?* London: Verso, 2009.

Butler, Judith, Zeynep Gambetti, and Leticia Sabsay. Introduction to *Vulnerability in Resistance,* edited by Judith Butler, Zeynep Gambetti, and Leticia Sabsay, 1–11. Durham, NC: Duke Univ. Press, 2016.

Caiani, Fabio. "'My Name Is Yalu': The Development of Metafiction in Ilyas Khuri's Work." *Middle Eastern Literatures* 10, no. 2 (2008): 137–55.

Chedid, Andrée. *The Sixth Day.* 1962. Reprint. London: Serpent's Tail, 1987.

Chehabi, Houchang. *Distant Relations: Iran and Lebanon in the Last 500 Years.* London: Center for Lebanese Studies and Tauris, 2006.

Choucair, Julia. "What Is Oligarchy?" Public Source, Feb. 18, 2020. At https://thepublicsource.org/what-is-oligarchy.

Chulov, Martin. "'You Think We Care about Masks?' Anger and Poverty Grip Lebanese City." *Guardian,* May 1, 2020. At https://www.theguardian.com/world/2020/may/01/care-about-masks-anger-poverty-grip-lebanese-city-tripoli-coronavirus.

Clark, Laurie Beth. "Ruined Landscapes and Residual Architecture." *Performance Research* 20, no. 3 (2015): 83–93.

Colla, Elliott. *Conflicted Antiquities: Egyptology, Egyptomania, Egyptian Modernity.* Durham, NC: Duke Univ. Press, 2007.

Connerton, Paul. *How Societies Remember.* Cambridge: Cambridge Univ. Press, 1989.

cooke, miriam. *War's Other Voices: Women Writers on the Lebanese Civil War.* Cambridge: Cambridge Univ. Press, 1987.

———. *Women Write War: The Centring of the Beirut Decentrists*. Oxfordshire, UK: Centre for Lebanese Studies, 1987.

Creswell, Robyn. *City of Beginnings: Poetic Modernism in Beirut*. Princeton, NJ: Princeton Univ. Press, 2019.

Dagher, Carole. *Bring Down the Walls: Lebanon's Post-war Challenge*. New York: St. Martin's Press, 2000.

Daher, Joseph. *Hezbollah: The Political Economy of Lebanon's Party of God*. Florence, Italy: European Univ. Institute, 2019.

Daoud, Hassan. *The House of Mathilde*. Translated by Peter Theroux. London: Granta, 1999.

Darwish, Mahmud. *Memory for Forgetfulness: August, Beirut, 1982*. Translated by Ibrahim Muhawi. Berkeley: Univ. of California Press, 1995.

———. *A River Dies of Thirst: Journals*. Translated by Catherine Cobham. Brooklyn, NY: Archipelago, 2009.

Darwīsh, Maḥmūd. *Dhākirah lil-nisyān: Al-Zamān, Bayrūt: Al-Makān, yawm min Āb 1982* [Memory for Forgetfulness: The Time, Beirut: The Place, a Day in August 1982]. Cairo: Dār al-Thaqāfah al-Jadīdah, 1989.

Dāwūd, Ḥasan. *Bināyat Mātīld* [The House of Mathilde]. Beirut: Dār al-Tanwīr, 1983.

———. "They Destroy and We Build." Translated by Issa J. Boullata in *Lebanon, Lebanon*, edited by Anna Wilson, 22–26. London: Saqi, 2006.

Ḍayf, Shawqī. *Tārīkh al-adab al-ʿArabi 1: Al-ʿAṣr al-jāhilī* [History of Arabic Literature: The Pre-Islamic Age]. Cairo: Dār al-Maʿārif, 1960.

De Certeau, Michel. *The Practice of Everyday Life*. Translated by Timothy J. Tomasik. Minneapolis: Univ. of Minnesota Press, 1998.

Deeb, Lara. *An Enchanted Modern: Gender and Public Piety in Shiʿi Lebanon*. Princeton, NJ: Princeton Univ. Press, 2006.

———. "Exhibiting the 'Just-Lived Past': Hizbullah's Nationalist Narratives in Transnational Political Context." *Comparative Studies in Society and History* 50, no. 2 (2008): 369–99.

Deeb, Lara, and Mona Harb. *Leisurely Islam: Negotiating Geography and Morality in Shiʿite South Beirut*. Princeton, NJ: Princeton Univ. Press, 2013.

Defense Update. "Dense Inert Metal Explosive (DIME)." N.d. At defense-update .com/products/d/dime.htm. Accessed Jan. 7, 2018.

Deleuze, Gilles, and Félix Guattari. *Kafka: Toward a Minor Literature*. Translated by Dana Polan. Minneapolis: Univ. of Minnesota Press, 1986.

Derrida, Jacques. *Acts of Literature*. Edited by Derek Attridge. New York: Routledge, 1992.

———. *Specters of Marx: The State of the Debt, the Work of Mourning, and the New International*. Translated by Peggy Kamuf. New York: Routledge, 1994.

DeSilvey, Caitlin. *Curated Decay: Heritage beyond Saving*. Minneapolis: Univ. of Minnesota Press, 2017.

———. "Observed Decay: Telling Stories with Mutable Things." *Journal of Material Culture* 11, no. 3 (2006): 318–38.

———. "Palliative Curation: Art and Entropy on Orford Ness." In *Ruin Memories: Materiality, Aesthetics and the Archaeology of the Recent Past*, edited by Bjørnar Olsen and Póra Pétursdóttir, 79–91. London: Routledge, 2014.

Diab, Youssef. "Scandal of Lebanese Politicians' Transfer of Billions of Dollars Abroad 'Confuses' Banks." *Asharq al-Awsat*, Dec. 29, 2019. At https://english.aawsat.com//home/article/2057301/scandal-lebanese-politicians%e2%80%99-transfer-billions-dollars-abroad-%e2%80%98confuses%e2%80%99-banks.

Di-Capua, Yoav. "Arab Existentialism: An Invisible Chapter in the Intellectual History of Decolonization." *American Historical Review* 117, no. 4 (2012): 1061–91.

Edensor, Tim. "The Ghosts of Industrial Ruins: Ordering and Disordering Memory in Excessive Space." *Environment and Planning D: Society and Space* 23 (2005): 829–49.

———. *Industrial Ruins: Space, Aesthetics, and Materiality*. Oxford: Berg, 2005.

———. "Waste Matter: The Debris of Industrial Ruins and the Disordering of the Material World." *Journal of Material Culture* 10, no. 3 (2005): 311–32.

Elias, Chad. *Posthumous Images: Contemporary Art and Memory Politics in Post–Civil War Lebanon*. Durham, NC: Duke Univ. Press, 2018.

Elsir, Amir Tag. *Ebola 76*. Translated by Charis Bredin and Emily Danby. London: Darf, 2015.

Embaló, Birget. "The City, Mythical Images and Their Deconstruction: The Image of Beirut in Contemporary Works of Arabic Literature." In *Myths, Historical Archetypes and Symbolic Figures in Arabic Literature: Towards a New Hermeneutic Approach*, edited by Angelika Neuwirth, Birgit Embaló, Sebastian Günther, and Maher Jarrar, 583–603. Stuttgart, Germany: Steiner, 1999.

Evans, Brad, and Bracha Ettinger. "Art in a Time of Atrocity." *New York Times*, Dec. 16, 2016.

Fakhr al-Dīn, Jawdat. *Al-Aʿmāl al-shiʿriyyah* [The Complete Works of Poetry]. Beirut: Al-Muʾassasah al-ʿArabīyah li-l-Dirāsāt wa-l-Nashr, 2006.

Fakhreddine, Huda J. "Defining Metapoesis in the 'Abbāsid Age." *Journal of Arabic Literature* 42 (2011): 205–35.

———. *Metapoesis in the Arabic Tradition: From Modernists to Muḥdathūn.* Leiden: Brill, 2015.

Financial Times. "Lebanon's Central Bank Governor: 'We're Not a Normal Country.'" Nov. 20, 2017. At https://www.ft.com/content/cf667768-c0bd-11e7-b8a3-38a6e068f464.

Fisk, Robert. "Relatives Let into Israelis' Jail of Death." *Independent* (United Kingdom), Feb. 2, 1995. At http://www.independent.co.uk/news/world/relatives-let-into-israelis-jail-of-death-1571094.html.

Flint, Julie. "Town Tells of Day of Torture." *Guardian*, Feb. 24, 1986.

Forty, Adrian. Introduction to *The Art of Forgetting*, edited by Adrian Forty and Susanne Kuchler, 1–18. Oxford: Berg, 1999.

Foucault, Michel. *The Archaeology of Knowledge and the Discourse on Language.* Translated by A. M. Sheridan Smith. New York: Pantheon, 1972.

———. "On the Archaeology of the Sciences: Response to the Epistemology Circle." In *The Essential Works of Foucault, 1954–1984*, vol. 1, translated by Robert Hurley, edited by Paul Rabinow and Nikolas Rose, 392–422. New York: New Press, 2003.

France 24. "Lebanon Approves Long-Awaited Economic Rescue Plan after Weeks of Unrest." Apr. 30, 2020. At https://www.france24.com/en/20200430-lebanon-approves-long-awaited-economic-rescue-plan-after-weeks-of-unrest.

Fregonese, Sara. *War and the City: Urban Geopolitics in Lebanon.* London: I. B. Tauris, 2019.

Gebhardt, Hans, Dorothee Sack, Ralph Bodenstein, Andreas Fritz, and Jens Hanssen. *History, Space and Social Conflict in Beirut: The Quarter of Zokak El-Blat.* Beirut: Orient-Institut; Würzburg, Germany: Ergon Verlag in Kommission, 2005.

Gessen, Masha. "The *New Yorker* Interview: Judith Butler Wants to Reshape Our Rage." *New Yorker*, Feb. 9, 2020. At http:/www.newyorker.com/culture/the-new-yorker-interview/judith-butler-wants-to-reshape-our-rage.

Gilbert-Sleiman, Betty. "The Reform of History School Textbooks in Lebanon: Collecting Conflict Memories in a Peace-Building Process (1996–2001)." In *Archives, Museums and Collecting Practices in the Modern Arab World*, edited by Sonja Mejcher-Atassi and John Pedro Schwartz, 121–38. London: Routledge, 2016.

Ginsberg, Robert. *The Aesthetics of Ruins.* Amsterdam: Rodopi, 2004.

Gordillo, Gastón R. *Rubble: The Afterlife of Destruction*. Durham, NC: Duke Univ. Press, 2014.

Gordon, Avery. *Ghostly Matters: Haunting and the Sociological Imagination*. Minneapolis: Univ. of Minnesota Press, 2008.

Gordon, Neve. "Outsourcing Violations: The Israeli Case." *Journal of Human Rights* 1, no. 3 (2002): 321–37.

Gregory, Derek. "'In Another Time Zone, the Bombs Fall Unsafely . . .': Targets, Civilians and Late Modern War." *Arab World Geographer* 9, no. 2 (2006): 88–111.

El Habre, Simon, dir. *The One-Man Village*. Mec film, 2009.

Hage, Ghassan. "Academia in the Revolution." Lecture at Jibrān Park, Beirut, Oct. 27, 2019.

———. "Introduction: States of Decay." In *Decay*, edited by Ghassan Hage, 1–16. Durham, NC: Duke Univ. Press, 2021.

Halabi, Zeina, ed. *Unmaking of the Arab Intellectual: Prophecy, Exile, and the Nation*. Edinburgh: Edinburgh Univ. Press, 2017.

Hammami, Rema. "Palestinian NGOs since Oslo: From NGO Politics to Social Movements?" *Middle East Report* 214 (2000): 16–19, 27, 48.

Hamori, Andras. *On the Art of Medieval Arabic Literature*. Princeton, NJ: Princeton Univ. Press, 1974.

Hamzeh, Ahmad Nizar. *In the Path of Hizbullah*. Syracuse, NY: Syracuse Univ. Press, 2004.

Harb, Mona. "Story of a Name." In *Beyroutes*, supplement of *Beiroutes: A Guide to Beirut* 22 (2010): 71–75.

Harb, Mona, and Lara Deeb. "Culture as History and Landscape: Hizbullah's Efforts to Shape an Islamic Milieu in Lebanon." *Arab Studies Journal* 19, no. 1 (2011): 10–41.

Harlow, Barbara. "Prison Memoirs of Political Detainees." In *Resistance Literature*, 117–54. New York: Methuen, 1987.

Hartman, Michelle, and Malek Abisaab. Introduction to Nawal Qasim Baidoun, *Memoirs of a Militant: My Years in the Khiam Women's Prison*, translated by Michelle Hartman and Caline Nasrallah, edited by Malek Abisaab, 1–28. Northampton, MA: Olive Branch Press, 2022.

Haugbølle, Sune. "Counterpublics of Memory: Memoirs and Public Testimonies of the Lebanese Civil War." In *Publics, Politics, and Participation: Locating the Public Sphere in the Middle East and North Africa*, edited by Seteney Shami, 119–50. New York: Columbia Univ. Press, 2010.

———. "The (Little) Militia Man: Memory and Militarized Masculinity in Lebanon." *Journal of Middle East Women's Studies* 8, no. 1 (2012): 115–39.

———. *War and Memory in Lebanon*. New York: Cambridge Univ. Press, 2010.

Ḥāwī, Īliyyā. *Imru' al-Qays: Shā'ir al-mar'a wa-l-ṭabī'a* [Imru' al-Qays: Poet of Women and Nature]. Beirut: Dār al-Thaqāfa, 1970.

Hayek, Ghenwa. *Beirut, Imagining the City: Space and Place in Lebanese Literature*. London: I. B. Tauris, 2014.

Hell, Julia, and Andreas Schönle. Introduction to *Ruins of Modernity*, edited by Julia Hell and Andreas Schönle, 1–14. Durham NC: Duke Univ. Press, 2010.

Hermez, Sami Samir. *War Is Coming: Between Past and Future Violence in Lebanon*. Philadelphia: Univ. of Pennsylvania Press, 2017.

Herscher, Andrew. *Violence Taking Place: The Architecture of the Kosovo Conflict*. Stanford, CA: Stanford Univ. Press, 2010.

El-Hibri, Hatim. *Visions of Beirut: The Urban Life of Media Infrastructure*. Durham, NC: Duke Univ. Press, 2021.

Hirsch, Marianne. "The Generation of Postmemory." *Poetics Today* 29, no. 1 (2008): 103–28.

———. "Introduction: Practicing Feminism, Practicing Memory." In *Women Mobilizing Memory*, edited by Ayşe Gül Altınay, María José Contreras, Marianne Hirsch, Jean Howard, Banu Karaca, and Alisa Solomon, 1–24. New York: Columbia Univ. Press, 2019.

Hirsch, Marianne, and Nancy K. Miller. *Rites of Return: Diaspora Poetics and the Politics of Memory*. New York: Columbia Univ. Press, 2011.

Hirsch, Marianne, and Leo Spitzer. *Ghosts of Home: The Afterlife of Czernowitz in Jewish Memory*. Berkeley: Univ. of California Press, 2010.

———. "What's Wrong with This Picture? Holocaust Photographs in Contemporary Narratives." *Journal of Modern Jewish Studies* 5, no. 2 (2006): 229–52.

Hirst, David. *Beware of Small States: Lebanon, Battleground of the Middle East*. New York: Nation Books, 2010.

———. "South Lebanon: The War That Never Ends?" *Journal of Palestine Studies* 28, no. 3 (1999): 5–18.

Hoag, Trevor L. "Ghosts of Memory: Mournful Performance and the Rhetorical Event of Haunting (Or: Specters of Occupy)." *Liminalities: A Journal of Performance Studies* 10, nos. 3–4 (2014): 2–22.

El-Hokayem, Emile. "Hizbullah and Syria: Outgrowing the Proxy Relationship." *Washington Quarterly* 30, no. 2 (Spring 2007): 35–52.

Holstun, Jim. "Antigone Becomes Jocasta: Soha Bechara, *Résistante*, and *Incendies*." *Mediations: Journal of the Marxist Literary Group* 29, no. 1 (Fall 2015): 3–42.

Holt, Elizabeth M. *Fictitious Capital: Silk, Cotton, and the Rise of the Arabic Novel*. New York: Fordham Univ. Press, 2017.

———. "Resistance Literature and Occupied Palestine in Cold War Beirut." *Journal of Palestine Studies* 50, no. 1 (2021): 3–18.

Hout, Syrine. "Recounting Memories of Resistance in 33 Days." *Arab Studies Quarterly* 38, no. 2 (2016): 481–99.

Human Rights Watch. *Flooding South Lebanon: Israel's Use of Cluster Munitions in Lebanon in July and August 2006*. New York: Human Rights Watch, Feb. 2008. At https://www.hrw.org/reports/2008/02/16/flooding-south-lebanon/israels-use-cluster-munitions-lebanon-july-and-august-2006.

———. "Torture in Khiam Prison: Responsibility and Accountability." Oct. 27, 1999. At https://www.hrw.org/en/news/1999/10/27/torture-Khiam-prison-responsibility-and-accountability?print.

———. *Why They Died: Civilian Casualties in Lebanon during the 2006 War*. New York: Human Rights Watch, Sept. 2007. At https://www.hrw.org/sites/default/files/reports/lebanon0907.pdf.

Huyssen, Andreas. *Present Pasts: Urban Palimpsests and the Politics of Memory*. Stanford, CA: Stanford Univ. Press, 2003.

———. *Twilight Memories: Marking Time in a Culture of Amnesia*. New York: Routledge, 1995.

Al-ʿĪd, Yumnā. *Al-Kitābah taḥawwul fī al-taḥawwul: Muqārabah li-l-kitābah al-adabīyah fī zaman al-ḥarb al-Lubnāniyyah* [Writing Shifts in Transition: An Approach to Literary Writing at the Time of the Lebanese War]. Beirut: Dār al-Ādāb, 1993.

Ingold, Tim. "The Temporality of the Landscape." *World Archaeology* 25, no. 2 (1993): 152–74.

International Crisis Group. "The Beirut Blast: Accident in Name Only." Aug. 7, 2020. At https://www.crisisgroup.org/middle-east-north-africa/eastern-mediterranean/lebanon/beirut-blast-accident-name-only?fbclid=IwAR1F_MWKzPJvz9megfW3UbkfwFhISxXnkT8G2LJolCdH4OPIyuEFEsAgXzk.

"Interview de Souha Bechara." In Jean Khalil Chamoun, dir., *Arḍ al-nisāʾ* [Women beyond Borders]. Aflām Miṣr al-ʿĀlamīyah/Arab Film Distribution, 2003.

Jaber, Hala. *Hezbollah: Born with a Vengeance*. New York: Columbia Univ. Press, 1997.

Jaber, Rabee. *Amerika*. Translated by Charlotte Woillez and Simon Corthay. Paris: Gallimard, 2013.

———. *Berytus, une ville sous terre*. Translated by Charlotte Woillez and Simon Corthay. Paris: Gallimard, 2006.

Jābir, Mundhir Maḥmūd. *Sharīṭ al-Lubnānī al-muḥtal: Masālik al-iḥtilāl, masārāt al-muwājahah, maṣā'ir al-ahālī* [The Occupied Lebanese Border Strip: Occupation Routes, Paths of Confrontation, the Fate of Its Occupants]. Beirut: Mu'assasat al-Dirāsāt al-Filasṭīnīyah, 1999.

Jābir, Rabī'. *Amīrkā: Riwāyah* [America: A Novel]. Casablanca, Morocco: Al-Markaz al-Thaqāfī al-'Arabī, 2009.

Joreige, Lamia, dir. *Huna wa rubbamā hunāk* [Here and Perhaps Elsewhere]. 03 productions, 2003.

Journal of Palestine Studies. "Palestinian Emigration and Israeli Land Expropriation in the Occupied Territories." 3, no. 1 (1973): 106–18.

Kacandes, Irene. *Talk Fiction: Literature and the Talk Explosion*. Lincoln: Univ. of Nebraska Press, 2001.

Kanafani, Ghassan. *Fi al-adab al-Sahyuni* [On Zionist Literature]. 1967. Reprint. Nicosia, Cyprus: Rimal, 2015.

Khalaf, Samir. *Civil and Uncivil Violence in Lebanon: A History of the Internationalization of Communal Conflict*. New York: Columbia Univ. Press, 2002.

Khalili, Laleh. *Heroes and Martyrs of Palestine: The Politics of National Commemoration*. Cambridge: Cambridge Univ. Press, 2007.

———. *Time in the Shadows: Confinement in Counterinsurgencies*. Stanford, CA: Stanford Univ. Press, 2012.

Khankan, Nathalie. "Re-perceiving the Pre-Islamic Nasīb." *Journal of Arabic Literature* 33, no. 1 (2002): 1–23.

Khatib, Lina. "Lebanese Cinema and the Representation of War." In *Film in the Middle East and North Africa: Creative Dissidence*, edited by Josef Gugler, 134–46. Austin: Univ. of Texas Press, 2011.

Khayyat, Munira. *A Landscape of War: Ecologies of Resistance and Survival in South Lebanon*. Berkeley: Univ. of California Press, 2022.

Khayyat, Munira, Yasmine Khayyat, and Rola Khayyat. "Pieces of Us: The Intimate as Imperial Archive." *Journal of Middle East Women's Studies* 14, no. 3 (2018): 268–91.

Khayyat, Yasmine, and Rola Khayyat. "Ruminating on Ruins in Beirut." *Jadaliyya*, Aug. 7, 2020. At https://www.jadaliyya.com/Details/41537.

Khoury, Elias. "The Novel, the Novelist, and the Lebanese Civil War." Fourth Farhat J. Ziadeh Distinguished Lecture in Arab and Islamic Studies, Department of Near Eastern Languages and Civilization, Univ. of Washington, Seattle, 2006. At http://depts.washington.edu/nelc/pdf/event_files/ziadeh_series/2006lebanon-eliaskhoury.pdf.

———. *Yalo*. Translated by Peter Theroux. New York: Archipelago, 2008.

Khrais, Bilal. "Lebanon's Women Warriors." *Al Jazeera*, Apr. 24, 2010. At https://www.aljazeera.com/videos/2010/4/24/lebanons-women-warriors.

Khūrī, Ilyās. "Al-Riwāya wa-al-riwā'ī wa-al-ḥarb" [The Novel, the Novelist, and the War]. *Al-Mulḥaq al-thaqāfī li-al-nahār*, Jan. 22, 2006, 14.

———. "Saramāġū: Al-Wabā' wa al-'ama al-abyad" [Saramago: Epidemic and White Blindness]. *Al-Quds al-Arabi*, Apr. 20, 2020. At https://www.alquds.co.uk/-ساراماغو-الوباء-والعمى-الأبيض/.

———. "Al-Wabā' wa al-adab al-'arabī al-ḥadīth" [The Epidemic and Modern Arab Literature]. :24, Apr. 6, 2020. At https://24.ae/article/560736/%D8%B3%D9%8A%D8%A7%D8%B3%D8%A7%D8%AA%20%D9%83%D9%88%D8%B1%D9%88%D9%86%D8%A7?fbclid=IwAR30odTaq08kznMC01W10-8yB1x6kmm0wMsLdeVNnVjXpys9p77O4e7LtxA.

———. *Yālū: Riwāyah* [Yalo: The Novelist]. Beirut: Dār al-Ādāb, 2002.

———. *Zamān al-iḥtilāl* [The Age of Occupation]. Beirut: Mu'assasat al-Abḥāth al-'Arabiyyah, 1985.

Kifah, Hanna. *Feminism and Avant-Garde Aesthetic in the Levantine Novel: Feminism, Nationalism, and the Arabic Novel*. New York: Palgrave Macmillan, 2016.

Kilpatrick, Hilary. "Literary Creativity and the Cultural Heritage: The Aṭlāl in Modern Arabic Fiction." In *Tradition, Modernity, and Postmodernity in Arabic Literature: Essays in Honor of Professor Issa F. Boullatta*, edited by Kamal Abdel-Malek and Wael Hallaq, 28–44. Leiden: Brill, 2000.

Klemm, Verena. "Different Notions of Commitment (*Iltizam*) and Committed Literature (*al-Adab al-Multazim*) in the Literary Circles of the Mashriq." *Arabic & Middle Eastern Literature* 3, no. 1 (2000): 51–62.

Kosmatopoulos, Nikolas. "Unhatching the Egg in Lebanon's 2019 Protests: Activism, Purity and the Real-Estatization of Civil Society." *South Atlantic Quarterly* 120, no. 2 (2021): 446–55.

Kwon, Heonik. *Ghosts of War in Vietnam: Studies in the Social and Cultural History of Modern Warfare*. Cambridge: Cambridge Univ. Press, 2008.

Labban, Mazen. "On the #BeirutBlast: Organized Abandonment and the Environmental Violence of Capital." *Capitalism Nature Socialism* 31, no. 4 (2020): 18–22.

Labīd ibn Rabī'ah. "The Mu'allaqah of Labīd ibn Rabī'ah." In *The Mu'allaqat for Millennials: Pre-Islamic Arabic Golden Odes*, translated and edited by Suzanne Pinckney Stetkevych and Khalid Stetkevych, 202–52. Olaya, Saudi Arabia: King Abdullazizz Center for World Culture (Ithra), King Fahad National Library, 2020.

Lambert, Léopold. "#PALESTINE /// The Right to the Ruin: Civilizational Absence in the Post-Nakba Landscapes." *Funambulist* 14, no. 6 (2013): 39–48.

———. *Weaponized Architecture: The Impossibility of Innocence*. Barcelona: dpr-Barcelona, 2012.

Lang, Felix. *The Lebanese Post–Civil War Novel: Memory, Trauma, and Capital.* New York: Palgrave Macmillan, 2016.

Larkin, Craig. *Memory and Conflict in Lebanon: Remembering and Forgetting the Past.* Abingdon, UK: Routledge, 2012.

Larkin, Craig, and Ella Parry-Davies. "War Museums in Postwar Lebanon: Memory, Violence, and Performance." *Nationalism and Ethnic Politics* 25, no. 1 (2019): 78–96. Reprinted in *Power-Sharing after Civil War: Thirty Years since Lebanon's Taif Agreement*, edited by John Nagle and Mary-Alice Clancy, 78–96. New York: Routledge, 2022.

Launchbury, Claire. "Staging Khiam: Documentary, Theater, and Archive in Postwar Lebanon." *Contemporary French and Francophone Studies* 18, no. 5 (2014): 514–22.

Launchbury, Claire, Nayla Tamraz, Roger Celestin, and Eliane Dalmolin. "War, Memory, Amnesia: Postwar Lebanon." *Contemporary French and Francophone Studies* 18, no. 5 (2014): 457–61.

Lefebvre, Henri. *The Production of Space.* Translated by Donald Nicholson-Smith. Oxford: Blackwell, 1992.

Ma, Yo-Yo. "Bach Project." N.d. At https://bach.yo-yoma.com. Accessed Sept. 11, 2018.

Al-Majlis al-Thaqāfī li-Lubnān al-Janūbī [Cultural Council of South Lebanon]. *Al-Muqāwamah fī al-ta'bīr al-adabī* [Resistance in Literary Expression]. Beirut: Dār al-Farabi, 1985.

Makdisi, Saree. "Beirut, a City without History?" In *Memory and Violence in the Middle East and North Africa*, edited by Ussama Samir Makdisi and Paul A. Silverstein, 201–14. Bloomington: Indiana Univ. Press, 2006.

———. "Laying Claim to Beirut: Urban Narrative and Spatial Identity in the Age of Solidère." *Critical Inquiry* 23, no. 3 (Spring 1997): 661–705.

Al-Malaika, Nazek. "Cholera." Translated by Husain Haddawy. In *The Poetry of Arab Women: A Contemporary Anthology*, edited by Nathalie Handal, 176–82. New York: Interlink Books, 2001.

Merhej, Karim, Kareem Chehayeb, and Christina Cavalcanti. "How the Lebanese Government Disabled Hundreds of People—and Then Left Them to Pay for Its Crime." Public Source, Aug. 5, 2021. At https://thepublicsource.org/disability-justice-beirut-blast.

Mervin, Sabrina, ed. *Les mondes chiites et l'Iran*. Paris: Karthala, 2007.

Mitchell, W. J. T. *Picture Theory: Essays on Verbal and Visual Representation*. Chicago: Univ. of Chicago Press, 1994.

Mounzer, Lina. "In Lebanon, a Pandemic of Hunger." *New York Times*, May 6, 2020. At https://www.nytimes.com/2020/05/06/opinion/lebanon-protests-coronavirus.html.

Al-Musawi, Muhsin Jasim. *Arabic Poetry: Trajectories of Modernity and Tradition*. London: Routledge, 2006.

———. *The Postcolonial Arabic Novel: Debating Ambivalence*. Leiden: Brill, 2003.

Al-Mutanabbī. *Sharḥ dīwān al-Mutanabī* [Explanation of al-Mutanabī]. 4 vols. Edited by ʿAbd al-Raḥmān al-Barqūqī. Beirut: Dār al-Kitāb al-ʿArabī, 1986.

Nagle, John. "Ghosts, Memory, and the Right to the Divided City: Resisting Amnesia in Beirut City Centre." *Antipode* 49, no. 1 (2017): 149–68.

Nahrnet. "Beit al-Madina to Recall Horrors of Civil War." Oct. 17, 2008. At www.middle-east-online/com/english/i?d=28346.

Naṣrallah, Jad. "'Bayt al-ʿAynkabūt' yunsaj fī al-Ḍāḥiya wa-l-iftītāḥ al-rasmi masāʾan." [The Spider's Web Has Been Woven in Ḍāḥiya and Its Official Opening Is This Evening]. *Al-Akhbār* (Lebanon), July 25, 2007.

Navaro-Yashin, Yael. "Affective Spaces, Melancholic Objects: Ruination and the Production of Anthropological Knowledge." *Journal of the Royal Anthropological Institute* 15 (2009): 1–18.

———. "Diversifying Affect." *Cultural Anthropology* 33, no. 2 (2017): 209–14.

———. *The Make-Believe Space: Affective Geography in a Postwar Polity*. Durham, NC: Duke Univ. Press, 2012.

Neville, Brian, and Johanne Villeneuve. "Introduction: In Lieu of Waste." In *Waste-Site Stories: The Recycling of Memory*, edited by Brian Neville and Johanne Villeneuve, 1–26. Albany: State Univ. of New York Press, 2002.

Nora, Pierre. "Between Memory and History: Les lieux de mémoire." *Representations* 26 (1989): 7–24.

Norton, Augustus Richard. *Amal and the Shi'a: Struggle for the Soul of Lebanon.* Austin: Univ. of Texas Press, 1987.

———. *Hezbollah: A Short History.* Princeton, NJ: Princeton Univ. Press, 2007.

———. "Hizbullah and the Israeli Withdrawal from Southern Lebanon." *Journal of Palestine Studies* 30, no. 1 (2000): 22–35.

Nucho, Joanne Randa. *Everyday Sectarianism in Urban Lebanon: Infrastructures, Public Services, and Power.* Princeton, NJ: Princeton Univ. Press, 2016.

Packer, George. "We Are Living in a Failed State." *Atlantic*, June 2020. At https://www.theatlantic.com/magazine/archive/2020/06/underlying-conditions/610261/?fbclid=IwAR2xhGtnq2Czvmll99fir3pZcmzHHJYZMyATYqo4kbxUZCLKa9_ZEXHTnfw.

Perec, George. *Species of Spaces and Other Pieces.* Edited and translated by John Sturrock. London: Penguin, 1997.

Public Source. "About." N.d. At https://thepublicsource.org. Accessed Feb. 1, 2020.

Qabbānī, Nizār. *Ilā Bayrūt al-unthā . . . ma' ḥubbī: Muqaddimah wa 5 qaṣā'id* [To Beirut, the Woman . . . With My Love: Introduction and 5 Poems]. Beirut: Manshurāt Nizār Qabbānī, 1981.

Qāsim, Na'īm. *Hizbullah: The Story from Within.* Translated by Dalia Khalil. London: Saqi, 2005.

Qiblawi, Tamara. "75% of Lebanon Needs Aid after Coronavirus, and Hungry Protesters Are Back on the Streets." *CNN World*, Apr. 29, 2020. At https://edition.cnn.com/2020/04/28/middleeast/lebanon-hunger-aid-coronavirus-intl/index.html?fbclid=IwAR18oIvQUWpwG1foDuT9ufZxYqVEr5j5H9DELPFOXxWs3aqp0ixzT7UN1Ww.

Quilty, Jim. "Prison. Museum. Ruin." *Daily Star* (United Kingdom), Aug. 24, 2006. At http://mobile.dailystar.com.lb/News/Lebanon-News/2006/Aug-24/43009-prison-museum-ruin.ashx.

———. "Putting Flesh and Bones on the Specter of Dahiyeh." *Daily Star* (United Kingdom), June 8, 2007.

Raad, Walid. The Atlas Group (1989–2004). Online archive, mixed media, n.d. At www.theatlasgroup.org/. Accessed May 29, 2018.

Raḥbānī, Ziyād. *Shī fāshil* [A Failure]. Beirut: Mukhtārāt, 1994.

Rancière, Jacques. *The Future of the Image.* Translated by Gregory Elliot. 2007. Reprint. London: Verso, 2009.

———. *The Politics of Literature.* Translated by Julie Rose. Cambridge: Polity, 2011.

Rose, Mitch, and John Wylie. "Animating Landscape." *Environment and Planning D: Society and Space* 24 (2006): 475–79.

Ruhayem, Rami, and Paul Adams. "The Inferno and the Mystery Ship." *BBC News,* Aug. 8, 2020. At https://www.bbc.co.uk/news/extra/x2iutcqf1g/beirut-blast.

Saade, Bashir. *Hizbullah and the Politics of Remembrance: Writing the Lebanese Nation.* Cambridge: Cambridge Univ. Press, 2016.

Saad-Ghorayeb, Amal. *Hizbu'llah: Politics and Religion.* London: Pluto Press, 2002.

Sabag, Randa Chahal, dir. *Civilisées* [A Civilized People]. Canal Plus, 1999.

Saghieh, Nizar. "Dhākirat al-ḥarb fil-niẓām al-qānūnī al-lubnānī" [Memory of the War in the Lebanese Legal System]. In *Memoire pour l'avenir,* edited by Amal Makarem, 240–55. Beirut: Éditions Dar an-Nahar, 2002.

Said, Edward. *Beginnings: Intention and Method.* New York: Basic Books, 1975.

Sajīn al-Janūb [Prisoner of the South]. Munīr Bū Samrā, 2000.

Salem Manganaro, Elisa. "Bearing Witness: Recent Literature from Lebanon." *Literary Review* 37, no. 3 (Spring 1994): 373–81.

———. *Constructing Lebanon: A Century of Literary Narratives.* Gainesville: Univ. Press of Florida, 2003.

Salloum, Jayce, dir. *Untitled Part I: Everything and Nothing.* France/Canada, 2001.

Samak, Muḥammad Ṣāliḥ. *Amīr alshi'r fī l-'aṣr al-qadīm Imru' al-Qays* [Prince of Poetry in the Ancient Era: Imru' al-Qays]. Cairo: Dār Nahḍat Miṣr, 1974.

Samman, Ghada. *Beirut '75.* Translated by Nancy N. Roberts. Fayetteville: Univ. of Arkansas Press, 1995.

———. *Beirut Nightmares.* Translated by Nancy N. Roberts. London: Quartet Books, 1997.

———. "Lebanon? It Left and Never Returned." *Sawt Beirut International,* Aug. 21, 2021. At https://www.sawtbeirut.com/press/لبنان؟-ذهب-ولم-يعد/.

Al-Sammān, Ghādah. *Kawābīs Bayrūt* [Beirut Nightmares]. Beirut: Manshūrāt Dār al-Ādāb, 1976.

———. *Rasā'il Ghassān Kanafānī ila Ghāda al-Sammān* [Ghassān Kanafānī's Love Letters to Ghāda al-Sammān]. 1992. Reprint. Beirut: Dār al-Taliya, 1993.

Sawalha, Aseel. *Reconstructing Beirut: Memory and Space in a Postwar Arab City*. Austin: Univ. of Texas Press, 2010.

Schwedler, Jillian. "Thinking Critically about Regional Uprisings." *Middle East Report* 292–93, no. 3 (Fall–Winter 2019). At https://merip.org/2019/12/thinking-critically-about-regional-uprisings/.

Seigneurie, Ken. "Introduction: A Survival Aesthetic for Ongoing War." In *Crisis and Memory: The Representation of Space in Modern Levantine Narrative*, edited by Ken Seigneurie, 11–32. Wiesbaden, Germany: Reichert, 2004.

———. *Standing by the Ruins: Elegiac Humanism in Wartime and Postwar Lebanon*. New York: Fordham Univ. Press, 2011.

Sells, Michael. *Desert Tracings: Six Arabian Odes by ʿAlqama, Shānfara, Labīd, ʿAntara, al-Aʿsha and Dhu al-Rūmma*. Middletown, CT: Wesleyan Univ. Press, 1989.

Serrano, Richard. *Neither a Borrower, nor a Lender: Forging Traditions in French, Chinese and Arabic Poetry*. Oxford: Legenda, 2002.

Shams al-Dīn, Muḥammad ʿAlī. *Al-Aʿmāl al-shiʿriyyah* [The Complete Works of Poetry]. 2 vols. Beirut: Al-Muʾassasah al-ʿArabiyyah li-l-Dirāsāt wa-l-Nashr, 2009.

Sharara, Waddah. *Dawlat Ḥizbullah: Lubnān mujtamaan Islamiyah* [The Hizbullah State: Lebanon as an Islamic Society]. Beirut: Dār al-Nahar, 2006.

Sharif, Hasan. "South Lebanon: Its History and Geopolitics in South Lebanon." In *South Lebanon*, Special Report no. 2, edited by Elaine Hagopian and Samih Farsoun, 10–11. Detroit: Arab American Univ. Graduates, 1978.

Shringarpure, Bhakti. *Cold War Assemblages: Decolonization to Digital New York*. Milton Park, UK: Routledge, Taylor & Francis Group, 2020.

Sinno, Nadine. "The Greening of Modern Arabic Literature: An Ecological Interpretation of Two Contemporary Arabic Novels." *Interdisciplinary Studies in Literature and Environment* 20, no. 1 (2013): 118–32.

Snaije, Olivia. "Seeing Yourself Re-made as Fiction." *Daily Star* (United Kingdom), Feb. 2, 2011. At http://www.dailystar.com.lb/Culture/Film/Feb/02/Seeing-yourself-re-made-asfiction.ashx#axzz1PJ051RPc.

Sontag, Susan. *Regarding the Pain of Others*. New York: Farrar, Straus and Giroux, 2003.

Sperl, Stefan. *Mannerism in Arabic Poetry: A Structural Analysis of Selected Texts*. Cambridge: Cambridge Univ. Press, 1989.

Stamatopoulou-Robbins, Sophia. *Waste Siege: The Life of Infrastructure in Palestine*. Stanford, CA: Stanford Univ. Press, 2020.

Stetkevych, Jaroslav. *The Zephyrs of Najd: The Poetics of Nostalgia in the Classical Arabic Nasīb*. Chicago: Univ. of Chicago Press, 1993.

Stetkevych, Suzanne Pinckney. *Abu Tammam and the Poetics of the Abbasid Age*. Leiden: Brill, 1990.

———. *The Mute Immortals Speak: Pre-Islamic Poetry and the Poetics of Ritual*. Ithaca, NY: Cornell Univ. Press, 1993.

Stewart, Susan. *The Ruins Lesson: Meaning and Material in Western Culture*. Chicago: Univ. of Chicago Press, 2020.

Stoler, Ann Laura. *Along the Archival Grain: Epistemic Anxieties and Colonial Common Sense*. Princeton, NJ: Princeton Univ. Press, 2009.

———. *Duress: Imperial Durabilities in Our Times*. Durham, NC: Duke Univ. Press, 2016.

———. "Imperial Debris: Reflections on Ruins and Ruination." *Cultural Anthropology* 23, no. 2 (2008): 191–219.

———. "Introduction: 'The Rot Remains': From Ruins to Ruination." In *Imperial Debris: On Ruins and Ruination*, edited by Ann Laura Stoler, 1–36. Durham, NC: Duke Univ. Press, 2013.

Stone, Christopher. "Ziyad Rahbani's 'Novelization' of Lebanese Musical Theater or the Paradox of Parody." *Middle Eastern Literatures* 8, no. 2 (July 2005): 151–70.

Sullivan, Helen. "Dispatch: The Making of Lebanon's October Revolution." *New Yorker*, Oct. 29, 2019. At https://www.newyorker.com/news/dispatch/the-making-of-lebanons-october-revolution.

Al-Tahir, Ahmad Makki. "Imru' al-Qays." In *Dictionary of Literary Biography*, vol. 311: *Arabic Literary Culture: 500–925*, edited by Michael Cooperson and Shawkat M. Toorawa, 212–24. Detroit: Thomson Gale, 2005.

Al-Ṭāhir, Aḥmad Makkī. *Imru' al-Qays: Amīr shu'arā' al-jāhiliyyah* [Imru' al-Qays: Prince of Pre-Islamic Poets]. Cairo: Dār al- Ma'ārif, 1968.

Taussig, Michael T. *Shamanism, Colonialism, and the Wild Man: A Study in Terror and Healing*. Chicago: Univ. of Chicago Press, 1987.

Taylor, Diana. *Disappearing Acts: Spectacles of Gender and Nationalism in Argentina's "Dirty War."* Durham, NC: Duke Univ. Press, 1997.

Touhouliotis, Vasiliki. "Weak Seed and Poisoned Land: Slow Violence and the Toxic Infrastructures of War in South Lebanon." *Environmental Humanities* 10, no. 1 (2018): 86–106.

Traboulsi, Fawwaz. *A History of Modern Lebanon*. London: Pluto Press, 2007.

Trigg, Dylan. *The Memory of Place: A Phenomenology of the Uncanny*. Athens: Ohio Univ. Press, 2012,

Trouillot, Michel-Rolph. *Silencing the Past: Power and the Production of History*. Boston: Beacon, 2001.

Tsing, Anna Lowenhaupt. *The Mushroom at the End of the World: On the Possibility of Life in Capitalist Ruins*. Princeton, NJ: Princeton Univ. Press, 2015.

Umam Documentation & Research. "About Us: Mission Statement." N.d. At http://www.Umam-dr.org/index.php/mission-statement. Accessed Aug. 20, 2019.

———. "The Collection." N.d. At http://www.Umam-dr.org/en/home/categories/13/our-collection. Accessed Oct. 20, 2020.

———. Memory at Work: A Guide for Lebanese on Peace and War. Database, n.d. At https://www.memoryatwork.org. Accessed Oct. 19, 2010.

———. *The "War" through Its Memorials: Photo Exhibition in Progress*. Haret Hreik, Lebanon, June 12–29, 2009. At https://umam-dr.org/event_detail/77/77/.

Vázquez, Miguel Ángel, and Robert G. Havard. "Poetic Pilgrimages: From Baghdad to Andalucía, Abū Tammām's *Lā anta anta wa-lā al-diyāru diyāru*." In "The Arabic Literature of al-Andalus," special issue of *Journal of Arabic Literature* 34, nos. 1–2 (2003): 122–37.

Volk, Lucia. *Memorials and Martyrs in Modern Lebanon*. Bloomington: Indiana Univ. Press, 2010.

Volney, Comte de (Constantin-François de Chassebœuf). *The Ruins; or, A Survey of the Revolutions of Empires*. Translated by James Marshall. With an introduction by Jonathan Wordsworth. West Yorkshire, UK: Orley, 2000.

Walcott, Derek. *Collected Poems 1948–1984*. New York: Farrar, Straus and Giroux, 1987.

Warner, Michael. *Publics and Counterpublics*. New York: Zone Books; Cambridge: MIT Press, 2002.

Wehr, Hans, and J. Milton Cowan. *A Dictionary of Modern Written Arabic: (Arabic–English)*. Wiesbaden, Germany: Harrassowitz, 1979.

Weizman, Eyal. *Hollow Land: Israel's Architecture of Occupation*. London: Verso, 2012.

———. *The Least of All Possible Evils: Humanitarian Violence from Arendt to Gaza*. London: Verso, 2012.

Williams, Raymond. *Marxism and Literature*. Oxford: Oxford Univ. Press, 1977.

Wilson, Anna, ed. *Lebanon, Lebanon*. London: Saqi, 2006.

Wilson-Goldie, Kaelen. "Contemporary Art Practices in Post-war Lebanon: An Introduction." In *Out of Beirut*, edited by Suzanne Cotter, 81–89. Oxford: Modern Art Oxford, 2006.

———. "Walid Raad and the Atlas Group." Bidoun, n.d. At https://www.bidoun.org/articles/walid-raad-and-the-atlas-group. Accessed June 9, 2012.

World Bank. "Targeting Poor Households in Lebanon." Factsheet, Apr. 21, 2020. At https://www.worldbank.org/en/news/factsheet/2020/04/21/targeting-poor-households-in-lebanon?fbclid=IwAR0jK7XL5VZXd4USaP_AOBve0zo44Y6PpkFH6lVRLkHS9r9AWc6iGTDLP_w.

———. "World Bank: Lebanon Is in the Midst of Economic, Financial and Social Hardship, Situation Could Get Worse." Press release, Nov. 6, 2019. At https://www.worldbank.org/en/news/press-release/2019/11/06/world-bank-lebanon-is-in-the-midst-of-economic-financial-and-social-hardship-situation-could-get-worse.

Young, James Edward. *At Memory's Edge: After-Images of the Holocaust in Contemporary Art and Architecture*. New Haven, CT: Yale Univ. Press, 2000.

———. *The Texture of Memory: Holocaust Memorials and Meaning*. New Haven, CT: Yale Univ. Press, 1993.

Zeitlyn, David. "Anthropology in and of the Archives: Possible Futures and Contingent Pasts; Archives as Anthropological Surrogates." *Annual Review of Anthropology* 41 (2012): 461–80.

Zimmerman, Emma. "A 'Tottering Lace-like Architecture of Ruins': The Wartime Home in Elizabeth Bowen's *The Heat of the Day*." *Literary Geographies* 1, no. 1 (2015): 42–61.

Index

Yasmine Khayyat is assistant professor of Arabic language and literature at Rutgers University.

Printed in the USA
CPSIA information can be obtained
at www.ICGtesting.com
CBHW031322150524
8605CB00002B/45

9 780815 637936